Creating a Peaceable Kingdom

How to Live with More Than One Pet

Creating a Peaceable Kingdom

How to Live with More Than One Pet

CYNTHIA D. MILLER

Animalia Publishing Company
Yuba City, CA

To Alessandra and Rebekah
I love you up to the moon and back a hundred million times!

Individual Sales. Animalia publications are available through most
bookstores or can be ordered directly from Animalia Publishing at the
address below.

Quantity Sales. Special discounts are available on quantity purchases
by corporations, associations, and other organizations. For details,
contact the "Special Sales Department" at the Animalia Publishing
address below.

Animalia Publishing Company
P.O. Box 1390
Yuba City, CA 95992
(916) 755-1318   Fax: (916) 755-2695
Toll Free: (888) 755-1318

Miller, Cynthia D.
        Creating a peaceable kingdom : how to live with more
        than one pet / Cynthia D. Miller. - 1st ed.
        Includes bibliographical references and index.
        ISBN 0-9649413-6-8
        1. Pets - Multiple pets. 2. Pets - Care. 3. Pets - Behavior.
        4. Dogs. 5. Cats. 6. Pet birds. 7. Rabbits. I. Title
        Library of Congress Cataloging in Publication Data:
        95-083688   636.0887

Illustrations by Susan Gross
Design by Janèl Apple

Printed in the United States of America by Quebecor Printing

10 9 8 7 6 5 4 3 2 1

Contents

Chapter 2

Chapter 3

Chapter 4

Chapter 5

Chapter 6

Chapter 7

Acknowledgments

Writing a book has many emotional peaks and valleys — periods filled with exhilaration and more than enough moments of deep self-doubt. Without the unfaltering support and vision of my editor, Sharon Goldinger, I may have given up. I want to thank her for her enormous skill, precision, patience, and "telling me like it is." I learned more than I would have ever dared hoped to.

Special thanks to Michele Weaver and Karen Neilsen for always assuming I'd finish this book and believing in me. A warm thanks to Karen for her input on the aesthetic qualities of this book and for reading the worst first draft ever written by the human hand. Thanks for your enthusiasm!

Thanks to Kenny Yartz for making his way through the same first draft and still finding good things.

I'd like to acknowledge all of the people who spent their valuable time offering their thoughts and experiences in taking care of multiple animal companions. Their input was invaluable.

Hugs and kisses to my husband and girls who had to patiently wait their turn far too often. And finally, to the animals who have generously taught me the lessons that make my life surrounded by the animal-kind the most fulfilling life I could ever imagine.

Preface

More and more people are sharing their homes with animals. In the United States, fifty-three million homes are shared with critters of all kinds, with an average of two pets per family. With this many people caring for animals, it is easy to understand the seemingly unquenchable thirst for knowledge regarding these wonderful creatures.

I have been an animal lover my entire life. Books I've read, movies I've seen, and my thoughts, dreams, and conversations have always been filled with animals. My book reports and papers were on animals. "Save the Deer!" was a popular declaration used by some to tease my exuberance. (This was due to my vocal disfavor of hunting, which didn't go over well in my small rural town.)

Although I dearly loved animals, a dog and eventually a cat were all I was allowed when I was young. So instead I dreamed — dreamed of running one of the largest, fanciest canine training and breeding establishments in the world and building an aviary housing hundreds of exotic and not-so-exotic birds. I wanted to be like Snow White with birds perching on my head, arms, and hands, and critters at my feet, contently following me.

Then I was on my own but still stifled because I rented for many years. After my husband and I bought our first house, I was able to flex those "must-have" muscles. Oh boy! Was I in deep! With a house full of animals, the responsibility was overwhelming.

I've since learned many important and valuable lessons about keeping multiple animals healthy and happy. I had to learn the hard way because there was nowhere to turn. I could find no resources explaining how to introduce my dog to my cats — no information to help me make friends of two rabbits that sent each other into a rage simply by seeing each other.

I've spent extensive time and effort educating myself. I was determined to have a house full of multiple species sharing the same space in harmony. I knew in my heart I could create a peaceable kindgom under my roof.

I'm offering you a guide, a compilation of my education. I've spent many hours discussing problems, cures, and joys with people all over the United States — people who have taught me so much. Both research conducted on animal behavior and my own experiences are presented. My quest for a concentrated source of information on the dynamics of a multi-animal household led me to the conception and fulfillment of this book. I hope you find it both enjoyable to read and helpful in creating your peaceable kingdom.

Creating a Peaceable Kingdom

How to Live with More Than One Pet

Introduction

Something enchanting happens to us when we share our lives with animals. If we completely relinquish our emotional selves (letting go of control and feeling our emotions), we bond with the creatures we care for. We experience magic.

To be fully alive, to experience existence in its most fulfilling realm, people need to be with nature. There must be a portion of our lives that can breathe the wildness of the universe. This connection with nature is so ingrained in our genetic makeup that without it we are never truly whole. We may have productive, full, and even happy lives, but without an attachment to nature there can never be complete spiritual contentment. This is why we plant gardens, take vacations in the country, and have animals share our homes.

Although most animals we keep as pets are domesticated and have been developed to depend on humans for survival, they are not human. They are beyond the invention of mankind. They are a reminder of our emotional spirit — wildness revisited. We are analytical, cognitive creatures and as such rely entirely too much on our brain — our thinking mind. Animals are emotional and instinctive — they feel and experience their lives at the most basic level. In this way, they are "wild."

Animals remind us of our ability to feel. In order to relate to our wild side, we must experience the intense emotions that transcend words — the ones, that for a fleeting moment, freeze time and make anything other than our feelings nonexistent.

This potency of emotional experience is continually expressed in our animal friends — the profound disappointment in a dog when he has to stay home from a daily run, the contentment a cat expresses when stretched out in a sunbeam, and a rabbit's pure enjoyment of play as he spins and jumps around

the room. There is no doubt that a bird is singing (or screaming) his sincere appreciation of being alive. As animal lovers and guardians of animal companions, we know emotions are felt by the creatures, and we are comforted and gratified to be sharing our world with them.

This expression of emotion offers us many benefits of friendship. The loyalty of our animal companions is incomparable. They appreciate us, regardless of our ability, or lack thereof, to fit into the mold of perfection in either looks or manners. We are the most important people in our pet's world. We are special. No matter what mistakes haunt us from our past, our animal companions won't judge or criticize us. We are not penalized or shamed by our shortcomings. We are rescued from loneliness and taught about giving, receiving, caring, and letting go with profound honesty.

As animal lovers, we often find ourselves caring for more than one pet and managing the dynamics of multiple personalities — a mix of animal and human. Suddenly routine care becomes consuming, and the joys may be diminished under the weight of responsibility. If we understand animal personalities and how they interrelate with each other, as well as manage obligations, our home becomes our private peaceable kingdom — a slice of nature, a piece of heaven.

Each animal contributes to the peace of the kingdom, sometimes testing this harmony and then relinquishing to the dynamics of the group. The relationships are compelling and powerful — alive. The alliance between people and animals is synchronized, and harmony is achieved.

This book is intended as a guide to give animal lovers the basic information necessary for a well-managed and joyful multi-animal family. The emphasis is on attitude. Establishing a peaceful, organized environment with minimum work and maximum delight is a pleasure and an attainable goal. Each of us has the ability to create a harmonious household; we simply need the tools.

Throughout the writing of this book, my goal has been to create a user-friendly reference tool for the multiple pet caretaker. The style of organization I chose is intended to help the reader find the most relevant information needed. Because animal caretakers are a diversified group — having different pets with different needs at different times — significant information that requires repeating is contained in a number of sections. For example, you may find information in the rabbit section that is important for your dog or a suggestion in the cat section that can assist you in your interactions with your bird. Please bear with the way I have chosen to provide information. My attempt is not to bore you with repetition but to provide thorough information pertaining to various animal household situations.

In an effort to avoid the term "it," suggesting our animal companions lack identifiable personalities, I alternate the pronouns he and she at each chapter. Any use of colloquial terminology or terms of endearment is meant in fun, admiration, and respect.

I have also avoided referring to animal guardians and caretakers as "owners." Although the law and our registration papers say otherwise, we do not own our animal friends. We accept responsibility for their care, but we cannot possess the spirit of the creatures — we are partners in a symbiotic existence, relying on each other and building eternal relationships based on emotional devotion and sincere compassion.

There are few absolutes in the care of animals; some may argue there are none. The rule is that there are exceptions to the rules. I am sharing with you the information to guide your actions. It is the frame work from which you can build on. Each of your companions is an individual, so follow the clues each gives regarding the success of your care.

When we take on the responsibility of multiple animals, we create a lifestyle in which our creatures are a significant part of our existence. A peaceful, content multi-animal household does not occur without effort — sometimes great, sometimes small.

As caretakers of a peaceable kingdom, we are the maestros. Dictatorship stifles the soul of the orchestra and extinguishes the heartfelt expression of the players. Yet lack of guidance precedes chaos. When we view ourselves as the conductors of a multiple-animal household, we can look upon our responsibility as leading an organized and harmonious concert of diverse individual personalities. Each of us is a proficient, gentle leader giving rise to a harmonious symphony of spirit.

The appendix provides information on organizations you may wish to contact. In addition, a glossary of terms used throughout the book is also provided.

Some information is presented as noted below:

SPECIAL ADVICE FOR THE MAESTRO

This grey box alerts you to valuable hints that are unique to caretakers of multiple animals. Think of them as notes for the symphony.

I hope you find this book useful in the management and enjoyment of your multiple animal family and that you refer to it again and again.

1

Adopting an animal means accepting the challenge of providing a healthy, emotionally satisfying life for a sensitive, intelligent creature. Devoting yourself to supplying a quality life is a gift and an obligation.

Are you ready for another pet?

You've decided to adopt another animal, but are you prepared for the responsibility? Adding one more animal to your household may make the difference between pleasure and frustration. One more pet needing your attention, one more mouth needing to be fed, and one more voice adding to the noise may be one too many and upset the balance. But how do you know? Start by reminding yourself of the obligation to your animal kingdom; it may have become so routine you have forgotten the extent of devotion.

Begin by indulging in extensive soul-searching. To help in this quest, an overview of the responsibilities of caring for animals is presented in this chapter. Consider each area and evaluate your ability to fulfill these needs. Adopting an animal means accepting the challenge of providing a healthy, emotionally satisfying life for a sensitive, intelligent creature. Devoting yourself to supplying a quality life is a gift and an obligation.

The animals highlighted in this book require a large degree of affection. These creatures thrive on attention and require regular portions of it to maintain their physical and mental well-being. It is unfair to fill your home with precious creatures and then discover that you are unable to give them the care they deserve. It is crucial, therefore, to perform this thorough self-examination and to honestly contemplate the questions posed in this chapter before adopting a pet. The questions assume you already have at least one pet and are planning to add another to your household, although the same questions are just as important if you are contemplating your first pet.

Why do I want another pet?

The first step in deciding if you are ready is to have a clear picture of why you want to add another animal to your household. There are as many reasons as there are animal lovers. Even a reason that seems "wrong" at the onset may be completely justified when you take the right approach to your decision-making process.

The secret to a successful human/animal relationship is to be certain that the reason justifies the responsibilities. You will have another creature to clean, train, groom, and spend your hard-earned cash on, so make sure you understand why you feel the desire to adopt another. Every pet, no matter how wonderful, entails some level of sacrifice on your part. Are you prepared to make additional sacrifices?

What is your motivation? What kind of pet are you visualizing? Do you want a cute little puppy to

---

MAKING A COMMITMENT

Commitment is a learned trait — people learn it from experience, and children learn it from their parents. When you adopt an animal, inviting the creature into your life and your home, you are making a promise to her, ensuring you will care for her for the rest of her life. Too often there is no long-term commitment. If the relationship becomes uncomfortable or difficult, some simply give up instead of making an effort to fix the situation.

If you get to the point where your situation is not working, ensure that you have truly given your best effort. Are you willing to part with your pet too soon?

Your pets sense that they are at your mercy. They are sensitive and know what you are feeling often before you do. If you have not made a mental or emotional commitment to their life, they will be anxious and uncertain, which makes their health less stable. They may feel more vulnerable and may be unable to learn appropriate behaviors. Your animals depend on you for security and stability — prove to them you are worthy of their trust.

wrestle with? Is it spring, which always makes you long for a fluffy, tiny lop-eared rabbit?

Is your canine friend getting older and you'd like a young puppy to raise with your existing pet? A puppy sometimes rekindles the puppyhood of an older dog, or the puppy may become a source of irritation to the more mature animal. (More on this in the next chapter.) If you compete in sporting events, you may be considering adding another dog for training. You may have a lap dog, but you'd love to have a dog to take on your morning run. Your cat seems especially lonely, and you think she would benefit from having another cat for company. You have always wanted a cockatoo; you now have experience with animals and feel you are ready to bring one home.

If you currently have one species of animal, such as a dog, and you're considering adopting a kitten, there are reasons why one animal would offer you something the other cannot. Wishing to share your life with a myriad of personality characteristics is a common trait of animal lovers. If you already have a dog and you're thinking of adopting another dog, it may be more difficult to identify the "why."

EXPECTATIONS

Why do so many people adopt a pet of the same species as the one they have? There are many good reasons, but sometimes it is because of a perceived failure of expectations. Whether you realize it or not, you have an ideal image of how you want your pet to be. Athletic, social, beautiful, quiet, or expressive may be some of the pictures of the perfect pet you were hoping to have. Do you have expressed or repressed disappointment at your companion's inability to fit this dream? If you feel your present animal is not living up to your preconceived vision of companionship, think this through before getting another pet.

The Disappointments

Give your current animal every opportunity to realize her potential. Are you giving her the affection and attention she needs? By failing to properly train your pet, have you missed an opportunity to shape her behavior? Seek the help of a behaviorist or trainer. Is there an area you are neglecting? For example, full-

spectrum lighting greatly improves the condition of a bird's feathers, thereby making her more beautiful, and increasing her health and mental well-being. It will require research and contemplation on your part to discover where improvements need to be made.

Maybe it is a physical characteristic that bothers you so terribly, such as the dog slime stains on the wall (yes, the ones that can't be reached without a stepstool) and the permanent ones embellishing your original art piece. I learned this the hard way. After a good head shaking, our dog leaves "Mike-slime," as we call it, eight feet up the wall. There is nothing that we can do to eliminate it — we tolerate it. We have learned to allow our dog access to water only outdoors and keep a towel handy just to wipe off drool. We can laugh it off and show our friends how impressive it is for a dog to get drool eight feet in the air.

Increase Your Knowledge

To better understand your pet, read books, watch shows on television, and talk to neighbors, trainers, and veterinarians. You may learn new ways of communicating and training your pet. Learning about characteristics of the species or breed can give you new insights into why she is behaving in a particular way and at least allows you to realize that your pet is not the only one exhibiting that behavior. If the caretaker of a sighthound feels unloved because the dog won't cuddle in his or her lap, the discovery that this lack of demonstrative affection is not a rejection encourages the appreciation for the dog's natural expressions.

Your Attitude

Consider the interactions between you and your animal companion. What are the dynamics of your relationship? Does she respond to your requests? Are you assuming that she will respond this way? Animals are more intuitive than people. If you treat her as a failure, she feels your disappointment and responds to you accordingly. Do not expect the worst before your pet has even had a chance to try and please you. Expect the best, and be prepared to put some work into it; you may be pleasantly surprised.

Appreciate your animal companion and accept her for who she is. It is unfair to expect her to fulfill your previously conceived image of the "perfect" pet. Too often, people find it easier to "try again" with another animal rather than investing the effort into the companion they presently have. Acknowledge her individuality and see the glory in her personality. Find the joy in the characteristics of her identity that you do appreciate and concentrate on those. Learn to adjust your expectations to this reality. Your commitment is to the individual, not the ideal.

THE DYNAMICS OF DIVERSE PERSONALITIES

Sometimes a particular personality balances another personality, and this can be quite rewarding. The independent, sophisticated nature of your cat is fascinating, but cuddling and wrestling with your dog are physical and emotional comforts in a busy life. The sweet whistles of your canary are balanced by your interactive, boisterous amazon. The eternal puppyhood of my mastiff, Mike, is in direct contrast to the seriousness of my Bouvier des Flandres, Retta. I enjoy being entertained by the naiveté of a bouncing 190-pound "puppy." I also enjoy the intelligent, intuitive interaction of my "nobody's-fool" Bouvier. Retta reminds me that I need to constantly relearn and expand my knowledge of the canine mind. Mike reminds me that a good laugh at a clumsy, good-natured ball chase is a wonderful stress relief.

Some traits can be credited to the breed or species. If a dog that digs is not what you want, choose a breed that does not have a reputation for digging. Adopting a terrier means sacrificing your yard, providing an outlet for the digging, or investing time and effort in trying to train her not to dig. If the loud voice of your macaw infuriates you and your neighbors, another bird with a loud voice is not for you.

A COMFORT IN DIFFICULT TIMES

People will often add a pet to their home during a difficult time in their life. During a traumatic event such as a move or a divorce, many people desire the comfort of an animal. Boredom can also stimulate the desire for a "new" companion. However, once the crisis has passed, these pets have "served their purpose" and many end up in the animal shelter. This does not mean you should not adopt a pet at these times. Often unconditional affection can be a great comfort in difficult times, and the caring devotion required by an animal can be a welcome distraction. These adoptions can be the beginning of a wonderful friendship if the commitment is realized.

I am a restless person, and once during a mellow (boring) time in my life, I decided to begin breeding birds. I wanted excitement and challenge. Without a moment's reflection on my lifestyle, I bought cage material, built cages, and purchased six assorted ringneck parakeets. I lived in a tiny house, so the birds were in a dark, overheated garage. A month later I bought a swamp cooler because the heat was so intense, and I was making plans to add skylights when my daughter was born. Because I had not considered the changes in my life after the baby and my home was insufficient in its current state, I had to admit my failure and sold the entire setup to a trusted breeder friend. Think hard first or pay hard later.

Do I have time daily to give attention and affection to another pet?

Every pet needs attention and affection. Some need it more than others by virtue of their species or because of their individual needs. Some pets, such as dogs or parrots, can become destructive and develop a neurosis from lack of interaction. Others, such as rabbits, suffer their loneliness in solitude. You must be informed, organized, and patient to care for a multi-animal household. If you spend only fifteen minutes a day of quality interaction with each of your ten pets, you will be spending at least two hours daily socializing with the animals. This doesn't take into account the care requirements, only what is necessary for emotional health. Does this time commitment fit into your schedule?

When you meet an animal that captivates you, ask how much time the person spends interacting with her. If the personality of the animal is vibrant and stimulating, you will find the caretaker and pet spend a great deal of time together. Animals that are bonded to their guardians make the most fascinating pets, and bonding takes a commitment of time and energy. (The bonding process will be further discussed in chapter 4.)

Understanding your companion's emotional needs comes from your own intuitive understanding of what your creature needs to be her emotional best. If you are observing your pet's actions, you will be able to tell when your affection is needed or when your animal requires time alone. You learn through experience what your animal companion is trying to tell you, and you learn to trust your intuition and observation.

Isolation and boredom can lead an animal to behavioral problems and stress-induced illnesses. Giving attention is a requirement you must be willing to accept without reservations.

Can I afford another pet?

Financial responsibilities can become a major burden when caring for multiple pets. The initial cost of the animal is often the only expense people consider; however, it is the long-term costs such as housing, food, supplies, and veterinarian care that should be thought through in advance. You can economize only so much without lessening your standards of care — you cannot skimp on nutrition or veterinary care without your pet suffering the consequences. The more animals you have, the more expenses you incur. Although this seems obvious, many people forget to consider this obligation.

Make a list of all the expenses involved so that you are prepared. Budget for equipment (cages, crates, brushes, beds, toys, and dishes), vaccinations, spaying or neutering, licenses, books and magazines, and memberships to organizations that interest you. Estimate high so you won't be faced with too many surprises and calculate replacing some of the equipment occasionally. Purchase the best equipment at the best price to be cost efficient.

Once you've finished your budget, you will better understand your financial responsibility. If you are honest and your budget shows that adopting an-

other animal will be financially difficult, postpone getting another pet. Future opportunities will be available, and you can save your money in the meantime.

HEALTH EXPENSES

Routine vaccinations, checkups, and emergency veterinarian visits cost money. Veterinary care will probably be your most substantial expenditure. You will experience tremendous guilt if you cannot afford to give your pet adequate veterinary care because of lack of funds. Ask your veterinarian about insurance for your pet, as described in chapter 7, or set up a savings account with a regular schedule of deposits for veterinary care.

If you have several pets of the same species, also consider that if one contracts a contagious illness, it will spread throughout your household. You'll experience elevated veterinary bills, as well as headaches and heartache, if the disease is serious or has no cure.

DAMAGE TO YOUR BELONGINGS

Animals can do quite a bit of damage to furniture, possessions, and your house. Can you accept the fact that things may have to be replaced because of damage caused by your growing pets? One excursion of a cockatoo can destroy a couple of table legs. A bored puppy can, in an hour, make stuffing from the quilt that your grandmother lovingly created. The new garden you spent two years and several thousand dollars on may be just the way you dreamed, but it can be ruined in one week with a canine juvenile in the backyard. I can personally vouch for this.

Once my mastiff, Mike, pulled a freshly planted tree out of the ground. I witnessed the action through the window. Furious, I tore through the house to the yard. My anger immediately subsided into amusement as I saw Mike — his cute innocent face with wrinkled eyebrows and drooping lips wrapped around the three-inch trunk, two feet of roots sticking out on one side of his head and two feet of flowering bush on the other. He was having fun and was totally oblivious as to why I would be running from the house in such a ruckus. He seemed to pause from his destruction to be sure he wasn't missing out on something more fun. I laughed and shrugged off the tree. "Oh, well," I thought, "another Mikey expense." Keeping a good outlook in even the most frustrating situations is an important characteristic of a successful caretaker.

With guidance, forethought, and a watchful eye, many destructive behaviors can be controlled, but damage will be done. Can you forgive your pet and accept partial blame, or will you hold it against her?

Can I get all my animals nourished with ease?

You must feed your animals quality, nutrient-loaded food regularly and in sufficient quantities. Each species of pet has different nutritional requirements, and it is your responsibility to research these requirements and fulfill them.

Those who study pet nutrition are acquiring a better understanding of the intricate and perplexing cellular system of animals. They are using this information to better inform caretakers about how dietary intake influences our pet's ability to attain optimum health. Use this knowledge by putting good nutrition into practice.

What your animals eat determines their energy and weight, and helps manage their bodily systems. Knowing the nutrient requirements of each of your animals is paramount. Begin by asking your veterinarian what he or she suggests. Then you can purchase and prepare the most useful and healthful food for your animal companions. Usually this means spending a bit more money for the superior cuisine.

Sound nutrition often takes a dedication of time. Feeding a household of animals can absorb a significant chunk of your day. Putting dry kibble in a dog dish may not take long, but cutting up fresh vegetables for a couple of parrots or mixing vitamins into cat food takes longer. Birds must have some sort of soft food daily, and this food must be taken out of the cage after a couple of hours to avoid ingesting spoiled food. If you work outside the home, this means feeding as soon as you awake and then removing the dishes before you leave. Cats have to be fed and then their dishes removed after a half-hour. Vegetables and greens must be freshly cut for your rabbits. Most pets must be

These two dogs are the best of buddies, lying paw in paw during quiet time (even if there isn't a lot of quiet time with two dogs).

fed twice daily. All water dishes must be checked twice a day. Although these tasks require a time commitment, an efficient routine can be easily established as discussed later.

Can I make sure all my pets get adequate exercise?

Even though smaller animals can get the majority of their exercise in the house, especially if you instigate games, playing outside is loads of fun and is important for physical and mental health. Bigger dogs must have time outside to exercise their bodies adequately. Will you be able to take them for regular walks or play sessions?

Most cats get their exercise throughout the day, and initiating a chase game with them can encourage extra physical activity. Birds need lots of toys and time out of their cage each day to get their exercise. Rabbits need time to run about, kick up their heels, and spin to their heart's content.

In a house with many different species sharing the same living space, exercise needs suddenly become a complicated consideration. A dog that chases your rabbit cannot be allowed in the house while the rabbit is out exploring. Cats that threaten the safety of your bird must be closed away in another room for a period of the day. The level of caution you have to employ is difficult to predict because of the varying personalities of the animals involved. If you give thought to problems that may arise before adopting a pet, you will be better prepared.

Do I have the time for additional cleaning?

The more animals that share your home, the bigger the mess. A vacuum is an absolute necessity for pet lovers! Vacuuming or sweeping every day around cages and litter boxes is a common chore. The more animals, the more hair, feathers, food, and dirt that get on your floors and furniture, and the more you must clean. No matter how diligent you are in brushing your pets and keeping your house clean, you will find hair everywhere.

If any kind of disorder or mess sends you into a frantic, uncontrollable cleaning frenzy, your personality may make keeping multiple pets difficult. You may find yourself resenting the animals who cause you anguish. If you think that you can successfully curb your urge to panic at a loose feather stuck to the couch or a cat hair on the kitchen table, then you can adjust and live happily with your animal companions.

It is a matter of priority. If you could not live with anything less than a house full of animals, then you understand that part of the compromise is relaxing your need for perfection.

Do I have time for daily grooming?

Grooming every day keeps your pet's skin and coat in their best condition, but it also has many other benefits. Grooming time can also be bonding time. Even animals that barely tolerate a brush in the beginning will learn to enjoy it and appreciate the human contact. Grooming alerts you to any physical changes that occur as well as to any parasites or pests that may be invading your pet and home.

All animals need some amount of grooming; some need more than others. Shorthaired animals require less grooming, but even they need a quick brush over. Birds require little daily grooming, but they need diligent wing clipping and baths. If you have two longhaired cats and two longhaired dogs in full coat, you have a large commitment to daily grooming. Do you really need to bring home that adorable scruffy-haired puppy your friend has? Think about how much time you spend grooming and decide if you really want to spend more time on this chore each day.

Is my home large enough to accommodate another pet?

Every animal needs a private and quiet corner of her own to rest and find solitude. Provide a warm and cozy place for each pet.

Do you have room for another generously sized cage for a bird? A parrot cage can take up a large space and fill a small living room. Parrots also need a play stand to spend time out of and away from their cage.

Rabbits also need a cage. Litter boxes have to go somewhere. There must be adequate places for the animals to eat so that they can do so peacefully and without feeling threatened.

Every creature deserves her right to privacy, and so do you. Is there a place for you and your family members to have a quiet moment alone without furballs or feather dusters? No matter how much you appreciate your animals, there will be times when you need your own private moments. Be sure you leave yourself a special spot in your animal-filled home.

Am I willing to take my neighbors' comfort into consideration?

One dog may bark occasionally, but two or more dogs barking and getting each other excited create significantly more noise. If you plan to let a cat outdoors, you must consider your neighbors' feelings. If your neighbors are active gardeners, they may resent deposits left in their flower gardens. Do your neighbors keep their automobiles immaculate? A feline with dirty feet warming her paws on the hood of a recently driven vehicle may make your neighbors furious. Do you think your noise-sensitive neighbors will enjoy awakening to the raucous jungle sounds heralding the beginning of your macaw's day?

Your life will be easier and more pleasant if your neighbors are on your side. Prove to them that you are a responsible pet owner. Take their feelings into consideration before purchasing another pet that may affect their lives, and cordial relationships will prevail.

If a neighbor is pushed to the point of complaining, then you can assume the problem is serious. People don't usually complain until they cannot cope with the problem anymore. You may not be able to repair the damage. Be careful and think of how your neighbors feel. If you are the owner of a noisy or troublesome pet, you can be taken to court. This kind of headache and bad feelings can be avoided. Think ahead.

Is another pet acceptable to my landlord?

RENTING REGULATIONS

Read your lease carefully. You may have to pay an additional deposit for each pet, and the deposit may or may not be refundable. There may be a provision in your lease stating what kind and how many pets are allowed. If you are interested in an animal that deviates from these qualifications, be prepared to explain to your landlord why you should be allowed to break the rules. Be honest about what kind of animal you are thinking of adding to your family and how you expect to care for the pet. Show your good intentions by explaining your dedication to responsible pet care. If you already have a pet and have set a good example with her care, show this as proof.

My husband and I looked a long time for our first house to rent. We wanted to have a dog, and there were few advertised places allowing pets. One day we drove by a home with a "for rent" sign. We loved it — it was cute and in a good neighborhood, and it even had a big fenced yard. But the owner said no pets. We talked to him, convincing him of our good intentions. He decided to give it a try

and charged us a large deposit. We did not disappoint him, and after two years we got our full deposit back.

If you own or rent a condo, you must abide by the regulations of the complex. Referred to as CC&Rs (covenants, conditions, and restrictions), these can limit the number and size of animals allowed. They can also restrict the activities of your animal companions at the complex. Sometimes the CC&Rs are vague, so check them thoroughly.

GETTING PERMISSION

Do not purchase a pet before clearing it with your landlord. Get permission first! You may have no notice to get rid of your pet if you break the rules. Adopting a pet and then having to part with it because you didn't get permission first is unnecessary.

Have the manager or landlord write a separate agreement stating what pets you are allowed to have and any conditions that apply. You may be able to have the pets added to your lease. Both of you should sign or initial the addition. Be specific; verbal agreements will not help you if a new manager takes over, and you could lose your right to keep your animals.

When you move from a rented home, be certain to make any repairs and replace any damaged property. Set a good example of what responsible pet ownership can be and you make it easier for the next animal lover to get permission to keep pets. You will create a good recommendation for yourself if, despite your creatures, you leave the home in great condition.

YOUR OWN HOME

Owning your own home does not guarantee you can have any animal or any number of animals you want on your property. Laws govern what animals you may have on any given parcel of land. When looking at property, do not ask the real estate agent about zoning regulations; go straight to the planning commission of the city.

Regulations change continually. City limits are stretching farther and farther into the country. Just because the people in the house before you had five dogs does not guarantee this is legally allowable. They could have been unaware of the regulation, or the laws may have changed recently. To avoid trouble, check the rules before you bring another pet home or move to your new property.

Will I be able to find someone to provide the best care for my pets in my absence?

The situations below will be discussed in later chapters, but your prior consideration will be of benefit.

DURING VACATIONS

Vacations are supposed to be a time of relaxation. Often the activities involved in preparing for a vacation leave you stressed. When you have pets, you have even more to worry about. You worry about what you can do to make your pets comfortable and safe while you are away because you know that vacation time is a source of anxiety for your animal friends.

It is more difficult to find a friend or family member to care for multiple animals. You may feel comfortable asking someone to care for one dog, but when you have several animals, creating dozens of extra duties, it hardly seems fair to ask. If a spur-of-the-moment weekend getaway is a part of your family's lifestyle, take this into consideration. With multiple pets, it can be very difficult to find adequate care on short notice. Understand this difficulty before adopting another pet.

IF SOMETHING HAPPENS TO YOU

A major concern for pet caretakers, whether they have one pet or ten, is who can take care of the animals if something happens. This is an unpleasant subject; however, it is important. Pause for a moment and think of what would happen to your pets if you weren't here to take care of them. Parrots are a special consideration because of their long life spans. If you adopt a macaw while you are in your thirties, she may, with good health, outlive you. Preparing ahead for the best possible placement for your precious animal companions is a demonstration of your devotion.

How will my other animals react to an additional pet?

When thinking of adopting another pet, don't forget to take into consideration the emotional well-being of the animals you presently live with. If you have an animal that is very anxious or shy, reacts to change unfavorably, and is easily stressed, you may have to postpone adopting another animal or decide against it completely.

What is going on in the life of your animal companions right now? A move, a rambunctious toddler, new furniture, a new job, or a member of the family moving in or out are all stressful situations. This may not be a good time to bring another animal into your home. Wait until things are calm and your present pets have had time to adjust to any changes before adding another pet.

My husband and I once adopted two puppies. One was planned, and one was a rescue. I had a daughter in diapers, a brand new baby, and two puppies to housebreak. I felt like I was up to my elbows in you know what all day. We finally found a wonderful home for the rescued puppy where even to this day I see her riding in the car with her caretaker. I felt much better, and I'm sure everyone else, human and animal, in the house felt calmer because I wasn't as frantic. Too much change meant it was not a good time to add a second puppy.

Some animals are more resilient than others. Their personalities may indicate they can, with a bit of patience, accept another pet. Other personality types may require much nurturing before they are able to accept another animal.

Don't forget the potential for jealousy; many undesirable behaviors result from it. If your present pet is exceptionally jealous, you may not want to add another pet until your animal has learned to accept other people and animals more openly. Follow the guidelines in the next chapter regarding introducing new pets to your kingdom. Make sure you give your first pet plenty of attention. She needs to know that her place in your heart is still there.

Your pet may like or dislike the new creature — you have no way of foretelling how their relationship will develop. Each animal has a unique personality. Like people, some animals can really irritate other animals. Knowing the animal you have and understanding her personality will help you find a pet she will accept, but is not a guarantee of instant friendship. You must do your best and be prepared. The following chapter will help you know what to expect.

Are the human members of my household willing to share their living space with another animal?

No matter how much thought you have given to how you can handle another pet, you must also think of everyone else's feelings. The same questions that you ask of yourself must be asked of the other humans in the home.

THE ADDED OBLIGATION

If the pet is to be primarily your responsibility, then you will be the one most devoted to her emotional and physical care. You may need occasional support from friends and family in the event of your absence or sickness. It's comforting to know that a helpful spouse or child will care for the animals if you are sick.

The other humans sharing your home will be living with the mess, noise, and lack of spontaneity. Your spouse may have had other plans for the savings account, and your children may not want to spend their weekends at dog shows.

When my husband brought home the previously mentioned, unplanned puppy, I felt resentful. I didn't need an added responsibility. I feel bad, even to this day, that I was unable to shower her with the affection she deserved. Strive to make it a positive experience for all by making sure every person is willing to adopt another pet.

JEALOUSY

Other family members may not be equally enthusiastic about your pet's wonderful qualities. If there is any resentment of the new animal, it makes life more difficult and can lead to a stressed-out pet

and human. Everyone in your home affects your animal's development. Each creature has the right to live in an accepting, nurturing environment.

Jealousy is another consideration. If your spouse or child already feels that your time is precious and in short supply, the addition of another responsibility will only add to the resentment. Many a spouse has heard the ultimatum, "Me or the beast!" However, the resentful person may be more subtle. I've seen people be mean and unaccepting to an animal because the pet seems to love someone else in the family more intensely. These situations are very emotional. They are often very complex and concern more than just the pet. In this unfair situation everyone suffers; unfortunately, it is not uncommon. Communicating in an open, honest discussion before bringing another animal home is the best way to avoid such heartache.

What exactly am I expecting from my relationship with this pet?

This is probably the most difficult question to answer; however, it is the most important. Understanding your motivation for bringing another pet into your home makes your choice more clear.

As mentioned above, involve your family in the adoption process. Each person has a vision of his or her "ideal" pet. Take all of these expectations into consideration when deciding what animal you want to share your home with. Ultimately, have each person meet the animal you intend to adopt before you bring the animal home.

WHAT IS "IDEAL"?

What do you expect to receive from this creature? What mental image do you have when you are contemplating a pet? Do you want a frisky dog who will greet you enthusiastically after a long day? Do you prefer a sedate, regal lounge mutt? You may prefer a pet that requires little training, or you may be looking for a challenge. You may be fascinated by the beauty of an Afghan hound or intrigued by the exotic qualities of a macaw.

You may have fallen in love with the gorgeous

YOUR ANIMAL'S PERSONALITY

The personality of your animal companion is influenced by these forces:

INHERITANCE —
The species and breed play a role in the characteristics expressed by the animal. Genetically programmed personality traits, as well as ones unique to the individual, are a gift from the animal's inheritance.

ENVIRONMENT —
Environment has been proven to influence the personality of humans; the same is true of animals. The more stimulating the environment, the more opportunity the animal has to express herself. Good health, clean living space, and stimulating toys are a necessity.

BOND WITH CARETAKER —
Only in a stable and secure environment are animals able to comfortably express themselves and share their world with humans. An investment of time and emotion on the part of the caretaker creates a trusting, meaningful relationship.

longhaired cat on a television commercial and have decided that is what you want. The intelligence of a movie wonder dog may have won you over. You may have considered owning a bird after you heard a friend's amazon sing her unique rendition of "The Farmer in the Dell."

EXPECTATION WORKSHEET

The best answer is to create a list. Write down your pet dreams and hopes; your list of desires should be as detailed as possible. Each quality you find interesting should be listed. Next to each positive qualification, list any negative features that come to mind. If you have any physical or financial limitations, these should also be listed. Don't get frustrated by the negatives you encounter. The revealing nature of this exercise is finding solutions to these possible problems.

Are you going to do your part in realizing your expectations? If an obedient dog is important to you, be willing to invest time in training and shaping the dog's behavior. If you want a rabbit that is oozing with personality and character, plan to interact with her often and regularly. Your contribution is what makes the difference between an animal that "exists" in your house and a true companion.

Next to each negative item on your list, think of a solution or a compromise. Is there a sacrifice you need to make? See the sample expectation worksheet below for examples. Are you willing to follow through with your end of the bargain? The perfect relationship does not happen without effort, but the strong bond created with your animal friend feels like magic. Careful consideration of what you want from your pet reveals what you must do to make the relationship work.

Be honest. Have realistic expectations. Animals are sensitive, and they want your approval. They deserve your acceptance of them as individuals. Even with your best intentions, they may not be exactly what you dreamed. They will be the natural combination of their genetic inheritance, their environment, your guidance, and most importantly, your affection and compassion. In other words, a trusting life is in your hands.

EXPECTATION WORKSHEET

Use this sample worksheet to stimulate your thoughts about your ideal animal companion of any species. Create your own worksheet using the criteria important to you.

What I'd like in a canine companion

1 — playful spirit
2 — take along on long-distance hikes
3 — low energy level in the house
4 — good with children
5 — requires little grooming
6 — healthy; low veterinary expense
7 — protective; alert to strangers
8 — obedient

Possible challenges

1 — too much energy and too playful
2 — high energy level
3 — not enough energy for activities I'd
    like to pursue
4 — no possible challenges
5 — must be able to handle cold,
    heat, high altitudes
6 — even healthy dogs need veterinary care
7 — too aggressive or dominant
8 — can learn undesirable behaviors;
    bored if not mentally challenged

Solutions to challenges

1 — engage in daily play or exercise sessions
2 — give her regular exercise
3 — avoid the lazy breeds
4 — research breeds that are good with
    children; teach children respect for dog;
    introduce them slowly; keep a watchful
    eye on the interactions
5 — find breeds adaptable to these environments
6 — choose a breed with few genetic faults;
    find a breeder who has dogs with a healthy
    lineage; provide good preventative care
7 — invest time and money in good training;
    choose a reputable breeder with dogs of
    stable temperament
8 — provide extensive training to alleviate boredom

A word about rescues

Sometimes a new pet is added because your heart goes out to a needy animal. An abandoned and mistreated creature might discover that her wandering path ends at your nurturing arms. You caringly spay her, ending the link to more suffering. You nurse her back to health and lovingly demonstrate to her that you can be trusted and devoted. The pet becomes a member of your family, and although you did not plan for her arrival, she adds a dynamic dimension to your life.

Rescuing an animal is a wonderful way to acquire a lifelong friend.

Animal lovers often have big hearts, and with these big hearts comes the desire to help animals in need. There is, however, such a thing as rescuing too many pets. Caution is necessary when your emotions are strong. Providing even one creature with the life she deserves and the affection she needs takes time and energy.

If you don't feel that rescuing one animal and providing her a loving home is enough, and you want to help more, then offer your assistance in alternative ways. Donate money, time, or your expertise to animal rescue groups, shelters, education, and special clinics. Giving with your heart is valuable; you don't have to offer your home to so many pets that their (or your) quality of life is compromised.

VISITING A SHELTER

Shelters are difficult places to visit. You may feel the overwhelming urgency of the animals' situations and feel it is your responsibility to save them all. There is no possible way for one person to save them all, and the guilt or desperation you feel from this inadequacy may keep you from visiting a shelter. But this is the worst way to deal with these feelings. You are not expected to save them all; you can only do your share. Your share may be one life, and if you can save that one life, you should feel personal satisfaction and pride in your action.

*Success may
come to the
impulsive, the
unknowledge-
able, or the
unconcerned, but
true happiness
more often comes
from planning
and forethought.*

Creating your own
peaceable kingdom

As a human caring for a kingdom of animals, whether this kingdom includes two pets or a dozen, you are required to be master, referee, protector, psychologist, and nurturer. Appreciation of this responsibility and its intrinsic rewards are your motivation. If you are up to the challenge, you can meet or exceed the needs of your animal friends and keep their lives safe, happy, and full of devotion.

Success may come to the impulsive, the unknowledgeable, or the unconcerned, but true happiness more often comes from planning and forethought. If after you answered the questions posed in the previous chapter with complete honesty and sincerity and you feel that adopting another animal would be a positive addition to your household, then your experience will be exceptional.

The importance of attentiveness

As your household develops and settles into a more predictable pattern (if a house full of pets is ever predictable), your attentiveness may decrease as you take your pets' interrelationships for granted. The success of a multi-animal household depends on your careful attention to the safety and stress level of all the animals. Even pets that have gotten along for years may suddenly quarrel. Social status may be tested, especially when an animal is vulnerable because of illness, stress, or age. As your pet gets older, he may become more cranky, sore, or just plain intolerant. You must respect his need to be left alone, and you must be able to protect your other pets from harm. Many wonderful friendships have developed between various species, but the wisest caretakers are the most watchful and cautious.

This is not meant to frighten you, only to impress the importance of your awareness. Your expectations will come to fruition, so keep your thoughts positive. Do not assume the worst — assume the best, but don't wear blinders.

An increase in stress

Having several pets in your home could increase the stress level of many animals. Some are forced to live with others that would be their natural prey or predator. Most take to this lifestyle with ease, but others may be constantly anxious. If your dog stands by the rabbit cage and barks excessively, especially when you're not home, your rabbit will feel vulnerable and may become susceptible to illness. Fortunately, you can take measures to prevent much of the stress. If you keep the anxiety level low and the animals under control, you will increase the positive influence on the environment.

Part of the challenge of multi-animal households is ensuring that all animals are safe and content in spite of the complex mixture of instincts and personalities. Part of the joy is witnessing the friendships that develop among the different species. If you think positively and only encourage good behaviors and attitudes, you will be rewarded by the camaraderie created in your peaceable kingdom.

Before bringing your new companion home

After you make the decision to adopt another animal, preparations for his care and how he will relate and interact with your existing animal family must be considered. Your goal is to keep the peace and introduce pets in a safe, docile environment.

PLANNING FOR PEACEFUL INTRODUCTIONS

Until you have the new addition in your household, you cannot be sure how relationships will develop. Animals have unmistakable, distinctive personalities (have I said this enough?), and they have their own likes and dislikes. If two animals decide that they will not get along, there may be constant battles, ranging from cold war to physical scrimmages. You will be called upon to referee, and you must act quickly and fairly to decide how to remedy the situation. Some quickly, and almost immediately, accept the new addition with curiosity and approval.

MAKING A COMMITMENT

The peaceful coexistence of a multi-animal household requires three commitments.

Accepting of Each as an Individual

The knowledge that each animal is an individual and has a distinct personality is vital in a multi-animal household. Recognize each of your animal companions as unique and appreciate the complexity and interconnection of the group.

Maintaining a Positive Attitude

Always possess a positive attitude. Emotions spread like wildfire, so spread enthusiasm, tenderness, and sensitivity. Negative thoughts, no matter how repressed, will be felt by all. Know there will be peace and balance, and they will exist.

Being Faithful to Your Determination

Determination and dedication to your ideal will assure the realization of a peaceable kingdom. Your commitment to each individual creature and your tenacity in creating a harmonious group will give you the endowment of a maestro. Do not waiver in your quest, and you will be rewarded.

If you intend to make changes in the environment (such as adding cages or equipment) or in the current routine (feeding at a different time or changes in behavior expectations), then these alterations should be initiated before bringing home the addition. Giving your current animals a prior opportunity to adjust to these changes lessens the negative impact on their lives when the new pet comes to live in the home.

Keep in mind that it is easier to introduce animals to each other if none of them are adolescents. Adolescence is a time for rebellion, activity, and feistiness. None of these qualities contribute to successful introductions, but great friendships can be developed despite them.

JUST IN CASE, BE PREPARED

Be prepared to face any problems due to conflicting personalities, and have a plan ready to enact if you need to deal with these challenges.

Have a number of alternatives and solutions in mind. Do you have room in your house to keep the animals separated until they can tolerate each other's company? Are you equipped to set up a dog-free area if your dog threatens your other animals? If you must, can you trust that everyone in your home will be diligent about keeping the animals in their respective environments? Do you have the patience and persistence needed to train the animals to respect each other? If they can coexist peacefully when you are present, can you provide a system to keep them apart when you are not around? If there is nothing you can do to help the animals get along better, are you willing to find a good home, no matter what it takes, for the "troubling" animal?

Tough decisions and difficult solutions may be required. There is nothing more heartbreaking than to live with creatures that are intolerant of each other, especially when your feelings for them both are strong. I hope you'll never have to face this predicament.

A STOP AT YOUR VETERINARIAN'S

Bringing home a new animal may introduce a health risk to your resident pets, so a stop at your veterinarian is in order. Your current animals have had their vaccinations, and because of your dedicated concern, you know they are healthy. However, some more sensitive or compromised creatures should have a health exam by your veterinarian before you adopt another animal to be sure they will weather the transition in their best health. Be faithful to necessary quarantines, and get your new pet to your veterinarian as soon as possible.

The Theory

A stop at your veterinarian's for a health check on the way home is a wise safety precaution especially if you have pets of the same species at home. Your new pet may inadvertently bring a disease or parasite into your household, so ensure that the new animal is healthy from the beginning. If you adopted a pet who had a prepurchase veterinary exam by the seller and you have a copy of a health exam record, then you can wait for a couple of days to take the pet to your own veterinarian. If you do not have another animal of the same species at home, you can save the veterinarian checkup for sometime in the next few days.

Although another stop on the way home may make the animal a bit more nervous and makes the trip a bit longer, having your new creature adapt to change in his environment only to put him in the carrier and take off again can be more stressful.

The Reality

Arranging for a veterinarian appointment on the trip home can be a difficult venture and herein lies the fault of a perfect theory. Coordinating your most opportune time for picking up the animal, the seller's schedule, and the appointment load and working hours of your veterinarian can be frustrating, perhaps impossible. The physical location of all involved may make the organization of a veterinarian stop a long excursion. Give it a try, but don't panic if you cannot organize it. If this doesn't work for you, ask the seller to take your chosen animal to your veterinarian prior to your picking him up. You may need to offer a small fee for doing so. Otherwise, take him to your veterinarian as soon as you can, keeping the new pet separate from the other animals in the interim.

TIPS ON CHOOSING A NAME

- Choose a name that does not rhyme with a command or sound like a rebuke.

- Choose a name you can take pride in sharing with people. (If you are embarrassed to call your pet "Tinkles" in public, choose another name.)

- Choose a name that is easy to say and rolls off of the tongue. Animals seem to prefer names that end with a "y" sound.

- Choose a two-syllable name rather than a longer one, or use a nickname.

- Remember that the name you choose will have a psychological impact on the way you and other people view your pet. A big, brawny dog named "Killer" will naturally make the people who meet him feel threatened and untrusting. Not a good way to keep your pet socialized.

- In a multiple animal family, be careful to choose names that are different enough to avoid confusion. "Muffy," "Duffy," and "Fluffy" may never be sure who you are calling for.

- Don't worry about changing the name of an adult animal. If your new pet comes with a name that you don't like, he will learn to adjust to one you choose. Just don't expect him to know immediately that you are referring to him when you use the new name; he will need to learn it as if he were a baby. Sometimes changing the name of an animal is beneficial, especially when the name has negative connotations to you or the creature. If the name has been used as a reprimand, he will probably react favorably to a new one.

POSITIVE THINKING

Although some people may view this as too metaphysical for their belief system, the truth is that it is a simple and easily understood dynamic that manifests itself in all relationships.

You get what you expect. Your pets will live up to your expectations. If you assume you will have trouble housebreaking your puppy, then inevitably you will. If you assume that your bird will bite you every time you attempt to remove him from his cage, he will oblige.

If you are sure about your choice of pet, the animals will know. If you have no doubt the new cat is going to coexist peacefully with your present cats and you imagine only the best, you will experience ease in developing the relationships.

Sometimes this idea is referred to as "self-fulfilling prophecy." Animals, like children, will live up to your expectations. It doesn't matter what you say or do; it's what you think and visualize that influences their behavior. Many people believe animals can "see" your thoughts. This could be likely because animals are so much more intuitive and in tune with their senses. To those who are paying attention, this certainly seems to be true.

It is not clear what makes this true. It may be subtle body language. It may be because animals rely so heavily on their intuition and they sense apprehension. It may even be that you have unknowingly trained your pets to behave in a particular manner through your actions. You must communicate positive thoughts to your pets.

When I trained my very sensitive mastiff, I could not for an instant let negative thoughts enter my mind. If he was having a difficult time and I couldn't figure out why, I'd stop and realize I was thinking he would not be able to perform the exercises. I hadn't even noticed I was thinking negative thoughts. I cleared my mind and visualized him performing the exercises correctly. He did. Good trainers do this whether or not they are aware of their skill to clear their minds and therefore clearly see the results they desire.

Although you may need to remind yourself occasionally in the beginning, clearing your mind of negatives is quite successful and becomes less difficult with time. Practice and you will find it really helps the dynamics of a multiple animal family remain more serene.

Multiple dogs

• • • • • • • • • • • •

If you are not home for long stretches of time, two dogs can keep each other company. However, two dogs can also more than double your trouble. Their play can become rough and cause damage to your house and yard. More than one dog can also mean twice the fun, noise, etc.

BARKING

The comfort of your neighbors must be considered because many problems are magnified with multiple dogs. More than one dog adds to the volume level, and if you live in a neighborhood where the homes are close to each other, this can become a significant problem. Some breeds bark more than others, so research the breed you are considering. If you are considering a mixed-breed dog, spend enough time with him to get an idea of his own noise level.

If your present dog is not a barker and you have never had this problem, remember that another dog may create a noisemaking situation. Even if the new dog is not a barker, the two dogs together may increase the excitement level so greatly that they just can't help themselves. Perhaps they make noise only when they are playing, but it can still be irritating to those around you. Neighbors who value their silence are not going to think it's cute when your two rascals enjoy a joyful, albeit noisy, romp! If the new dog tends to be one that barks at the slightest sound or odor, you may find your more peaceful dog joining in as he wonders what the fuss is about. He may not join in, but do you want even one dog that makes too much noise?

If you live on isolated property where you don't have to worry about neighbors, you must still consider how you and your family, including other pets, feel about increased volume levels. Can you handle the added commotion of another dog?

If you choose a breed of dog that doesn't have a reputation for barking, take note if he howls or makes other noises. These vocalizations can be quite irritating and aggravate anyone who lives within audible range.

FIGHTING

Another problem that arises in multi-dog households is fighting. Some breeds or individual dogs tend to fight more than others. If the breed you have an affection for is one that has a tendency to be dog-aggressive, be prepared to deal with this problem.

As long as the animals you plan to keep together are well bred and have normal canine temperaments, some generalizations can aid you in making your choice. Large dogs usually will not fight smaller dogs, and males will generally not fight with females. However, some dogs will fight any dog regardless of size, age, or sex.

Every effort should be made to find another dog that will become good friends with your present pet and avoid this trouble from the onset. Having two dogs that want to continually fight is an unpleasant experience. If you find yourself in this predicament, the best advice is to find a suitable home for one of the canines. Will you always be able to keep the disagreeing canines out of each other's way? You can never be certain.

People can be hurt, and hurt severely, during a dog fight. Consequently, dog fights should not be taken lightly. You want to promote harmony in your household by having animals that are friends or will at least tolerate each other. Keep in mind that the reason you want to have animal companions is for the enjoyment. Being constantly on guard and worried about your pets can be stressful to you and them.

TRAINING

Your present dog should be well trained before adding another canine. Being able to control using basic obedience commands is essential. Every dog should be obedience trained using a gentle, mutual-respect training method. If you have not given your pet any reason to doubt the sincerity of your motives or any reason to be resentful or distrusting, you will not lose control simply because there is another dog in the house. Adopting a dog that has been bred for stable temperament gives you a better chance of a peaceful home. Dogs have been bred for thousands of years to serve mankind; if you give him no reason to waiver in his loyalty and you have a dog with a sound mind, you should have minimal problems dealing with more than one dog.

PACK BEHAVIOR

If you have two dogs and are adopting a third, you may find that the two gang up on the new addition. When two dogs create a united front against the newcomer, intervene and take charge immediately to make the transition work. The situation can become quite dangerous.

Many sources on canine social order warn about pack behavior. It is true that with two or more dogs you have a pack on your hands, but it isn't going to resemble a mad, rabid pack on the hunt. Your pets are going to be trained; as previously mentioned, they will know you are master because you have shown them that the best thing in the world is to look to you for guidance. When the dogs know that you make the rules, they live by your standards. They will work out a pecking order among themselves, and they will continue to respect your authority. Dogs are more prone to developing pack behavior against their caretakers if they are left alone most of the time with little human interaction. Make sure they see you as master before they spend extended time alone together.

GENDER

Some people have had great success mixing any number or combination of sexes. Others swear that in order to keep peace, there are certain mergers that should be avoided. If you presently have a female, adding either sex, especially a puppy, appears to bring out the mothering instinct of many dogs. If you have two female dogs, adding a male can create tension and fighting as the females "discuss" who will receive the interests of the male. Two intact (unneutered) males are always more difficult but not impossible. Two females can be quite a pleasure but only if they are compatible and you're determined they will tolerate each other before adopting. If you spay and neuter, one animal of each sex is the most frequently recommended combination. Peaceful coexistence always depends on three keys — the unique personality of the animal, your attitude, and your determination to make it work — not just the gender of the animal.

AGE

Getting another dog of a different age will generally make things easier in the future. If both dogs are adolescents, they can be quite unruly. It can be a lot of work raising two teenage hoodlum canines. These dogs will also grow old together, and you will be spending more money on veterinary bills and time nurturing them in their later years. The hardest part of having two or more pets the same age is knowing that you will lose your pets within a couple of years of each other. This future trauma will be difficult and sad.

Although there are no set rules, some trainers suggest that the best age difference is around three years. This difference seems to make the balance of dominant and submissive positions evolve naturally. The development of friendships can be more difficult with a larger age span.

Consider your individual situation and choose the age that best fits your animal kingdom. Of course, many successful friendships between dogs of different ages have developed.

Two Puppies Are a Handful

One of the most distressing situations dog caretakers can get themselves into is adopting two puppies of the same age or from the same litter. Training one puppy takes hard, dedicated work; training two puppies is twice the work! Housebreaking is only the beginning of the frustration. You will have two creatures that have endless energy, are capable of vast destruction, and have absolutely no idea of the social graces of a human household. It's not impossible to train more than one puppy at a time, but your feelings of fun will be diminished.

If you know that you want two dogs, get a puppy and raise him with all of the manners that you would expect your little canine buddy to possess, and then add another. The older dog may demonstrate the proper way to earn your attention and admiration, and your new little charge may learn the ways of your home more quickly. You will be less stressed and thus more capable of enjoying your puppy. You will also have practice and feel like an old hand at puppy raising.

Another Viewpoint

That having been said, many attached dog buddies are ones that were raised together from puppyhood. If you know you want two dogs and two puppies from the same litter have complementary personalities, you may find great joy in raising the pups together. Their bond will be strong. Some devoted people claim that raising two puppies at once is easy. They will probably not cry during the night, will keep each other company, and have instant playmates, giving you a break. If you already have a number of pets, have children, or work many hours, your schedule and lifestyle may not permit raising two puppies with ease. But if your lifestyle is more flexible or less demanding, this can be a rewarding experience.

Dog-to-dog introductions

When introducing dogs to one another, be sensitive and alert to signs of stress or incompatibility. Supervise the interactions until you can be certain that the dogs have developed a good relationship. Recognize a balance between too much roughness and the natural behavior of dogs working out a social order. Allow them the opportunity to relate to each other as dogs will, but be sensitive to excessive behavior. During this adjustment period, it is important that you are patient and cautious. Rely on your intuition to assess the progress of the friendship.

ATTENTION

The key to establishing a peaceful and fun environment, and building friendships in the process, is to keep your first buddy confident in the knowledge that he is important. Letting your attention diminish because of the new family member produces jealousy in your first dog, which may create aggressive behavior and anxiety.

In "dogdom" there is no equality; there is a definite hierarchy, with one dog higher than the other. Your new dog will not suffer any psychological blow because you give the first dog more attention. As long as each animal receives plenty of affection and care, you should express to your first pet the special place that he holds in your heart. Showing your dog affection when the new dog is around helps make this point.

DOMINANCE ISSUES

The definite hierarchy in the social order of dogs means one will be in charge while the others form a ladder of authority behind him. This social ranking is flexible and varies according to the location, physical condition of the animals, perceived value of a possession, time of day, time of year, other people or animals present, and a myriad of other situations.

Upon attentive observation, you will discover that in some situations one of your dogs is more dominant and at other times is more submissive. One dog may be dominant when outside in the yard and more submissive indoors. One dog may be in charge of all food stuff but relinquish control over all toys.

This social order also changes with the age and health of the animals. As your dogs age and go through difficulties in life, you must be sensitive to new problems arising in their relationships. Bringing in a new animal companion, or the departing of one, will alter the dynamics of the group, so this is an especially important time to be aware.

Sometimes the dominance order of your dogs appears out of sync with your expectations. Your new dog may come into your home and take over your resident dog's superior position. Or more likely, you will feel that your resident dog is being intolerant and unkind to your new dog. You should not intervene. Feeling sorry for the lower-ranking dog and stepping in to create a democracy will only create problems. Your dominant dog should have his ranking reinforced by being fed first, going through the door first, and receiving your attention first. If he takes a toy or other item from the lower-ranking canine family member, let him have it. This can be difficult for our equality-based mind-set, but it is a necessary contribution to the peace of your household. You cannot change the social status of your dogs, and an attempt to do so will cause the dominant dog to feel threatened. Attempts to secure his position will result in fights amongst the dogs, so respect their social order.

If you have adopted a puppy, your adult dog will try to show the pup manners, and this should be accepted. If the adult gets too rough, then you should intervene, but let the two animals work out a system of hierarchy that is best for them. If your adult dog slaps the pup with a solid paw and turns him on his back, don't worry. The adult is just reminding the puppy who is in charge. Once the puppy understands this (usually just a couple of times will do it), then your adult dog will have established his superior ranking. If your adult dog is well adjusted and has a healthy mind, he will not get too rough with the baby. An adult will walk away rather than injure a puppy.

KEEPING ORDER

Although the dogs must develop their own social order amongst themselves, they must remember that you are still in charge. Demonstrate to them that your authority is not to be challenged. This means being fair on reprimands as well as affection. Any misbehavior, regardless of who started it, must be handled equally. If there is trouble, any dog that participates is disciplined. When play gets too rough, all must be placed in a "down-stay" position or separated until calm is once again restored. Make the rules, and then back them up with necessary action.

When you decide to bring another canine into the dynamics of your household, your dog must accept this. Do not let your pet for an instant think that the relationship is up to his discretion. Do not force the new dog on him, but make sure he understands that he has no room to question your actions. You brought this new family member into the home, and he must accept him. Even if the present dog does not want to interact and build a friendship with the new addition, he must cordially tolerate the existence of the newcomer.

If one dog is continually getting into mischief, he may be expressing a need for more attention. Keep an eye on the individual animal's behavior and use your intuition to let you know when one pet is not getting enough of your affection.

FORMAL INTRODUCTIONS

Think positively and be straightforward in your introductions. Act with authority and confidence. Remember, what you feel and think translates to your actions, even if subconsciously, and your animals sense your emotions.

Neutral Territory

If you can, introduce the dogs outside of your current dog's territory. If adopting a puppy, talk to the breeder about taking your adult dog to the breeder's home to make introductions. Take just the puppy you have decided on to a part of the property away from the other dogs. Here you can introduce them while they are busy checking out the new surroundings. If this is not possible, introduce the dogs in neutral territory such as a park or friend's yard. (If you are getting a puppy and he has not completed his vaccinations, it is important that the place where you introduce the dogs is free from contamination.)

A secure, fenced area where the two dogs can run works best. Psychologically, dogs tend to be more receptive and less worried about defending themselves when they are off leash in an open area.

If adopting a dog from a shelter, don't take your dog to the facility. You will have to be a good judge of canine character and predict the compatibility of the animals. With the help of a friend, take the two creatures to a neutral place for their first meeting. Again, a park or a friend's yard is ideal.

Adult and Puppy

If you have purchased a puppy and already have an adult dog at home, the adjustment should be easy. As previously mentioned, your established canine friend should be well trained (any dog in a multi-animal household should be reliable and consistent in following obedience requests) and should look to you to guide his behavior. Your new puppy will be rambunctious and may find it difficult to leave the more mature dog alone. A large dog or overzealous adult may accidentally harm the more vulnerable puppy during play. Be attentive and end any negative interaction before it has a chance to upset either dog.

Separate the dogs, and then introduce them to each other slowly in short sessions while you are present. Keep the stronger dog leashed so you can gain control if necessary, while verbally supporting the weaker dog. Keep your attitude positive during these meetings. Don't assume the worst, and don't make a war out of a battle. The more tense or excited you become, the more anxious the animals will be. Stay relaxed and keep a loose hold on the leash.

Confine the puppy for periods throughout the day to allow your established pet a break from the overwhelming energy of the puppy. While the puppy is confined, engage your established dog in an activity that he particularly enjoys. Remind him he is important, and give him the confidence and assurance to deal with the little devil once he is released.

As with any animal-to-animal introductions, you can use distraction to ward off problems before they become uncontrollable. Don't use frightening distractions — a toy, ball, someone calling the animals, or acting silly will distract them.

If your current dog is mature, sick, or physically weak, protect him from the rough play of a puppy. The younger, more vibrant dog may also try to dominate the established dog. This can be dangerous, and you must maintain control of the situation.

Praise the dogs when they are behaving in a hospitable manner. Offering food rewards may instigate competitive behavior, so avoid food treats while they are getting to know one another.

The First Meeting

Introducing two adult dogs may be more complex than introducing a puppy and adult. Opposite-sex introductions tend to go a bit smoother than same-sex introductions. Also, if the dogs are neutered or spayed, you will have an easier time.

If you cannot find a secure, open area for the introduction, keep them on a loose lead. Let the dogs relax while meeting. Tugging on the dog's neck creates tension and aggression. The leash is only a reminder for your dog that you are in charge, and it gives you some control when needed. A tight leash doesn't solve problems; it creates them. You can place your dog in a down-stay if he is wary of new animals or is overly playful. Once you see that everything is going well, you can release your dog from his down-stay and let him and the new dog explore and play. Supervise the interaction, and end it anytime one of the animals becomes tense or tired. Keep everything

as positive as possible from the beginning and prevent hard feelings from developing.

If you presently have more than one dog, introduce each dog to the addition separately. It would be quite stressful and could result in a "gang" mentality if all dogs were thrown together to get to know one another.

BODY LANGUAGE (GETTING TO KNOW YOU)

You can use the dogs' body language to assess how the introduction is progressing. When two dogs first meet, they make contact with their noses. They can immediately tell if the other is a friend or foe. They will follow nose-to-nose contact with a sniff of the anal region. The self-confident dog will readily allow other canines to smell his anal area. If the two dogs meet, stand next to each other, sniff each other's behinds, and wag their tails, they are accepting each other, and their relationship is off to a good start. They may work things out quickly, but keep an eye on them to analyze the possibility of a developing friendship.

If one is timid and one is stiff or has his hair up, then watch them closely. If one dog is showing signs of submission (crouching, rolling on his back, tucking his tail, or lowering head and ears), then they have established a power hierarchy. Just watch for oversubmission and overdominance. If one dog is pawing at the other one and the other is showing no signs of submission but is instead getting irritated or expressing dominance, watch closely; you may need to separate them. Any sign of mounting behavior should be discouraged. Mounting is not only sexual but also a demonstration of dominance. If one dog submits to the more dominant dog, then everything will be fine. If both dogs want to be in charge and call the shots, then they could be heading for a fight.

If a dog fight breaks out, the first thing you should do is the hardest — stay calm. Yelling and frantically trying to separate them will only encourage their excitement and can get you seriously injured. To break up a dog fight, separate the dogs by grabbing a back leg or the base of a tail and pull them apart. This way you will less likely get bit. If you have a hose or water, spray or splash them to get them apart. Give your companion time to calm down, and never give the instigator attention, even negative attention. Don't try to reprimand, sweet talk, or in any other way interact with your pet until he is completely calm and relaxed. He will be too excited and may not be reliable in his actions.

ONCE AT HOME

When you bring the new dog home, he will be entering the territory of your present dog. Some disagreements may arise, depending on the territoriality of your current pet. Watch the animals closely, taking the introductions in small, controlled stages and going only at the pace the dogs dictate. Only allow them time together when you can supervise. Keep up this pattern for a couple of days. It may be necessary to continue this level of supervision for a week or so. This is a good technique to ensure that everything is going smoothly, and it keeps you in control.

Be fair to the animals and provide them each a place to feel secure and unintimidated in your home. Your first dog should be able to relax in his spot without worrying that he needs to protect it.

FOOD AS A TOOL

Because food is so important, you can use mealtime as a tool for building a relationship between your dogs. The level of peace accompanying mealtime can also be used as a gauge to determine the amount of acceptance growing between the animals.

Begin by feeding them at the same time in the same room but at different corners. If all goes well, maintain this schedule a couple of weeks before asking for more closeness. One dog may finish before the other and try to take over the food dish. Be sensitive to any stress the animals may be experiencing. Never ask for more closeness than the dogs are comfortable with. If necessary, separate them with a gate.

If even seeing each other causes anxiety, you may have to feed them in different rooms until their relationship is more tolerable. If you must go to these extremes, you will be working with challenging dynamics. However, if you've been careful in your choices, you will probably not experience this level of discord.

Later they may willingly share their food, and then you know you have a strong friendship blooming.

ONE LAST WORD

If nothing you do has helped the two dogs get along, you must take action; read the section "If it just isn't working" in chapter 5. If you are careful about the breed and characteristics of the dog you choose, prepare your environment carefully, and have well-behaved and obedient pets, you should have little difficulty. Most importantly, you must be committed and truly believe that the two animals can live together peacefully. Assist the dogs in developing a good friendship with patience and perseverance. Support each dog by expressing your affection fairly and consistently.

Caring for more than one cat can be quite a pleasure. Cats often welcome the companionship of another of their kind.

Multiple cats

Having two or more cats in one home is not much more trouble than having one. The main criteria, other than your time, is having enough room for each cat to find a secure, quiet place all his own. If you are able to provide this, then living with multiple cats will be a rewarding experience.

If you have more than two cats, you need to add another litter box. If you have two or three cats sharing the same litter box, you must clean out the waste at least twice a day and scrub it thoroughly once a week. Multiple cats make a bigger mess at the litter box, and they also make a bigger mess eating and cost you more in food.

If you believe you could easily handle these things and you don't have a problem providing additional time for loving and grooming, then adding another cat to your household will probably be a pleasant experience for you and your feline friend.

FELINE SOCIAL ORDER

Cats do not have the same kind of dominance contests that dogs do. Cats have an autocratic ranking system: each is "top cat" of his territory. They like to know and claim territory, but often this is as simple as a window sill. They allow other cats to share the spot if they so desire, but the others will be there by the grace of the "top cat." The ruling cat of the territory — be it the immediate area, the room, or the floor of the house — even considers *you* under his sovereignty. This system is fluid and the cats often rearrange and redefine territory. One of my cats changes his territory every few weeks (for example, a box, the top of my dresser, or a pillow on the bed). Each cat needs his own territory to be psychologically healthy, but this is an easy requirement for you to fulfill if your home is large enough for the number of cats who share it.

Cats mark their territory by scratching or spraying. They also rub a special gland of their chin or forehead on the periphery of their chosen territory. They repeat the same path daily, walking the rim, and renewing their boundary claim. They get bored of the same area and enlarge the edges of their territory again and again. If they are allowed outdoors, your cats may claim your yard and expand to include your neighbor's yard or the whole block. You may witness any level of this territoriality in your furry friends.

SHARING FOOD

Because a rigid social order or hierarchy does not exist with our domestic cats, multiple cats can share one dish. Placing each cat's serving on a different edge of the plate gives them space. I prefer to offer enough plates for each and let them work it out among themselves. With only a couple of cats, it is not much work to offer each a plate. If you give them something especially tantalizing, such as a piece of meat, you will find that they will more forcefully defend their share, so make sure each gets the same amount.

I adopted one cat, Mendy, when she was around ten years old; she still will not eat with the cats I had first. They accept her, but she just gets too stressed to eat in the same area, so I feed her in her own spot. Sometimes it's better on the animals if you don't push an issue, especially when it is an uncomplicated one.

BALANCING DIFFERENT PERSONALITIES

If you already have a cat and want to adopt another, consider the personality of your current cat when finding the best feline friend for him.

If your cat likes to nap and hang out at the highest areas of your house, look for a cat that likes to lay low so they won't compete for the same prime rest areas. If your cat is a snugly ball of fur that demands extensive affection and your time is restricted, adopt a cat that is a clown and enjoys the entertainment value of life with humans versus the cuddle value. If your current feline resident is older and beginning to slow down a bit, a calm, loving mature cat would create less stress and be easier on the delicate senses of the older cat. The same would be true if your cat is sickly or has a physical limitation.

If you have a cat who lounges around most of the day, inactive to the point of obesity, consider a playful, young kitten that will interest your couch potato in a game of chase. If the cat you live with is driving you crazy because he is so energetic and constantly inviting you to romp, another cat with the same energy level will keep him entertained and out of your way. A new cat may even tire out the little devil. If you want to add a cat to a home that already has cats, a playful, calm, and easygoing cat will readily adapt. Other personality types require more patience but will also adapt and be a joy.

Cat-to-cat introductions

Introducing two cats to each other often takes patience. Cats who have outgoing personalities easily adapt to new situations, but generally cats take more time than other animals to become accustomed to alterations in their lifestyle. Cats are sensitive enough to changes that you would be doing yourself and your resident cats a favor by having someone other than a family member bring home an animal addition. This saves you from being the bad person who brings home the "intruder." It may appear extreme, but many cats are so sensitive that this eases their emotional acceptance of the newcomer.

Give your cats time to feel comfortable with their new situation. The new cat probably needs several weeks to feel at ease, and your first cat may find it difficult to accept a new member in the family. Be understanding and sympathetic.

CONTINUING ATTENTION

As when introducing dogs to one another, maintaining your present level of attention and affection to your first cat is essential. Helping your cat feel confident that his place in the home has not been reassigned can be accomplished by lavishing attention on him and reminding him how much you love him. Always say hello to your established cat first. It helps the acceptance process if you also tell your cat how wonderful "his" new friend is. Even if he doesn't understand English, he will sense the meaning of your words through your voice and will at least appreciate some encouraging verbal praise.

SHARING ESSENTIALS

In the beginning, you need to provide a separate litter box in a different location for the new kitten. After the cats have gotten to know one another and are comfortable with each other, they can share a litter box. Keep your resident cat's litter box in the same spot with the same litter to lessen his anxiety.

If the new cat has been using a different litter material than you are presently using, offer him a litter box with the familiar litter. This can help ease the transition and increase the confidence in elimination habits. Purchase both kinds of litter, and give each cat the kind he is accustomed to.

Changing the food that the cats have been eating can also cause anxiety. Purchase the same food that the previous owners have been feeding your new addition. Later, after the cats have settled into a routine and the acclimation period is over, you can begin making changes that make life easier on you. Adjustment is stressful, so reduce the trauma by not changing everything at once.

QUARANTINES

Be certain the cat you are adopting does not have an undiagnosed contagious disease or illness. If you take your new pet to the veterinarian on the way home, make sure he or she knows you have other cats. If your veterinarian suspects trouble, you will be advised on the best course of action. He or she must wait until the results of blood panels and other diagnostic tests have been performed to get a clear picture of your cat's health, so quarantine your new pet by keeping his food and litter separated. Food and litter boxes are where contaminants are more likely to be transmitted. Think of the quarantine as an extra safety precaution until you are assured all is well.

I learned this safety precaution the hard way after I brought Mendy home. It was the next week when I took her to my veterinarian for a routine visit to get an idea of her health and update her shots, and I was a bit concerned about her bloated stomach.

My veterinarian suspected Mendy had Feline Infectious Peritonitis (FIP), a highly contagious disease that presently has no cure. I was suddenly confronted with the possibility of losing all my cats. I was angry with myself for allowing them to interact before securing the health of all involved. I was fully aware of the concept of quarantine because of my involvement with birds, but I had failed to apply the same logic to my other animals.

After many tests, some patient waiting (with all the animals separated), and a good-sized veterinary bill, Mendy wasn't seriously ill. I was relieved and smarter.

INTERACTION AMONG THE FELINE RESIDENTS

Before you bring home another cat, make sure that all the cats' claws have been trimmed. If the cats end up brawling, you want to diminish the possibility of injury.

Assume your present cat will accept a newcomer. If you allow your cat outdoors, you may have witnessed him chasing away any strange cats. This should not be taken as a sign of your cat's inability to relate to a new friend. He may eventually find an addition you bring into the house to be a playmate and friend.

Take It Slow

Some cats immediately interact, challenging each other and deciding who will be boss. Others investigate briefly and then act as if the new cat has been there for months. Because most cats need quite a bit of time to adjust to new situations, some may hide and act fearful for days or weeks. Try not to pressure these creatures. Give them time and patience. Try to coax them out with loving words and special treats, patience, and sensitivity.

If the new cat stays in one particular room and hides, shut the door to that room and give him some time to build up his confidence and get curious about what's happening on the other side of the door.

Cats separated in this manner may first become acquainted by sniffing each other through the crack under the door. After a couple of days or a week or so, remove the cat from the room if you can without force. Confine the other cats in a room and let the frightened one out to explore so he can accustom himself to the smells of the other cats. If the established cats are closed off in the same room where the frightened one was confined, they will get a chance to check out the newcomer's smells.

Another tool for sharing the odors among the resident felines is a towel. Rub a towel on each cat, especially after grooming. Using the same towel on each cat transfers their scents amongst each other. Getting them used to the scent of a strange cat goes a long way in creating friendships.

Becoming Friends

When things seem to be calming down, let all the cats wander around the house together. If there is still some disagreement or anxiety, let them mingle for only a couple of hours. Increase the time at each subsequent visit as they relax around each other. This visiting should be supervised until you are sure they each respect one another.

Encourage your cats to become friends by creating a situation in which they need to look to each other for guidance — give them a new experience to explore together. Add something new to the room where they like to hang out, such as a new scratching post or climbing tree. Add a potted catnip plant for them to enjoy together. Take them for a ride in the car; crate each cat separately but place the crates next to each other. The strangeness and somewhat scary adventure of going for a car ride can encourage the cats to turn to each other for comfort. This strategy also works with rabbits.

It may take months before complete acceptance is realized; it may take minutes. Here is another situation in which your intuition as caretaker is the guiding force in your quest for peace and harmony.

If you persevere and let the cats develop their own social structure while providing them with plenty of space to retire from each other, they will develop a peaceful relationship. They may even find that they enjoy each other's company and become great friends.

Multiple birds

Pet birds are demanding and delightful creatures. Birds, especially parrots, require consistent patience; they are intelligent, emotional, and sensitive animals who need your devotion and loyalty.

Those who own birds are a special kind of people, and it seems many who have one want another. There are so many different kinds of birds, and they are all beautiful and have traits that are unique to their species. Throughout history, some people have had the urge to "collect" birds. Be forewarned; before you know it, you may get in too deep. One or two birds are wonderful; dozens can take over your life.

If you don't have a bird, start by adopting only one and live with this individual creature for a year or two. Understand the emotional complexity of your feathered charge, and give your lifestyle and your future lifestyle much consideration.

This isn't meant to scare loving, capable caretakers into bird rejection. It is only meant to remind you that pet birds are sensitive and demanding. Certainly it is possible to have more than one bird if you realize what will be required to do so. If you are willing and ready, birds are wonderful animals that thrive in loving homes.

CONSIDERATIONS TO PONDER

Birds are messy with their food, newspaper, feathers, feather dust, and water. Each bird must have ample time out of his cage each day. This means providing a perch area for every parrot. Parrots need to share your mealtime (more on this in chapter 4), and having more than one parrot somewhere close to your dinner table when you eat may create bad feelings with the people of the house. Would two or more birds next to the table have some people feeling like guests in an aviary? How do you and everyone in your family feel about this?

You can expect a bird to be noisy a couple of times a day. It is unrealistic to have a feathered friend and expect silence. Making a ruckus is a bird's way of being alive. When a couple of birds begin competing with one another, you greatly increase the decibel level of your home. How about your neighbors? They may not be bothered by the sweet chirping of a few songbirds, but many parrot species are loud — very loud — by nature. Even seemingly spacious distances between houses become closer with the cry of a macaw or cockatoo.

MATE AND FRIEND

If you plan to get your bird a mate, you then become a breeder. This is another responsibility altogether. You will need to invest much time and effort into research and have the help of a trustworthy, experienced friend who is already breeding and raising birds.

If you want to get another bird to keep your present pet company but don't plan to breed them, there are several considerations to keep in mind. Most avian experts would not put two different species in the same cage or put a small bird in with a larger bird. If you want to try to pair two birds together, a very large cage will be necessary.

If you are able to create a situation where two birds can live happily together in one cage, they may not find you as emotionally necessary. Although some birds in breeding situations may seek interaction with their human, even while raising babies, this is the exception and not the rule. If you are consistent in your affection, your birds may still turn to you for attention even though they have each other to fulfill their emotional needs.

This lack of dependency on your attention creates less intense demands on your time, but you can lose your bird as a pet if he decides he would rather not have anything to do with you and focuses his attention on his feathered buddy. They may even unite in an effort to rid "their" home of the "intruder" — you.

A bird does not rely only on another of his kind for company. Having other pets in the house, as long as the animals don't pester or frighten the bird while he is in his cage, will keep him company throughout the day and provide distraction and entertainment.

Bird-to-bird introductions

PREPARING YOUR RESIDENT BIRD

Sally Blanchard, a highly respected bird behaviorist, suggests a wonderful way to prepare birds for the introduction of newly adopted birds. This method also works with other animals in your household. Before bringing home your new addition, arrange his cage as it will be when he moves in by placing it in the appropriate spot and furnishing it with perches, dishes, and toys. Put food in the bowls, such as seed or pellets, to help the other creatures in the house get used to the smells.

Your present pets can then become accustomed to this strange addition to the living space. Your resident bird will be curious and intrigued by the new presence. By the time the genuine feathered creature makes his appearance, your resident bird will be less traumatized. The effort you make before you bring the new bird home desensitizes your present bird, and you will soften the change by exposing him first to the physical difference and then to the realization of another bird sharing your affection.

QUARANTINE: AN ASSURANCE OF HEALTH

A new addition should be separated from your present bird to safeguard the health of both birds. A quarantine for at least thirty days is a must. During this period, keep them strictly segregated. Wash your hands thoroughly with antibacterial soap between interactions with each bird and change your top layer of clothing after handling each bird. Keep all dishes and equipment separated.

Before bringing your new feathered friend into your home, have an avian veterinarian perform all necessary laboratory procedures. Trying to save money now can cost you later if you introduce an illness into your home. At the end of the quarantine period, have the entire process repeated. Also having your resident bird checked by your veterinarian is a good safety precaution to assure that both of your birds are in optimum health and ready for the stress of introductions. Once both birds get their health clearance from your avian veterinarian, introductions can begin.

INTRODUCTIONS

Introduce the birds slowly and cautiously. Keep them in separate cages, but let them see and hear each other from a safe distance. Placing their cages across the room from one another or in close rooms allows them visual and auditory contact. Once they are accustomed to having another bird around you can allow them to be closer.

Eventually the two birds can be in the same room in side-by-side cages. Move the cages closer and closer to each other as the birds adapt. Some people immediately put the cages next to each other, but this may cause too much stress for sensitive birds, and you won't know how yours will respond until he is placed in these circumstances. For precaution and ease of adaptation, start off slowly and take your time.

Meeting Each Other

When the birds have gotten a chance to become accustomed to one another, place each on separate play stands in different areas of the same room. Be there to supervise, making sure that one bird does not force himself on the other too soon. Keep an eye on the stress level and place an anxious bird in his cage allowing him to relax. If you do not push the birds too quickly and keep your energy level low, your bird will eventually accept the newcomer. How long this takes will depend on the personality of your birds. Never force them to interact or tolerate each other beyond their levels of acceptance.

Your birds may become great feathered buddies and enjoy each other's companionship when they are on the play stands for free time. They may cuddle and play or tease and taunt, and their interactions will delight you. Never forget the three keys of the peaceable kingdom (accept each as an individual, maintain a positive attitude, and be faithful to your determination) when dealing with multiple birds, and you will discover a special relationship on whatever level the birds decide is best for them.

If It Does Not Get Better

If the birds will not befriend each other and cannot tolerate even being in the same room, take measures to keep them apart. Keep them in separate cages in separate rooms. Allow them each their own free time on the play stand. This means creating a schedule and making an effort to assure that each bird gets plenty of playtime.

Jealousy is often the culprit that keeps the birds from tolerating each other. You can do much to ease this by continuing to give them as much attention as normal, maybe even a bit more than usual for your resident bird. Keep your mental images positive; birds are incredibly sensitive to your emotions and thoughts. Give the birds treats while they are behaving on their play stands. Ignore any attempts to win your attention by birdie antics and misbehaviors. Stay in control of the situation by doling out affection as reward for good behavior.

Multiple rabbits

Rabbits have complex social structures with a definite hierarchy system. Because their social life is so complex, it can be a challenge to find two rabbits that are compatible with each other. But many multiple rabbits become quite good friends, and rescue homes exist where a dozen or more rabbits have established mostly peaceful complex societies. A multi-rabbit household can be successful using the keys of a peaceable kingdom.

Rabbit-rabbit relationships aren't the only ones that can develop. Rabbits have been notorious for developing quality friendships with cats (see the "Cats and rabbits" section later). Some people who have lived with rabbits for many years believe that a rabbit-cat relationship is less stressful for the rabbit. Because of the inherent hierarchical relationship between rabbits, it is often easier for a rabbit and a cat to be friends than a rabbit and another rabbit.

DIMINISHING AFFECTION?

Some rabbit guardians claim that two rabbits are not as affectionate toward the people in their lives. This may be in part because the owner does not spend as much time with the pets, knowing that they are not as lonely. Experience in many multiple-rabbit households has demonstrated that rabbits still want your love and attention as long as you are consistent with your affection.

The other factor that keeps your rabbit interested in your interaction is establishing a great relationship in the beginning. If you and your resident rabbit have been great television cuddle-bunnies, adding another rabbit will not lessen his desire for quality snuggle time with you.

BALANCING DIFFERENT PERSONALITIES

If you want to have two rabbits, the most successful combination is a spayed female and a neutered male. Two unneutered males will fight aggressively. Two unspayed, unrelated females will also fight but will be less aggressive than their male counterparts. If you know you want to get two rabbits at the same time, purchasing two females from the same litter, raising them together, and getting them both spayed when they are old enough work out quite well, and there are usually few problems in the friendship.

If you don't have the rabbits spayed and neutered, you will have many baby rabbits. The rate of rabbit reproduction is legendary and factual. Having a litter of rabbits contributes to the vast number of throw-aways. Additionally, the care, time, and money needed to raise a litter of healthy babies are great. It is a large responsibility with many possible hardships.

The difficulty in raising two babies at the same time is the same as raising two baby animals of any kind. It is more work getting two animals accustomed to your lifestyle. Training is more intense when you are trying to keep two baby rabbits from chewing stereo speaker wires at different ends of the living room. Two rabbits learning how to use their litter box will make twice the mess. These are considerations to think about before bringing home two adorable baby rabbits.

Rabbit-to-rabbit introductions

ASSURING THE HEALTH OF THE RABBITS

Before allowing your rabbits contact with each other, have them visit your veterinarian. If you know your resident rabbit is healthy, take the new adoption to the clinic for a thorough health examination. Have your new rabbit tested for contagious diseases before you bring him home.

A quarantine period of thirty days is a smart practice. Use this period to observe the health and personality of your new friend. Don't stick him in a back room and forget him though; he needs your reassurance and affection. Between feeding, caring, and cuddling with one rabbit, thoroughly scrub your hands with antibacterial soap and change your shirt. Make sure each rabbit has his own food and water bottle or dish.

EASING THE ADJUSTMENT PERIOD

Begin introductions by accustoming the rabbits to each other's presence. Place the cages in the same room so the rabbits are able to observe each other going about their daily business. Don't let them out together at this time; give them a week or so to get comfortable with each other in the safety of their cages. The new rabbit is going to need a few days to adjust, so don't disturb him too much by increasing his anxiety. Talk gently to both rabbits.

You may witness some territory claiming by one rabbit leaving his scent or dropping in areas he is claiming to be his own. Both males and females will exhibit this behavior. Just clean it up without a fuss. As the rabbits work out their relationship, the behavior will diminish, and responsible litter box habits will return.

The introduction of two rabbits can have many interesting beginnings. Rabbits are unique individuals, each with their own tastes in friendship. Their budding relationship can be spontaneous or can take months or years to develop. Patience and sensitivity are required during this period.

NEUTRAL TERRITORY

Prepare a neutral place for the rabbits' first physical interaction. Choose a room that can easily be closed off. The rabbits should be close enough to one another that they are forced to deal with each other. If the room is large, they can hide at different ends of the space and ignore each other.

Put both rabbits in the room together as you supervise and referee. Protect yourself from claws and teeth by wearing gloves and a long-sleeved shirt.

If they immediately begin to fight, separate them quickly. The next time you let them in the same room together have a harness and leash on each of them. Limit their exposure time to just a couple of minutes and be prepared to separate them. If their fighting only consists of a couple of nips and some chasing, let them work it out together. Step in and separate them only if there is hair flying or one of the rabbits is getting hurt or frightened.

ASSISTING THE FRIENDSHIP

Let the rabbits become friends at their own pace. If you do anything to intervene at this point, you will never be truly sure they have worked out their own relationship. Moving the rabbits and placing them next to each other is pushy and they may not be ready. So sit back and be patient.

Keeping your energy level low helps. Think in positive images; visualize the two rabbits sitting side by side napping in a warm corner, and your positive images will keep everyone calm.

As the rabbits become accustomed to one another, you can lengthen the time they spend together. Gradually increase this period of interaction until they are peaceful for a full hour. Once your rabbits are able to stay in the room together for this length of time without any confrontations, let them alone and leave the room. Be patient about taking this step; don't rush things. Check on your pets from time to time, making sure that everything is going well. This level of tolerance can take days, weeks, or months. Take each step slowly, increasing exposure as each rabbit is able to accept it with ease. Rely on your instinct to best determine when it is right to proceed to the next level of exposure.

CONFRONTING OBSTACLES

When problems arise, think of them as opportunities to improve and learn and the experience will be positive. Great animal guardians are creative individuals who are able to find solutions to an array of problems and discover the unexpected benefit of difficult situations. An obstacle is not a guarantee of failure, it is an exciting challenge in the adventure. Your thoughts determine if you will be frustrated and doomed or successful and happy.

BEING FRIENDS

If you are fortunate, the two rabbits may get along from the start. They may run to each other and be the best of friends from the first moment — grooming each other immediately. This is delightful if it happens, but remember it is still stressful for your animals. Even if they get along well from the beginning, limit their time together to twenty minutes. Give this schedule a couple of days to a week so the animals are not too stressed. Then go to the hour-long supervised sessions, eventually proceeding to unsupervised playtime.

More than likely, the introduction will fall somewhere between the two extremes of immediate acceptance and outright hostility. Your rabbits will probably be somewhat cautious, examining and investigating each other curiously. Their friendship will develop as they eventually engage in mutual behaviors, such as eating together and playing.

If they sit by each other and snuggle and groom one another, they are ready to share a home and sleep in the same cage. They are now officially rabbit buddies! Their interactions will be intriguing, and you will find that there is no love like bunny love.

Dogs and cats

The strained relationship between dogs and cats is legendary but not rooted in reality. Dogs and cats do not have the in-bred hostility that most people believe. Some breeds of dogs have a high predatory instinct and chase anything that is smaller or moving quickly, and frightened cats often move quickly. Some cat breeds or individual felines are high-strung and nervous, and just the sight of another animal can cause panic. Individuals may be hostile or just nervous around the other animal, but this is not a rule.

It is more important, and makes a greater impact on the relationships of different species, to take into consideration the individual temperament of the animals instead of making generalizations. Some dogs and cats just don't seem to like each other. Some cats will be aggressive or bossy or ignore a dog that just wants to be friends.

DIFFERENCES IN SOCIAL ORDER

To cats, physical place is all important. To dogs, social place is all important. This difference in emphasis helps your dog and cat get along better — they will not be competing for the same vital "place." As long as the dog accepts the cat's dominance over territory, and most readily do, they develop a system that works for them.

It is difficult for dogs and cats to understand one another. Their means of communication differ in many important aspects. A dog wagging his tail would be interpreted as friendly and playful if the recipient of that communication understood the meaning. To a cat, a wagging tail is a signal of hostility or rage, or a warning of aggression. A dog will lift his paw gesturing that he wants to play, but a raised paw to a cat is a threat. You can see that the possibilities of miscommunication between cats and dogs are great.

If a dog and cat are raised together, their wonderful intelligence and intuitive senses help them understand each other. If they can communicate among themselves, you will not be needed as a mediator as often.

ADULT DOG AND KITTEN

If you are introducing an adult dog to a kitten, you will find that a good-natured, well-trained dog accepts the cat as a member of the family quite easily. Be careful to protect the kitten from the exuberance of your dog because a playful canine can accidentally injure or unnecessarily frighten the kitten. Show your dog that you expect him to be gentle and move slowly around the kitten. Put your dog in a down-stay while the kitten and dog explore nose to nose. Supervise their interactions until the kitten is old enough to run and escape if your dog gets too pushy or rough.

The critical learning time for a kitten is when he is two to seven weeks old. This is the time he forms everlasting impressions of the world around him. Interactions during this time influence his opinions for the rest of his life. Encounters with dogs should be as pleasant and positive as possible; therefore, inquire about the experiences the kitten had before you adopt him.

Even positive experiences shared during this

critical time can be offset later in life by a bad experience. If your cat later has a near-death encounter with a dog, or even just a very scary one, it may make him shy of dogs and negate any of the positive influence he received earlier. Protect him the best you can in order to maintain harmony.

ADULT CAT AND PUPPY

Introducing an adult cat to a puppy can be hard on the cat. Puppies are rambunctious and full of energy. The puppy may chase the cat, so be prepared by first letting them meet each other while the puppy is on a loose leash. If the puppy is younger than twelve weeks his neck is not fully developed and using force on a collar can be dangerous, so use a halter. Keep the meetings between the two animals as short and friendly as possible.

Confining your puppy is necessary at times. This is good for your cat; it gives him time to roam about the house, surveying his territory. If you keep your puppy separated with a gate or in an exercise pen, your cat can safely investigate the puppy if he is so inclined.

The critical imprint learning time for puppies is between three and twelve weeks old. To give a puppy the best beginning with your cats, adopt one during this stage of his development (after he is eight weeks old, of course). He will be at his most impressionable age, and you can influence his attitude toward cats as well as other animals. Show him how wonderful cats can be and make his interactions with felines positive.

SHARED MEALTIMES

During their scheduled mealtimes, each animal needs to feel safe and relaxed while eating. An animal who feels like he needs to defend his food is under much stress. Initially, the animals should be fed in separate areas. If they become good friends later, they may eat together, but you will have to be a good judge of character. Your dog may "wolf" down his food, finishing before your cat. If your dog eyes him impatiently, it may make your cat nervous. They may be best friends and yet need separate eating areas. However, eating in the same room with comfort is a good

indication that the relationship of the animals is developing into a trusting and rewarding one. My cat eats on a three-foot-high ledge in the same room as the dogs. The height gives her a sense of security.

Cats and dogs have been known to eat from the same bowl (although not wise nutritionally), and many share water bowls. If it happens on its own, great; but never force this kind of sharing. Your animals may not reach that level of comfort but still be tolerant and trustworthy enough to stay in the house together unsupervised.

WHEN YOU ARE GONE

What do you do with your dog and cat when you are not home? The level of confidence you have in your pets' relationship is based on your observation of how peaceful their contact has been. Knowing your animals well enables you to gauge the quality of their interactions. If your cat is at a disadvantage because he is older, disabled, or sick, you should never leave him alone in the house with your dog. If there is any rowdiness, he may not be able to escape, and if you have multiple dogs, they may exhibit pack behavior, and your cat will be at risk. Leaving the house just to get the mail can be long enough for serious trouble to occur.

Keeping Pets Separated

If you feel the animals are best separated in your absence, especially at the beginning of the relationship, you must find a place where they can be secure. Lock them in separate rooms with access to water, a bed or good resting place, and a couple of toys. Your cats will also need a litter box. Unless you feel it is time for more togetherness, don't let laziness take over — separate them. Make sure everyone in your family and any caretakers, such as sitters, understand the situation and are dedicated to keeping peace by separating the animals.

Interaction

If your pets are getting along well and there have been no negative encounters, it may be time to increase their periods alone together. Rely on your intuition as well as your perception of the relationship. Inspecting the environment and examining the attitude of the animals after you return will give you an indication if the time you were away was uneventful. Does your cat seem anxious and flighty? Is your dog barreling toward the door, wagging his tail in excitement? Are there plants knocked over and pillows all over the floor? If so, there was a lot of activity while you were gone. Perform a thorough examination of your pets; check for any scratches or punctures. If there are no outwardly physical signs, there may be internal injuries from falls or hard bumps, so keep a close eye on the animals for a couple of days. At any sign of change in normal daily habits or personality, immediately take the animal to your veterinarian and explain the situation.

If your dog chases the cat in your absence, he probably has fun, and the behavior is rewarding enough to continue. Trusting him until you are certain he has learned differently is impossible. Go back to the beginning of introductions and start from scratch. Sign up for a refresher obedience course, or work at home for ten to fifteen minutes a day with the basic commands to gain control and remind your dog who he should be looking to for guidance.

Dogs and birds

. . . .

CAUTION

Dogs should not be trusted alone with uncaged pet birds. If you live with a dog and a bird, your bird should have a safe, secure cage. Even when there are a couple of people around watching your dog and bird, a split-second encounter can end in tragedy. Some birds rule the roost, bossing the dog around; however, this bird-dog combination is the exception. More often caretakers become too complacent and comfortable and lose a precious feathered friend as a result. A bird does not have a chance against a large or determined dog. Use absolute caution.

Aggressive dog breeds are even more of a threat to your bird. Birds can be noisy and irritating, even to a dog. If you don't have a dog, your neighbors or friends may bring their dog to visit. Never let your guard down. Even if your bird is a large, boisterous macaw, he can be injured.

Taking your pet bird outdoors without a carrier can get him into trouble. A strange dog or cat can quickly hurt or kill a bird that flutters from your shoulder. If the dog is particularly aggressive, he may even attack your bird while you are holding him. Don't assume that you know all the animals in your neighborhood. Strange dogs will roam from far away and surprise you. It is not worth the risk.

EMOTIONAL CONSIDERATIONS

Consider the emotional state of your resident bird before adopting a dog. If your bird has had a bad experience with dogs and is a sensitive creature, a dog may upset him terribly and cause unnecessary stress. Decide whether he can handle the antics of a dog beforehand.

If your bird's history is unknown, experiment with a trial run. Invite a friend and his or her bird-socialized dog over to see how your bird reacts. Make sure the dog is gentle and calm. If at any point the dog comes rushing over, banging or pushing at the cage of an anxious bird, you may have destroyed any opportunity for the bird's adapting to a dog. Make the experience a positive one.

A curious or nonchalant reaction by your feathered friend can indicate the possibility of a positive experience. On the other hand, if the bird panics and becomes nervous or agitated, you know the introduction will be difficult and possibly unsuccessful.

AGE COMBINATIONS

If adopting a puppy, show him how to respect a feathered creature. Allowing behavior that seems cute in a small puppy can encourage deadly behavior in a full-grown dog. Make your baby dog treat the bird as you want him to throughout his life.

By adopting an adult dog, you may have an idea of how the dog has reacted to birds in the past. If the dog has not had any negative experiences, there is a greater possibility he will treat the bird with respect. If you don't know your dog's history, you must approach the introductions slowly so that you can get a clear idea how his behavior may affect your bird.

If you are bringing a bird into an established dog household, many of the same rules apply.

Investigate, as much as possible, the history of the bird. Knowing if there have been any negative experiences in his life will help you predict his adaptability. A baby bird should readily accept your dog. Good bird breeders raise their baby birds to be accustomed to the sights and sounds of many different situations, dogs included. Even if he has never been around a dog before, a baby bird will become accustomed to one without much difficulty.

INITIAL INTRODUCTIONS

Begin by preparing your resident animal friend for the new arrival as suggested in the "Multiple Birds" section.

When making the first introductions, have the dog on the leash and your bird in its cage above ground level. Walk your dog up to the cage and place him in a "sit-stay" position. The bird will be higher than the dog, which gives your bird a sense of security, especially with the cage as protection. Have treats available and reward your dog for being calm and gentle. Talk reassuringly to your bird. If your bird is territorial, he may lunge at the dog. Neither animal should have a bad experience, so if the initial introduction does not go smoothly, stop the interaction and try again later.

Once they begin relaxing and losing interest in each other, you know they have accepted the other as a permanent fixture in the environment. You can allow the dog to wander in the room on his own free will. However, remain sensitive to changes in the relationship; new stresses may surface later. As long as there is no aggression or taunting, their friendship will probably be stable.

SUPERVISING FREEDOM

Your bird will spend time outside of his cage on a play gym or stand, and your dog must know to respect the space of your feathered friend. As long as your dog has manners, doesn't eye the bird with roasted turkey in his mind, and sees that you are always there to supervise, there should be no trouble in letting the bird out with the dog in the room.

Your dog and bird should not interact physically. Again, there are exceptions to the rule, but this is an area in which caution cannot be overempha-

sized. Discourage your feathered friend from leaving his stand, especially if there are other animals in the house. If the bird flutters from his perch and runs around on the floor, take extra precautions. Every time your bird leaves his play stand, calmly, without fanfare, place him in his cage for five minutes. Then let him out again. He wants to be with you, and he'll catch on shortly.

UNIQUE FRIENDSHIPS

Dogs and birds can develop interesting forms of interaction, and they may actually build a repertoire of games to play together. Many talking birds have even put Fido through his obedience lessons. The dogs often obey! Birds can also tease unsuspecting dogs or cats by dropping food and toys on them. Some birds go out of their way to lure the pitiful animal over to their perch or cage to do the dirty deed. Birds are intelligent animals that despise boredom; a good-natured dog or cat can provide quite a bit of entertainment for a creative bird.

Dogs and rabbits

Rabbits are dogs' natural prey, so great care must be taken in developing a relationship between these two animals. The quick movement of a rabbit triggers the hunting and herding instincts of dogs, and once a pursuit is on, it is difficult to stop. If your dog experiences the "thrill" of the chase, it will be almost impossible to completely trust your canine's ability to restrain himself. Many dogs and rabbits get along, and there are even dogs and rabbits that live together freely in the house. The caring guardians of these pets have invested a great deal of time and energy into making the relationship work. Their dogs have solid obedience training with rigid adherence to control commands.

A couple of commands will make the introductions and ensuing relationships easier to monitor. "Leave it" is a valuable tool. You give the command and the dog stops what he is about to do and looks to you for direction. "Gentle" and "easy" both tell your dog that it is okay to continue (sniffing, licking,

This puppy and rabbit are investigating each other through the safety of a wire exercise pen. Both animals are being gentle, curious, and confident.

looking) but remind him that he must move slowly and cautiously.

If your dog does not know his basic obedience commands, he is not ready for new animals to come to live with you. This is especially true for introductions to an animal, such as a rabbit, that is so vulnerable to abuse. A well-trained dog looks to you for guidance, and even if he would chase a wild rabbit in a flash, he can learn that the rabbit you introduce as part of the family is not to be chased.

INVESTIGATING EACH OTHER

When introducing a dog to a rabbit for the first time, have the rabbit in his cage and the dog on a loose lead. Have small bits of treats available for your dog.

Keep your energy level low and calm and think in positive images. The experience should be as pleasant as possible for both the dog and the rabbit. Take your time and expose them to each other with strict supervision.

Walk the dog up to the rabbit while he is in his cage. Whenever your dog is being calm and gently inquisitive, reward him with a treat. If he is moving fast or is excited, place him in a sit-stay by the cage so that he can look in and smell the rabbit and the rabbit can come to the side of the cage if he wants.

Resist the impulse to correct your dog; you want him to associate the rabbit with good experiences, not bad. Use the treats to reward his good behavior, and make it difficult for him to be bad in the first place.

If it's not going well or your rabbit is nervous, take the dog away. Don't be discouraged or hold it against them. Just be patient and try again later. Some dogs and rabbits become quick buddies, but others need time to develop tolerance toward each other. Acceptance comes with your perseverance.

INITIAL INTRODUCTIONS

After a few weeks of this tolerance, it will be time to introduce the animals to each other without the cage. Choose a room where you have control over where the rabbit goes. The room should be big enough so that the animals don't feel trapped and yet small enough so they can't ignore each other. Recruit someone to help you, and have him or her hold the rabbit while sitting on a chair. The rabbit should be at nose level or higher than the dog. With the dog on a leash and you with treats, walk the dog up to the rabbit. If your dog is calm and gentle, reward him and let the two animals smell and investigate each other. If he is a bit excited, ask for a sit-stay.

If all is going well, let the rabbit down to scurry about. Place your dog in a down-stay, and let the rabbit play in the enclosed room. Give your dog treats and reward him for being good. If he begins whimpering or shaking from excitement, distract him with words, affection, a toy, or treats.

The next step in the process is to release your dog from the down-stay and let him wander about the room. Progress to this stage gradually and have patience. Keep the leash on in case of emergencies and until you are certain that he will not chase your big-eared friend.

If you have multiple dogs, introduce each dog individually to the rabbit, allowing each relationship to develop at its own pace.

SAFETY FIRST

Be diligent about your supervision in the first weeks and months of introductions. Supervise their time together and if you leave the house, even for a couple of minutes, place your rabbit safely in his cage or confine your dog. Only you can judge the safety of your rabbit. Your level of involvement in the interactions of your dog and rabbit will be based on your perception of the risk. The friendship they share may be one of simple tolerance or it can be a closer relationship. Your animals will decide. What you decide is that they will get along.

If you proceed slowly from the start, the reward will be a happy animal friendship.

Cats and rabbits

Cats and rabbits can become great friends. Of all the interspecies relationships mentioned in this book, the cat-rabbit friendship appears to be the easiest to introduce and the most considerable in attachment. As mentioned in the "Multiple rabbits" section, some rabbits seem to prefer the company of a cat to the company of one of their own kind.

A common scenario is the rabbit that bosses the cat around. Many rabbits rule the hutch when it comes to "Mr. Paws." Unless your cat is quite a bit smaller than your rabbit and at risk simply because of the size difference, or unless your rabbit is truly nasty, let the two of them work it out on their own without undue intervention.

Cats are predators and therefore may view rabbits as their prey. This is especially true if the cat is considerably larger than the rabbit. Take this into consideration when you are contemplating adopting an animal. Pets of equal size may get along easier, but this is not a rule, and many combinations of different-sized pets have become good friends.

The cat may chase the rabbit, and this can have terrible consequences if the rabbit gets extremely frightened. Read the "Dogs and rabbits" section, and use the same strategy for introducing animals under circumstances of being protected by the cage. This may be necessary if your rabbit is timid and shy or your cat is bossy. The rabbit will feel more secure and be more assertive because he will be defending his territory. They will be on a more equal level.

Before making physical introductions, freshly cut the nails of the animals to lessen the chance of injury. Recruit your helper again. He or she will hold the rabbit or cat; you will hold the other. You can have each on a leash if you feel they may need to be controlled. The leash should be attached to halters, not collars. Watch closely so they don't get the leashes wrapped around anything. The leash is not a correction tool; use it only in case you have to separate the two animals. If you are going slowly and the animals aren't showing signs of aggression, this is probably unnecessary. If the cat runs after the rabbit, again introduce the two by using the rabbit cage.

Choose a small room where they are visually reminded of each other but not so small that they cannot get away from each other. Sit on the floor while you and your helper are holding the animals. Overly anxious pets can get hurt jumping out of your arms from a high distance. If your pet gets scared and dashes from your lap, you may get scratched, so wear long sleeves and long pants.

Let the animals smell each other while they are being held. If all is going well, let them down to interact. They may begin to play together. Cats and rabbits often play chase, hide-and-seek, and follow the leader. If they are engaged in a chase game, decide if it looks friendly or if intervention is necessary. Are they trading who is chaser and who is being chased? If they are taking turns, it's a game. If either looks frightened, stop the game and separate them for awhile.

Some cats and rabbits share such deep friendships that they will sleep together, curled up in the rabbit cage or a cozy corner. If your pets are this bonded, you can leave them together unattended. They have definitely become loyal companions, and you will be filled with delight at watching their alliance grow and mature.

Cats and birds

CAUTION

Cats are predators, and birds are their natural prey. Evolution has designed cats to be effective bird hunters; consequently, you must take great care in the encounters between cats and birds. Direct, physical contact is not recommended because the risk is too great.

If a bird is scratched, evenly slightly, he is in danger. Immediately take your bird to your veterinarian if a cat's claws come in contact with his body. A cat carries the bacteria pasteurella, and an infection in a bird can be fatal. Your veterinarian must begin antibiotic treatment as soon as possible. Keep your cat's claws clipped so that even if you keep the bird and cat separate, you won't have to worry about the cat scratching the bird through the cage bars when you are unaware.

Testing your bird's tolerance to cats by bringing in a friend's bird-socialized cat is extremely valuable if you are unsure of the history of the animal. Observe how the presence of a cat influences the stress level of your bird. If your feathered friend has had a bad experience with a cat, he may become frightened. The stress of bringing a feline home may cause your bird to develop behavioral problems. Be kind and consider the emotional well-being of your creatures.

SECURITY

The size of the bird can determine the amount of danger involved. Budgies and similar-sized birds are easy prey for a healthy cat. They often flutter about in their cages, attracting even the most lazy of felines. A cat stalks and hunts small birds, even while the birds are in their cages. This is a natural reaction and one that is difficult to discourage. The cat may stare at the bird, crouching low with his tail sweeping in expectation.

Save your bird from undue stress and keep the risk of injury low by keeping the cage out of the cat's reach. Hang the cage or keep the bird in a separate room. If either of these are not possible, make your bird feel safer by making sure he has room to hide from the eyes of your cat. Offer him a large enough cage so that he can escape to a far corner. Add a nest box or a "hidden" perch product. Placing the cage in a corner where the cat cannot get between the wall and the cage on two sides adds a sense of security. Of course, make sure the cage is securely latched. Do not assume your cat is unable to open the doors; if the reward is great enough, he will get into it.

Discourage your cat from hanging around the cage by telling him "go" and removing him from the area whenever you catch him there. If you never see your furry animal sitting mesmerized by the bird cage, realize he may be saving his hunt for the times when you're not home. That is just the way cats are.

If you have a large parrot, your cat may avoid him because he finds the bird too intimidating. Loud voices, assertive personalities, and large stature persuade most cats to keep their distance. If your parrot is aggressive and territorial, you may even have to worry more about the safety of your cat than the safety of your bird.

BOUNDARIES OF INTERACTION

Observe the reactions of both animals whenever they are close enough to interact, paying close attention to their emotions and attitudes. Safeguard any animal from undue stress. If the cat is threatened by the bird, he will probably just stay away from the area. If your bird is out on a play gym or perch, make sure you watch closely the entire time. You may have to put the cat in another room for the duration of the bird's free time.

If your bird is secure in his cage, the two animals may enjoy each other's company. As previously mentioned in the "Dogs and Birds" section, birds can often develop playful relationships with the furry creatures of the family. Dropping toys and food and calling to the pets to come visit are popular means of parrot entertainment in a multi-species household.

Developing a compatible relationship on opposite sides of the cage bars is safest for both bird and cat. This is one relationship that you must have complete control over at all times. This does not mean the two species cannot share a home and be an integral part of your peaceable kingdom, but a commitment to their safety is imperative.

Birds and rabbits

You probably won't experience too much interaction between your bird and rabbit, but you never know when problems or friendships will arise, so be watchful of any encounters between the two species.

Large parrots could injure rabbits. Rabbits, being curious creatures, may be too inquisitive for the bird in your family, and the bird may feel the need to protect his cage if a roaming rabbit gets close. As long as the bird does not reach the rabbit through the bars, all should be safe. If both animals are out of their cages, be careful that they do not chase each other.

Because rabbits tend to have a lower immunity to the bacteria in bird feces, the biggest risk for your rabbit is to get on your bird's play stand and come in contact with it. Change the paper frequently, and train the rabbit to keep from getting under the birds.

I have seen rabbits kept in the bottom of bird aviaries in the past, and although this is an extremely unsanitary habit, it does demonstrate the compatibility of rabbits and smaller birds.

Children and animals

Animals and children have a special relationship. Some of your greatest memories of childhood probably involve a beloved pet. Hollywood profits from this relationship, often portraying incredible feats of animal bravery and extraordinary powers of communication between animals and humans, particularly children. But movies and television leave out the difficult aspects of developing this relationship and veil problems confronting many caretakers. Mixing animals and children involves important considerations, but you can make it happen by being attentive and keeping a positive attitude.

Even if you don't have children, consider some of the possible difficulties. You may decide to have children at a later time when your animal companions are still a part of your life. Also consider your pet's interaction with children if you are frequently visited by youngsters.

BABIES

If you already have pets and are expecting a baby, prior preparation and a good dose of forethought will make the transition smoother. No matter what some people will lead you to believe, you do not need to

part with your pets because you are having a baby. You will only regret it in the long run if you don't try to make it work. If you are dedicated to keeping your pet and, yes, your baby also, creating a harmonious household is possible.

Preparation

Prepare your animal companions for the baby's arrival much like you prepare them for the addition of a animal friend. "Pretending" to have the baby around by using a doll, diapers, powder, and other baby items that have visual or olfactory qualities will help your animals adapt to the sensory stimulus of babies. If you don't mind investing time to make the transition as smooth as possible, talk, cuddle, and care for the doll. Your time and energy preparing your animals will be well spent.

If you plan to alter your creatures' schedule after the baby arrives, begin early in the preparation stage by gradually changing their routine. Associating increased changes in their life because of a sudden appearance of a baby will make the animals resentful or nervous towards the baby.

Make this major transition as stress-free as possible by providing your animal companions with the same standard of care they are accustomed to. A secure, stable environment and good health through nutrition, grooming, and cleanliness help your animals adjust to this enormous change. If you feel you are unable to supply your animals with the same good care, try enlisting the help of others. Ask your spouse to take over some responsibilities or hire a trusted friend or relative to help out for awhile.

Cuddle time is the most important "chore" to keep for yourself. Be the one who relishes affection on your creatures, just like the days before the baby arrived. This lessens jealousy and helps your pets accept the baby with less turmoil. The comfort offered by your animals will also help alleviate some of the natural anxieties that a baby creates.

Separation

It is not true that cats will suck the air out of babies! However, animals do like to cuddle with babies, and cats are known to climb in the crib with a baby and snuggle up. It is possible they may claim the crib as their own before the baby arrives and then protect their territory when you bring the bundle of joy home. To avoid this, watch carefully and keep the cats or any other animal from claiming any of the baby's items.

Keep a gate on the doorway to the baby's room unless you are supervising. The animals can see and smell the room but do not have free access with a gate. Your pets won't feel shut out. A closed door increases curiosity and anxiety. If you have pets that can get over the gate, try a screen door. Okay, I know, this seems excessive, but there are many benefits to using a screen door. A screen door allows you to see and hear the activity on either side. Your cats or flighted birds won't have access to the room and you won't have to climb over a gate. You can just open the door with one hand, which is much appreciated while carrying a baby.

Jealousy

The most common problem, and one you will probably experience, is jealousy. Your pets may feel demoted and threatened by the baby and all the excitement associated with the new arrival. Although this is a busy, exhausting time, give the attention and affection to your animal companions that they are accustomed to receiving. Don't alienate them; they have been a part of your life and deserve your continued interaction.

Caring for a new baby takes much effort, but avoid casting aside your pet's emotional requirements. Having a special toy or treats to share with your animal companion when you cannot immediately fill

his attention needs gives him something to do while he waits his turn. This also increases your pet's acceptance of having the baby around (He'll think, "The baby is here, so I get a treat or a toy. I like having a baby around.") rather than only giving attention when you are alone with the animal ("The baby is gone, so I finally get attention. I wish that baby were always gone.").

Your pets may also become protective of the baby, and you may need to be cautious when guests come and fuss over the new addition. If your friends and relatives agree to help you out, have them greet your animal friends first and in the same manner that they did in the past.

One Last Word

Until your child is at least seven years old, you should be present when animal and child are together. You never know what can happen, and keeping control of the interactions is the best insurance of safety. Keep your attitude calm and gentle. Each animal in the house will develop his own comfortable relationship with the baby, and the friendships will be long-lasting.

YOUNG CHILDREN

Young children are perhaps the most difficult because they are full of curiosity and exuberance and yet have difficulty understanding the vulnerability of animals. This period requires increased vigilance. Young children, particularly those under the age of three, must be watched carefully around animals. Children can hurt pets simply because they do not understand and do not have the physical ability to control many of their actions. The animals may hurt the children if they feel they are threatened and need to protect themselves. Animals may play rough without realizing the vulnerability of the child and injure or scare the toddler.

Children should learn to play quiet games with pets because playing rough and noisy games with or around animals can make them nervous and anxious. The constant commotion surrounding small children may simply be too much for some sensitive animals. Here again, researching the breed or species is important so that you will have one tool in predicting the ability of your pet to tolerate the small children in your life.

Children must be taught to be kind to all animals and respect the pets that share their home. They should know, for instance, that they should not bother a sleeping animal. As a parent and a responsible pet caretaker, you must explain to your children that each pet is an important family member and, as such, is allowed to have his own space and quiet time.

OLDER CHILDREN

As children get older, they can interact with the animals on their own. The older child can even groom your pets after you teach them the correct manner of brushing and the most kind, gentle way of petting. Children can also play games with the animals as long as the games keep both child and pet on at least equal levels, preferably with the child having more control. Games such as fetch are fun for both children and pets. Games where one participant becomes the dominant victor, such as tug of war, should be discouraged.

Children may even take on responsibilities such as feeding. The child should not be expected to be solely responsible for such an important task. The basic needs of your pets have to be met, and ultimately the adults are responsible.

Children and pets build long-lasting friendships. This is one spoiled puppy!

LEARNING THE LESSONS OF KINDNESS

Teach your children and other children who come in contact with your animals the correct way of relating with them. Teach them to be slow and quiet for your rabbit friend, to respect the independence of your cat, to be aware that roughhousing with the dog may get them knocked to the ground, and to not attempt coercion on an uninterested bird. The traits of kindness learned through your relationships with the creatures in your care are taught to children with patience and supervision.

Instead of giving a list of rules your children must follow, teach them to have an intuitive understanding of the animals in their lives. Show them by example and explanation. Encourage them and they will share with you a deeper understanding of your special creatures. This awareness of animal behavior will enhance your children's appreciation of the natural world.

3

The daily life in a multi-animal house-hold is an experience full of hard work, emotional peaks and valleys, and a continual exchange of love. In short, it is a challenging and invigorating adventure.

Daily adventures

The daily life in a multi-animal household is an experience full of hard work, emotional peaks and valleys, and a continual exchange of love. In short, it is a challenging and invigorating adventure. It can be mostly joyous or mostly trying — but it is always a combination of both. Caring for animals is a balancing act between responsibility and enjoyment where true happiness comes from the merging of both. If you find that life with your pets has become more of a burden than a delight, then it's time to reevaluate your situation and redesign your care strategy.

Have you accepted more responsibility than you can handle? If so, what can you do about it? Do you need to get more organized? Do you need to enlist the help of other family members? Can the kids take the dog out for exercise? Can your spouse take over the afternoon feedings? Do you need to take your pet to the groomers once a month to give yourself a break? Are veterinary expenses out of control? Maybe you need to upgrade your cleanliness standards or invest in more preventative activities. Do you need a vacation? Maybe you need to remind yourself of the positive things that you enjoy about your pets.

Having pets alters your lifestyle and is a substantial adjustment. Once in awhile, you may wish you could sleep in like your petless friends or that you didn't have to clean bird feces off perches this weekend. But you do. It's okay if, once in awhile, you find these feelings creeping through your consciousness. As long as you have fun with your pets and appreciate the friendship and happiness they bring you, you can savor the rewards of living with the animals.

In this chapter you will find ways of turning the daily grind of pet guardianship into a more enjoyable adventure. By understanding your pet's behavior and personality, you will be able to recognize problems before they become serious. More importantly, you will better appreciate each animal for her own individual style and lifeview. Keeping your home and your pet's environment clean keeps your animals and yourself healthy. You won't be overwhelmed by odors and pet messes. If a behavioral problem arises, learning how to seek and evaluate advice can best help you and your pet. Encouraging peaceful interactions between the souls of your home is vital in a multi-animal household.

Keep a keen eye on your charges, maintain a positive attitude about your environment, take care of the daily work with dedication, and you'll find life shared with animals is truly an adventure.

Observation

Observation is the key to understanding the behavior of your animals and is also the catalyst for recognizing changes. It is easier to let clues of ill health go unnoticed in multi-animal households and by knowing the normal behavioral patterns of your pets, you will be alerted to any irregularities that need your intervention. Paying careful attention to the nuances of behavior that make each creature an individual and keeping a record of each animal under your care are necessities. An accurate record can only be accomplished by your observation and awareness.

In order to fully comprehend the information you receive from your animal friends during your observation, you must process it completely. Simply coexisting with your pets all day will not give you a clear perception of their habits. Until questioned by an investigating veterinarian about changes in your pet's personality, you may not realize your lack of knowledge. You will only be able to give accurate testimony to the change in your pet by knowing each of them well.

By understanding the personality of each animal, you can learn to recognize when one is feeling out of the ordinary. A change in behavior must be acknowledged and investigated. When an animal begins acting out of character, it may signify illness or stress. Both of these situations should be addressed immediately. The change in behavior may be subtle, and if you are not aware of your pet's personality, you may not notice soon enough. Allow your vision, hearing, touch, and intuition to guide you.

You may need to occasionally remind yourself to be aware, but this kind of observation is not work. It can become second nature, adding a new and wonderful dimension to your relationship with your animal companion.

When you live with animals, there is much going on around you: interaction among themselves, the furniture, the toilet paper roll, the sunshine, and their toys. Animal lives are busy, active, beautifully graceful, and sedate. By acute observation you will learn many interesting quirks of your animal's personality. You'll discover the particular things that fascinate or intrigue your animal friend and discover the depth of character possessed by each creature that shares your home.

Pet record and observation book

Every pet in your household should have a record book in which you will record any information gathered from your observations. You can keep this information on your computer, but it is best if you have a hard copy kept in a binder. The record book becomes your data bank, so it should be easily accessible. If one of your pets is ill or you suspect that something isn't right, keep frequent observations in your record book. Take your notes with you to the veterinarian appointment. Your record book should accompany you and your pet when traveling. It will also prove invaluable to your pet sitter.

The record book must be well organized so that you can quickly find the information you need or the area where you need to make notations. You can have a separate book for each pet, but it is easier if you have one book where you keep all your animal information. If you need to evacuate your home in an emergency situation, the information can be quickly gathered if it is kept in one binder.

How large of a binder you need depends on the number of animals you have. If you have three or more pets, you need to get a three-inch, loose-leaf binder. A divider identifying each pet keeps you organized and facilitates quicker access.

INFORMATION NEEDED

As shown in the example, the first page of the record book should contain the information pertaining to your complete pet household. This includes the animal poison control phone number, the phone number for an emergency contact person, veterinarian phone numbers, and any major medical conditions of your pets. This page is also a quick summary of your animal household with name and short description of each creature. Include a copy of your emergency plan if you are incapacitated. See chapter 5 for more information on this necessity.

Each pet should also have a stat sheet similar to the example shown. This may seem like too much information, but when you need information quickly and all you have to do is pull out your book and flip to the page you need, you will appreciate your efforts.

The first page of your Pet Record and Observation Book is for quick reference and contains the most important emergency phone numbers.

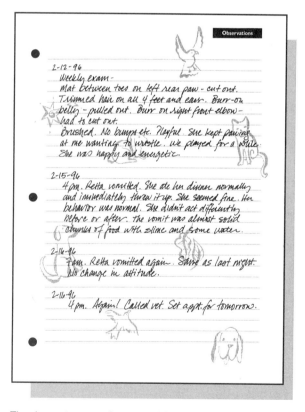

Identification

Name *Cody* Breed *Australian Shepherd*
Registered Name *Dream On's Ramblin' Blues*
Registration # *DL603700104* License # *3795-47*
Other Identification Registrations
Rabies # 960223

Describe Color *Blue Merle*

Describe Physical Characteristics
Dark patch 6"x7½" on right side. Brown eyes.
White - 7½" left rear, 6" right rear
8½" front left, 8" front right.
Tail - Docked.
Balanced blue merle on face with wide copper
frame, circling eyes and on ears.
Muzzle white. ½"x ¾" pink spot on left nostril.

The identification page of your record book should contain pictures of your animal companion and a complete written description of your pet's physical identification.

Identification Page

Each animal needs an identification page, such as the one shown, and it should include one recent, full-body photo. This photo can be used by emergency personnel to identify your pet in case something happens to you and can be put on posters if your companion becomes lost. For others to positively identify your pet, you need accurate information regarding her physical characteristics.

Take a close-up photograph of any distinguishing marks. Use your driver's license or other picture identification in the photo to show comparable size of the marks and to further identify the pet as yours. Pictures taken from every side of your animal give concise visual images. Put a date and name on the back of the photos (to avoid smearing or ruining the photos, write or type the information on a sticker

and stick it on). Update the photos regularly because your animal friends grow, change, and develop.

Write a meticulously detailed description of your companion. Record sizes in exact measurements. Your idea of large may be someone's idea of small. People comment how large my Bouvier is, and even though she is classified as a large dog, to me she is medium. Large is my mastiff who is almost twice her size. Make notes regarding coat or feathers, such as the length of fur, its texture, and how it conforms to the animal's body. Of course, also include the colors, how they blend, how much of each color, and the changes they make in different light. Any distinguishing marks deserve not only a picture as mentioned above but also a description. Be accurate and measure it.

Observations

2-12-96
Weekly exam -
Mat between toes on left rear paw - cut out.
Trimmed hair on all 4 feet and ears. Burr on
belly - pulled out. Burr on right front elbow -
had to cut out.
Brushed. No bumps etc. Playful. She kept pawing
at me wanting to wrestle. We played for a while.
She was happy and energetic.

2-15-96
4 pm. Retta vomited. She ate her dinner normally
and immediately threw it up. She seemed fine. Her
behavior was normal. She didn't act differently
before or after. The vomit was almost solid
chunks of food with slime and some water.

2-16-96
7 am. Retta vomited again. Same as last night.
No change in attitude.

2-16-96
4 pm. Again! Called vet. Set appt. for tomorrow.

The observation page of pet records book is for recording information from your weekly exam as well as notes on the health of your pet.

Observation Sheets

You will need blank copies of observation pages for each pet. Devise whatever is best and easiest for you, e.g., use lined paper or create something fancy. Sometimes I need to make simple notes consisting of a few words; other times, I need to record lengthy observations, and I prefer the lined paper for these.

Anytime you suspect your pet may not be feeling well or seems to be acting strange, immediately begin taking notes in your record book. Don't assume you will remember; you will probably forget the subtle beginning signs, so write them down as soon as you can.

When recording symptoms, make sure you give a good description. If your pet vomits, make note of the character of the vomit and the way your pet acted before, during, and after.

Is each animal eating her normal amount of food at the usual pace? A change in eating habits is one of the first signs that something may be wrong. Observe their elimination habits. If you let Fifi out the door and then forget her until she whines and scratches to come in, you may not discover her constant and difficult urination. If you never observe this behavior, you may miss the beginnings of a bladder infection. Has your cat been to the litter box twice in the last couple minutes? You may find signs of trouble such as blood in the box. This kind of observation may save her life by your getting prompt veterinarian attention.

A prey animal whose safety depends upon hiding any vulnerability, such as a rabbit or bird, is particularly subtle in illness manifestations. Keep an especially keen eye on their behavior and habits.

If you suspect one of your pets is sick, for the sake of precaution, separate her until she has seen your veterinarian and your veterinarian says she is okay.

Personality Awareness

Keeping observations in the record book is a good way to get to know an animal that you may not understand well. For example, if you have never had an iguana, it would be useful to keep track of how much she eats and when and what her attitude and personality are like. This will help you get a clear picture of the species as well as the individual.

If you have a budding adolescent parrot on your hands, an accurate observation record will give you more peace in the years to come. Record behavioral changes in your log because your bird will have a consistent series of temperamental shifts that correspond to her sexual cycle. She may have periods of aggression at the same time each year or after or during a particular environmental change. Keeping detailed records will alert you to the onset of this aggression or attitude change. You can then handle your parrot differently, as needed, without risk and with the understanding of one who is sensitive to nature's hormonal control.

Use your record book to keep track of aggression and behavioral cycles of other animals as well. If a situation or episode presents itself, make detailed accurate notes in that creature's section. Record what precedes the behavioral change and what succeeds it. What did she do? How did she act? Was she agitated and pacing? Mellow and lethargic? Was she panting and her eyes dilating? Whining, crying, or screaming in excess? Was it sudden and seemingly unprovoked and you have no clue as to why she behaved like she did? Did you feel that she needed rest or space or comfort, and did it work to settle her? Did it make her worse? More frightened? More worried?

Your intuitive creature may be warning you of subtle changes in weather or more momentous occasions, such as earthquakes. You may discover your animal is so sensitive to thunderstorms that even the next day she is a bit on edge and needs more space than normal. You'll learn not to push your pet when she is sensitive or anxious because you will know what signs to look for and what to expect.

THE ART OF COMMUNICATION

People sometimes forget communication is a two-way information exchange. It is easy to view communication as a one-way exchange. We are an information-hungry culture and have ready access to a multitude of specialized books, magazines, videos, and web sites. If we want to know something, we can find the answer at our fingertips, often with little effort.

Crowded classrooms have meant earning an education with little room for thought-provoking discussion. More important to your animal friends, the method of choice in relating to them has been to mold their behavior, with humans doing all the "talking" and very little "listening." This may be considered training, but is it communication?

True communication demands give and take. Each participant must reveal information and "listen" to the needs and desires of the other. When teaching acceptable behaviors to animal companions, you must understand how they perceive and relate to these expectations. When these behaviors contradict the animal's natural instincts or inherited impulses, you must acknowledge this conflict and have compassion when dealing with the problem.

A common example that illustrates this quandary is the dog that jumps. She may jump for many reasons. What is she trying to tell you? If you only take measures to stop the behavior without attempting to understand the reason behind the action, you have a frustrated dog that is unable to express her emotions. Stepping on her toes and kneeing her in the chest may convince her that jumping hurts, but she just wanted to tell you she missed you, or she wants to play, or she is anxious and has too much energy.

If you discover the reason behind the behavior, such as an excessive amount of nervous energy, you can give your pet an alternative. Distract her with a ball and a game of fetch when she wants to jump. Use your control commands to make her sit, stay, and drop. Soon she will bring you a ball when she is feeling high-strung and won't even consider jumping.

This is communication. You have a problem; I have a problem; let's find a compromise. The examples to illustrate this exchange are numerous and apply to all animals and people. If your animal companion consistently breaks a rule, you must consider why. It may be that your pet perfectly understands what you are asking but to refrain would close off a means of communication. To stop the unwanted behavior, you must offer alternatives. The lack of understanding may be yours, not your pet's. Help your animals better communicate with you by keeping your receptive understanding open. Exercise your listening and comprehension muscles to heighten your awareness of the difference between communication and telling.

Your weekly exam is the best way to keep an assessment of your animal companion's physical condition as well as assure that at least once a week your pet receives a thorough grooming. Remember to write about your exam in your record book.

MINI-CHECKUP

Once a week, conduct a mini-checkup for each pet. Any observations during these weekly assessments should be recorded in your record book.

This weekly ritual is important for the health of your pet. It is also a learning experience for the animal. She is required to stand still and accept handling and examination of her entire body, and this discipline of acceptance does wonders for her behavior at the vet's or groomer's.

Make a list of items you will be looking for when examining your pet. Check off each item as you perform the weekly examination, and add any conditions or special circumstances that you need to. During this once-weekly observation, perform a complete grooming job. This does not take the place of daily brushing; it is an important supplement and the foundation of observation.

Find a quiet place where there is good light and a low activity level. Soft classical music can make most animals feel more relaxed. Have your tools ready and laid out within your reach. Take your time; this should be a relaxing, positive encounter. Make it gentle and comforting.

The Weekly Exam

Begin your weekly session by running your hands over your pet's entire body, checking for any obvious signs of bumps, lumps, scratches, or "hot spots" by observing and touching. Some animals may not like this at first and squirm quite a bit, but they become more tolerant as they learn it is a positive experience.

If you find a lump or bump, part your pet's hair to examine the area. Is the bump a scab? Scabs should be left alone. Rub a bump between your fingers. How big is it? Write it down. Does it move freely between your fingers? Does it feel attached to tissue? If the bump is larger than half an inch and seems attached, make an appointment with your veterinarian. Record any findings in your record book. Keep an eye on the growth rate of the lump or any changes and be specific in your descriptions.

Make an allover body check for foreign matter. Ticks, fleas, and other pests will need to be dealt with immediately. Foxtails are also dangerous because they move in only one direction — forward. Foxtails can go in one side of your animal and work all the way through and come out the other side, causing damage the entire way. Check for other stickers and thorns. Use scissors to snip some of the more stubbornly attached debris.

Check your pet's ears, especially if the animal is frequently wet. Infections commonly occur in moist environments. Cut hair away from the ear of a dog who frequently swims and remove the hair from her ear canal. If you find odorous brown or black debris in the ear, there may be mites. Use mineral oil and a cotton swab to clean the outer ear, being careful not to push dirt farther in, and see your veterinarian. Ask for a liquid ear cleanser.

Finding the Time

The weekly observation and grooming session won't be lengthy, especially if you adhere to consistent regular grooming. With practice, you will learn how to perform the exam quickly and develop it into a habit. Once it is a habit, it will be part of your care routine and you will do it regularly.

If you have three or more pets, you may want to do each of them on separate days. There is no reason you have to do them all on one day, but if that works best for you, by all means do it. Make it easiest on you; that way it gets done.

Try establishing a special time set aside each week. For example, if every Thursday night you give your dogs a mini-exam, then it will more easily become habit.

When you are finished, offer your friend a treat and loads of praise. Record your observations in your record book immediately. Make notes of the physical exam, any trimming or cleaning you performed, and on your animal companion's mental attitude.

MINI-CHECKUP EQUIPMENT

Keep these items handy in a plastic box with a lid or in a plastic carrier. When it is time to give a pet her weekly examination, you won't have to waste time by repeatedly gathering your tools. Just grab the collection and take your pet to a quiet, relaxing place.

- Nail clippers and nail file
- Brushes and combs
- Mat breaker
- Flea comb
- Scissors
- Small flashlight
- 100% cotton swabs
- Toothbrush
- 100% cotton balls
- Towel
- Vitamin E oil or capsules
- Styptic powder
  (to stop bleeding)
- Treats
- Petroleum laxative
  (for cats and rabbits)

Organization — The gift of time

"I don't have enough time to do everything!"

"Oh, sure. I'll clean the rabbit cage every week, as soon as someone adds another day to the week!"

"How can I find time to spend with my pets when it takes so much time just taking care of their needs?"

These kinds of complaints are not limited to multi-animal households. In a high-pressured, must-have, must-do world, this time crunch is a reality felt by everyone. Go faster! Do more! You feel it, and it seems hopeless to try and make it go away.

Why then do some people get stressed and others seem to do it all and enjoy every minute? Time, or lack of it, affects you only in how you perceive it. Your perception of time limitations is what stifles your productivity or what gives you the freedom to live an active, fulfilling life.

Animal companions require cleaning, feeding, grooming, and playtime. In addition to the obligations to your pets, you probably have a job, children, creative ventures, home projects, civic duties, and friends. There must be time for pleasure and fun, also. The reason most people have pets is for companionship and affection. Leaving time for simply enjoying each other's company is important for their sake as well as yours.

Having control of your life and your immediate environment means keeping stress at a manageable level, being productive and efficient, and making time for the joys of life.

How can this possibly be achieved? Through organization. If you are organized, time multiplies. I will share with you some ways to get your animal responsibilities organized, and maybe these ideas will assist you in other areas of your life.

PERCEPTION OF TIME

You may think that your time constraints are unique, believing that no one has as much to do as you. No one can possibly understand what you go through in a day. If this sounds like you, you are letting an abstract concept — time — disrupt your life. Every person on the earth has twenty-four hours a day. Some people accomplish little in that period;

others reach incredible heights of personal fulfillment. How time affects you is up to you. How can you accomplish the "big" goals of your life while trying to get the "little" things done and still have time to enjoy yourself, your family, and your animal companions?

A Positive Attitude

Time can be positive if you keep a positive attitude. You can say to yourself that cleaning the bird cage is a real pain, time-consuming, and difficult — and (oh, no!) it needs to be cleaned! If you say this, it becomes your reality. If you can change your perception of the activity, you will be amazed at the difference.

Think of cleaning the bird cage as a positive activity that demonstrates the responsible attitude you have toward your feathered friend. You do it because you truly care for your bird's well-being and you want to keep her environment clean and safe. You know she can't tell you, but you understand that she appreciates a clean, neat cage instead of a dirty one.

You know it only takes thirty minutes from start to finish, and thirty minutes spent cleaning the bird cage is a good way to spend the time you may otherwise waste. It doesn't really take long, especially when keeping to a regular cleaning schedule. Cleaning the cage contributes to the prevention of disease and illness, keeps your feathered friend happy, and demonstrates your responsibility of and care for that creature.

Visualization

Visualization is an invaluable tool used by athletes to increase their performance. You too can use it to increase your productivity. Visualize yourself performing a particular chore you don't like to do such as picking up dog feces. While you see yourself doing this chore, imagine things that increase your enjoyment. Visualize the kind of day you like best. A crisp fall day, maybe. A nice bright sun, a cool breeze, the leaves' beautiful hues of gold, red, and green. Imagine the sweet smell of fresh-cut grass, hear the rustle of the leaves, and see the birds flocking to the bird feeder. See yourself quickly and efficiently doing the job.

Use this visualization to motivate and give you the "oomph" to get the job done painlessly. If you pick up on a regular schedule, you'll be finished in a short time. When you're finished, play with the animal who left you the mess. You've had a good excuse to be outside, enjoying your yard and the beautiful day, and the chore only took a few minutes.

This may seem a bit strange to some people, but coaches, athletes, doctors, psychologists, business executives, and others have found that the way they look at things changes their perception of them. Simply imagine the best; maintaining a positive attitude minimizes or erases negativity. Thinking of only the bad (terrible smell, land mines, heat, and flies) assures that is all you will experience.

TIME-MANAGEMENT SKILLS

If the food dishes aren't cleaned often enough, a breeding ground for bacteria and germs is created. If pets aren't groomed regularly, they may get mats of hair so thick and numerous that you have to spend hours cutting them out. If you can't find time to repeat your flea abatement program when required, you must start all over and your pets will suffer for it.

If you are having a difficult time getting everything done, and done properly, your problem may be one of poor time-management skills. Change this by altering some of your present habits and establishing new, more efficient ones. Those who study these things have discovered that habits take twenty-one days to develop. Until that period has passed, push yourself so you won't fall into your old habits too soon.

Even if you currently get everything done, try some of these skills and accomplish even more in less time. You may already be using some of these ideas, and your animals will greatly appreciate any extra time they can have with you.

Finding Time

The first step in organizing your time is to find out how you're currently spending it. One way to analyze your time efficiency is to keep a log.

Keep an accurate log of your activity for two weeks. Two weeks' worth of information is more telling than one, but for some people the thought of writing down everything they do for two weeks is overwhelming. If it seems more achievable to keep a log for one week, do it.

Every activity you do during the day should be recorded along with the length of time it takes to complete. Taking a shower, talking on the phone, and sitting and contemplating should be recorded in your log. You may need to set a timer or an alarm at different times throughout the day to remind yourself to take notice of your productivity and record your actions in your log.

Dividing the log into fifteen-minute segments and jotting down your activity at these increments give you an accurate, concise view of how busy you are during the day.

Once you've kept a record, you will know exactly how much time you really do have. You may be quite surprised at how much time is wasted in your day. This nonproductive time may be caused by lack of direction or lack of organization, or because you've spent too much time doing unnecessary things. You can get time efficiency under control. When it comes to managing a multi-animal household, there are specific things you can do to make it easier on yourself. This chapter is for those of you who want to be more efficient and productive.

Get Up Early

People who have pets are often early risers. Hungry animals rarely let a person sleep in too long. Getting up an hour or even a half-hour earlier can give you more time during the day. The early morning hours are the most quiet time, especially if you have a family.

Getting out of bed a half-hour earlier than anyone in the house enables you to complete the animal chores more efficiently. No begging cats under foot as you try to get breakfast for your three year old. No screaming birds as you try to take a shower.

Until you've tried this, you won't believe how much time you'll save. If it takes you an hour to get all the animal morning routines done, it will probably take you half the time if you start earlier. When there are fewer distractions, things get done quickly. When the house builds up steam and becomes a bus-

tling center of activity, you can be confident that your feathered and furred companions have been cared for, and then your attention can be focused elsewhere.

"I can't get up earlier! I can barely muddle my way through the morning as it is!"

If your head is foggy in the early hours, then the "care plan" described later will be especially valuable to you. The plan you create for your animal duties can be referred to as you go about your chores and give your morning direction. This also ensures you do everything that needs to be done.

Wake up at the same time every day, even on the weekend. This helps early rising become a habitual part of your life. Getting up earlier in the morning is, for most people, one of the hardest habits to form. Remember to push yourself, and in three weeks it will be much easier.

Consolidate

The quickest way to get everything done is to do as much as possible at once. Consolidating chores is effective and easy. Perform animal responsibilities in the least amount of steps; take the least amount of trips to and from the cage or animal area. Depending on the pets you care for and their accommodations and requirements, you can shorten the amount of time required to finish the animal duties by a considerable, or at least helpful, amount.

When you get the rabbit litter box out of the cage to dump it, is the cat litter box close? Dump the kitty litter clumps into the rabbit litter tray; then dump the rabbit litter tray contents in the garbage.

Take a stack of newspapers and a paper bag from cage to cage to replace the dirty paper. Don't make two or three trips to a cage, garbage, newspaper stack, and then back to the cage. Do it in one trip.

Use a tray or bucket to collect all the dishes in one sweep through the house. Use the same tray to put the full dishes back in the cages.

Use your creativity to discover other ways to consolidate chores. Use similarities in types of duties or physical location to guide you. Every moment counts; extra steps translate into extra time.

Watch Less Television

Until you keep a log of how you spend your time, you may not realize how much time you waste in front of the television. A glance to the television can suddenly turn into an hour-long viewfest.

If the television is on, you will be more likely to stop and watch. Even if you only watch a minute here and there, add these up and you could be wasting thirty minutes a day. That is enough time to scrub a cage, groom three cats, obedience train your canine friend, or cuddle and play with an animal companion. Everyday!

Even if you don't stop and watch television, it can influence your time efficiency. Television is distracting. I finally discovered it takes me twenty to thirty minutes longer to finish morning responsibilities when I turn on the television. I usually didn't stop to watch anything in particular; basically, I just moved slower. I listened to the shows, was easily distracted, and just didn't concentrate on what I was doing. I'd find myself wandering in the kitchen, thinking "What did I come in here for?" Now I get everything done at the same time each morning and have included a forty-five-minute run with my dog. The run helps me wake up and exercises us both in the process.

How? I did this by getting up a half-hour earlier, keeping the television off, creating a schedule, and keeping a good, upbeat attitude. It is possible!

Schedule your television time into the relaxing period of your day. Save it for unwinding at night or getting your second wind before the kids get home from school. The rest of the time, play music (upbeat or relaxing depending on the mood you require), be company to yourself, or visit with the people and animals in your life.

Organize

If your possessions are organized, it is quicker and easier to get the things you need. The optimum solution is to have all animal things organized together so they're easier to use. Keeping everything together in one place saves time and energy. Every second you spend by walking from one area to another or searching for the items you need is time wasted.

• **Get Organized** — Dedicate one afternoon to getting your pet care equipment organized. Begin by gathering all the items that pertain to your animal companions: food, extra sets of bowls, brushes, extra toys, blankets, carriers, and anything else.

Put everything together on the kitchen floor. Sort the items into categories of use — eating, training, grooming, bedding, and toys. By getting a good idea of the items you need to store, you can best find the perfect spot for each of them. Keep in mind the number of items and their size and bulkiness. Where is the best place to store all this stuff?

• **Get Rid of It!** — Begin by getting rid of anything you don't need. Don't keep it if you want it; keep it only if you need it. Even if you want all four leashes but only use one of them, why keep the rest? You have to store them, and maybe they would be more valuable donated to an animal rescue group, humane society, or your friend down the street who is using that one-inch-wide heavy leash on her toy dog.

Get rid of those cracked dishes, broken brushes, training devices you bought before you knew better, and the five collars your dog outgrew. They add to clutter and disorganization, which contributes to stress. Get rid of clutter and get rid of stress. Be brave, you can do it!

Once you have only the items you need, you will have a clear indication of what you must organize. You now have the items separated into categories and must search for the best place in your house to store them.

• **Your Kitchen** — Your kitchen will be the most challenging place to organize. Most people complain of too little space, but if your kitchen is organized, you would probably be surprised at just how much room you do have.

Find a convenient spot to store all the animal-related paraphernalia. You will be feeding your animals once or twice a day, so make it easy on yourself. The area needs to have counter access and should be close to the sink and refrigerator.

You will need many clear plastic containers, which will become the cornerstone of organization.

Buy these secondhand (just clean thoroughly and disinfect) or talk your friend out of the ones she's not using. Contribute to recycling by using coffee cans or other second-use items as storage containers. Clearly mark the containers to make it easy to identify their contents without opening them. You are finding time, and you don't want to open three cans to find what you need.

Every item should have its spot based on how often it is used. Things you need most often should be at the front of your storage area for quick access.

• **Organizing Your Feeding Routine** — In multi-animal households, an array of pet foods is inevitable. To keep them organized, you need a container for each kind of food. If you buy twenty- or forty-pound food bags, empty them into garbage cans in an area with adequate space. Storing animal food in bags is an open invitation for rodents and pests, so avoid attracting these determined criminals. I like plastic cans because they are easier to clean and won't rust, but hungry rodents can chew through them, so keep an eye on the condition of the can.

If pests are a continuing problem, you can store the food elevated off the floor. Special containers are available that store on the wall and have doors that release the food.

If the storage area, such as a garage or porch, is away from the dishes, feeding area, and kitchen, then you're wasting time. Store a couple of days' worth in the kitchen cabinet in a smaller container. Next time you go to the garage for something, you can refill the can. It's quicker, especially in the morning, to have the food with everything else.

If you feed your creatures canned food, keep a couple of days' supply in the kitchen. Keep a can opener by the cans. Dishes and mats not in use should also be kept here, as well as a second set of dishes for birds and rabbits.

Treats and nonperishable food items should also be kept together in the cabinet. Perishable foods should be kept in the same place in the refrigerator. Designate a drawer in the refrigerator just for animal food such as rabbit and bird greens and veggies and special foods for dog or cat diets. Pull the whole drawer out every morning when making food feasts.

The aim of all this kitchen organization is to be able to open a cabinet when you start your feeding regimen and have things flowing smoothly from one activity to another.

• **Storage Areas** — Find an underused cabinet or large drawer, preferably centrally located, that can be converted into your animal storage area. Purchase two clear plastic storage boxes: one for brushes, combs, clippers and other grooming supplies, and one for extra, rotated, or new toys. You may also need one for odds and ends such as extra carrier screws or pieces to other animal equipment. Make sure that they are large enough for all the items yet fit easily into the area you designated for pet supplies.

Store clean towels, blankets, and bedding in this cabinet. You can keep your pet care books in the same area if there is room.

Ideally, training equipment is stored by the training area or somewhere on the way to the training area. Leashes, collars, and clipboards can be hung on nails by the door. They are easy to grab and stay untangled and neat. Store your plastic pooper-scooper bag on a clip in this area. You can even clip the bag to the leash with a clothespin so you won't mistakenly forget it on your way out the door.

First-aid kits, medicines, shampoos, and any chemical products should be securely contained away from curious animals and children.

• **Carriers** — A carrier of appropriate size for each pet is a necessity. The carrier is used for fun trips and outings and to take your animal to the veterinarian. Crates or carriers keep your animals safe and secure when traveling and in emergencies such as fires or natural disasters.

The carriers should be easy to get to in a hurry. Don't let them get buried or shoved to the back of the basement or attic — they must be accessible. The best place for the carrier is as close as possible to the cage of the animal it belongs to. If there is a closet near the rabbit or bird cage, store the carrier there. Don't pile stuff on or in it.

Free-roaming pets may use their carrier as a bed if it's comfy and convenient. Leave the door secured open. If they use their carrier as a bed, you get two uses from one item. This kind of efficiency saves time, space, and money.

This area is well organized. It is directly outside the kitchen door and only steps from the counter used to prepare the animals' food. Dog food is kept in plastic cans, canned food is kept on top of the freezer, and other food is kept in clear plastic containers for easy access.

• **Other Organizing Ideas** — Cat litter scoops, extra litter, and a receptacle to put the clumps in should all be close to the litter box. A small can with a lid and disposable bag works if you clean it regularly. Cats don't like smelly areas, so if you leave it by the litter box too long, you may promote accidents.

Newspaper should be kept under or near cages for quick replacement. If you can't stand the sight of the paper or you have children or creatures who play with it, store the extra supply by the garbage where you dump the dirty paper. One more trip, a little more time — you have to decide which you prefer.

Once you have a place for everything and everything is in its place, you will experience the thrill of finishing pet responsibilities quickly and efficiently. Use the newfound time to cuddle or visit with one of your animal friends.

CREATING A SCHEDULE

Creating a schedule is a wonderful way to stay focused and to be effective when you are performing the duties of pet care. If you are easily sidetracked, somewhat foggy in the morning, or one of those people who gets more done with a "to do" list, creating a schedule is for you. Everyone who has two or more pets can enhance his or her efforts and become more efficient with a schedule. Call it your plan of attack, pet care strategy, or care program. Try it for awhile, and see if it doesn't help you keep focused.

A daily care list is a goal sheet for pet responsibilities. You need goals, even daily goals, to experience productivity and success. Having goals, whether for the day, week, or year, is not only for the proper, straight-laced, or stuffy. It will not stifle but rather free your spontaneity and creativity. It allows you to complete the "must dos" in a timely manner and have more time for those things you'd prefer to be doing. A good schedule alleviates stress.

How Do I Take Care of My Pets?

Take a little time and sit down with a piece of paper and a pen. Write down every chore and duty you perform for your pets' care; be as detailed as you can. Write down not just that you dump the litter box but that you get the scoop, go to the garage, get extra litter, grab a paper bag, walk to the box, clean it out, dump the bag, put the scoop back, and put the litter back. If it is easier, you may want to either walk through the motions (your animals and family may think you're crazy) or write them down as you do them. You will get a clear picture of all the steps that even the most simple chore demands.

Your task will be to cut back on the number of steps you perform for every chore. If you have followed the organization suggestions previously mentioned, you have already discovered a number of time-wasting practices and have organized the tools of your daily responsibilities.

What actions can you eliminate by organizing your equipment? What responsibilities can be consolidated into one trip? Are there any tools or gadgets that can make your chores more pleasant? Are there any tools or gadgets that you are currently using that are only making things more difficult? Do you often get sidetracked? Is the rest of your family demanding your attention during this time, causing you to take care of animal responsibilities for longer than necessary?

Most of the answers, along with suggestions for change, have been mentioned previously. Now is the time to apply these new time-saving skills to real life.

Fine-Tuning Your Schedule

Make a new plan of action for your schedule. A rough draft is best for now; just write it down in easy-to-follow steps. See the following example of a working schedule for ideas. Write it so it makes sense to you and is easy to follow. You may want a step-by-step listing or you may prefer just a basic outline to keep you on track.

The next morning, follow the schedule just as you have it prepared. Was it easy to follow? Did it make sense? Did it flow smoothly from one chore to another? Did you forget anything? The more animals that you have in your household, the more likely that something may have been left out.

Fix any area of the schedule that may work better another way. Play with the plan, fine-tuning it for a couple of days. When you think that you have a schedule you can live with, type up a nice copy, or have a friend type it for you. Hang the schedule where you can see it everyday; it should be easily accessible and completely in view. Hang it on the refrigerator or cabinet door.

The Value of Routine

With a schedule, you will find that completing all of the pet care responsibilities will be easier. You will be saved the frustration of standing in the kitchen at 6:00 A.M. thinking "Where do I begin? What do I need to do first?" The schedule helps you stay focused and complete your responsibilities quickly. You'll be assured you did not miss anything important. Once you have established a routine, you may not use the schedule every time, but you will have it when you need it. Keeping to an efficient routine becomes second nature, and you will soon find your responsibilities effortless.

ANIMAL CARE SCHEDULE

Morning
Put cat food on plates
Microwave it
Mix vitamins
Feed cat
Feed rabbit
Gather veggie dish
Change water in water bottle
Let bird out
Change bird paper
Gather bird dishes
Wash all dishes
Cut up veggies
Fill bird pellet, seed, and water dishes
Place food in bird cages
Give veggies to rabbit
File bird nails
Clean litter boxes
Place hay in rabbit cage
Brush rabbit
Put bird back in cage
Run with dog
Give bird a shower
Brush dog and check paws
Feed dog (1 hour after run)

Afternoon
Remove bird veggie dishes
Change bird paper
Refill seed and pellets if needed
Change water

Evening
Let bird out
Put cat food on plates
Microwave it
Mix vitamins
Feed cat
Feed dog
Give snack to bird and rabbit

Before Bed
Brush cat

```
┌─────────────────────────────────────────┐
│  TIME MANAGEMENT SKILLS SUMMARY          │
│                                          │
│    • Get up earlier                      │
│    • Consolidate chores                  │
│    • Watch less television               │
│    • Organize                            │
│    • Keep only what you need             │
│    • Have a place for everything         │
│    • Keep equipment together             │
│    • Create and use a schedule           │
│                                          │
└─────────────────────────────────────────┘
```

Cleanliness

Keeping your pets and their environment clean is the most beneficial effort you can make in keeping the health of your pets in optimum condition. Having a regular regimen of cleaning and adhering to a high standard of cleanliness should be priorities. This level of hygiene reduces your allergies and those of your guests. It also lowers the risk of other problems such as pests, mold, and the spread of disease.

Make your life as simple as possible. Establish a cleaning routine and stick with it. Letting your responsibilities slack will only make them harder to deal with down the road.

AIR QUALITY CONTROL

Hair, dust, dandruff, feathers, and feather dust are part of the substances inherent in the air of a home with animals. Depending on the sensitivity of the animals and the humans who share the household, this can be mildly troublesome or unquestionably dangerous. Many hazards and dangers that exist in your home are discussed in chapter 7. Airborne contaminants are prevalent in our chemical-laden society, and because your animal companions have quicker metabolisms and more efficient respiratory systems, they are at a higher risk of danger. In this section, organic components that form indoor air pollution will be discussed.

Hair

Depending on the hair type and the amount being shed, pet hair may be found everywhere. Even if you never let your pets on the counter, you will find hair there. It miraculously floats through the house, landing on the lip of Aunt Emma's water glass or in the cookie dough. Wiping counters and tables and vacuuming help cut down on the amount of hair, but it will still be there.

In order to get pet hair out of the carpet and furniture, you must have a strong attachment or power head for your vacuum. A rotating brush pulls the hair from the carpet fibers so that it can be vacuumed up. It's difficult to find a power head for a furniture attachment. If your furniture accessory doesn't have a rotating brush, use your vacuum on the furniture to get the bulk of the hair — yes, pick up the vacuum and use it on your couch. It works.

If you can't stand hair, then skip the furry animals altogether. If you really want to lessen the amount of hair, then choose a pet that does not shed a lot.

The best way to keep the amount of hair down is to keep your pets well groomed. A daily brush or comb does wonders to reduce the amount of hair on the floor, sofa, or your clothes. Of course, there are many benefits to daily grooming, and hair control is one of them. Grooming also reduces the amount of dandruff and dust by stimulating the natural oils on your pet's skin, which in turn benefits the condition of her coat.

Feathers

Birds present another problem: feathers. The downy feathers float through the air like the softest of "bunny fluff." The feather dust that birds cast off is more of a problem than the feathers themselves. This dust is especially pronounced in cockatoos but is not exclusive to them. The dust is an essential component to a bird's physiology, and if your cockatoo is not covered with dust, take her to see your avian veterinarian. You can wipe down the cage and furniture that surrounds the cage. Giving your bird a bath at least a few times a week also helps.

Filtering the Air

The best way to get some control over all of

this "air pollution" is to get an air purifier. If you have a number of animals, a large number of birds, or are especially sensitive to dust and hair, then a purifier is a smart way to go. The cost for good quality air purifiers has been coming down, and the technology has been improving.

Look for a purifier that works on one room at a time or investigate a whole-house ventilation system. A whole-house system pulls in air from outside, filters it, and then circulates this clean air through your home while pulling the stale or dirty air from inside. The complete exchange of air happens several times a day or even once an hour if necessary. See the bibliography for books that can lead you to sources and further research.

If your home has central heating or air conditioning, it can be a benefit. If you clean the filter frequently, it can keep your air cleaner; if you don't, it could be worse. The filter will need to be changed more often than recommended. The number of animals you have and the size of your home determine how often it needs to be changed. Check the filter frequently, and change it before it needs changing.

CAGES

Cages take a lot of work to keep clean. Thankfully, cage design has improved in recent years, and manufacturers have taken into consideration the animal guardian's limited time and concern over cleanliness. If you create a system for keeping cages clean and stick to a routine schedule for deep cleaning, a sparkly cage is an achievable reality.

Floor and Wall Protection

The walls and floor surrounding a bird or rabbit cage are highly abused territory. Seeds are smashed into carpet fibers. Feces are squirted with the force of a slingshot. Rabbit urine runs over the litter box and down the cage, splashes against the wall, and puddles on the floor. Fruit is flung madly from beaks, plastering walls and floors like cement. Protecting these surfaces is obviously necessary, and easy.

If you are renting your home, protecting the walls and floors is paramount. Food and waste are very difficult to clean off walls; some food can be-

come a permanent fixture. Set a good example for your landlord. Show how clean and responsible animal caretakers can be.

• **Protecting the Floor** — Every cage should have a protective cover directly underneath, extending one foot beyond the perimeter of the cage. Covering the floor with newspaper is a simple way but a messy one. Paper blows away, gets played with, and doesn't add much to the decor. Plastic sheeting is next best, although it can get ripped and be tripped over. Plastic runners, the kind you've seen in your grandmother's hallways, work well. These runners are inexpensive and have little cleats on the bottom so they stay in place on the carpet. They are clear so they won't clash with your color scheme and you can cut them any length that you want. Also, office supply stores and superstores carry heavy-duty, molded plastic protection sheets made to fit under a desk, and they can be cut to fit.

Taking it one step further, you can even create protection that complements your decorating style. For example, stick-on linoleum squares can be placed on a sheet of plywood that is custom cut to your cage.

• **Protecting the Walls** — The walls behind the cages must also be protected. The walls behind your rabbit's cage need protection generally toward the ground. Urine splashes are the most common form of rabbit messes on walls. Birds, on the other hand, are quite messy and can get food stuck on the wall from the floor to the ceiling. They can also, depending on the fury in which they dig into their Epicurean delight, strike walls that are a few feet away from their cage.

Clear plastic sheeting can be used behind the cage to safeguard the walls. This plastic quickly becomes unsightly but is inexpensive and easy to replace. A shower curtain can work the same way. You can buy ready-cut Plexiglas sheeting from hardware and home improvement stores. Use the strongest gummy-type picture hangers to attach Plexiglas to the wall; nails and screws can crack and split the plastic. To get fancier, buy a higher grade of Plexiglas from a plastic manufacturer and have it customized.

Look in the yellow pages under "Plastic."

These protective sheets must be cleaned periodically. If you use an inexpensive method, you may decide to replace it occasionally.

Deep Cleaning Cages

Deep cleaning each cage every couple of weeks is optimum for the health of your creatures. I understand this is a massive task when there is more than one cage. Scrubbing three cages every Saturday is quite a chore, but if you spot clean during your daily routine to get the biggest messes as they occur, you can be a bit more lenient about your deep-cleaning schedule. Cleaning a different one every other week is easier on your time and sanity and keeps the cages healthful. So relax, the clean-cage police won't arrest you if you are diligent with day-to-day cleaning and disinfect at least once every other month.

Bacteria can grow quickly on a dirty cage; there is just no way to keep this from happening. Even the most conscientious owner will not be able to get every last drop of feces and every bit of food from the nooks and crannies of the cage. If allowed to continue, this can start a cycle of health-related problems, so regular deep cleaning is necessary.

• **PreCleaning Preparation** — Remove your pet from her cage before you clean it. The time of day that she would normally be outside of her cage is a good choice. When the animal is out during cleaning, make sure that someone is there to keep an eye on her. You may get involved in cleaning and forget to check and see that all is going well. Using a carrier to confine your pet for part of the time may be a good solution. The job may take awhile, and you will have to wait for the cage to dry before your pet can return. Put her in the carrier while you are actually scrubbing the cage and then let her out while it is drying and you can show her some attention.

Completely vacuum the cage. Before the cage is disinfected, every piece of debris must be removed.

• **Cleaning** — How you go about cleaning the cage will depend on its size and the weather. If the cage is small, you can place it in the shower or tub. Soaking the cage in hot water first will make the actual scrubbing less labor-intensive. If the cage is large, it will be more of a burden to deep clean.

While shopping for a cage, make sure it has wheels or casters, which will help you when it comes time to clean. Don't buy a large cage you cannot easily move.

Large cages are easiest to clean in the warmer months when the cage can be taken outdoors. Wash the cage by pouring buckets of hot water over it or wiping with a heavily saturated sponge. Let this soak for awhile. If it is really warm, the cage will dry quickly, so it may take a couple of soakings to loosen everything up. I have a friend who cleverly places her cage in the middle of the yard while the sprinklers are on. By the time the yard is watered, the cage debris is loose enough to make cleaning a breeze.

Next comes the elbow grease. You can use a soap product if you wish, but choose an environmentally safe product for the least toxicity. Use a stiff-bristled brush, and scrub the inside, outside, walls, bottom, door, and top — everything because your pet gets messes everywhere. A small brush, such as a toothbrush, will get the tighter and smaller areas. Rinse the soap thoroughly from the cage.

Using a wire-bristled brush will remove paint along with the waste. Loose paint can be ingested by your pet. The paint protects the metal from rust and bacteria, so the less you scratch the painted surface, the better. Steel wool and other porous cleaning pads will also scratch. If your pet's cage has scratches, use a nontoxic paint to touch up the blemishes.

Repaint metal trays if they become rusty or pitted. Prepare the tray for painting following the paint manufacturer's suggestions. Paint the cage outdoors, and make sure it is completely dry before using the cage. Because moisture is the culprit that causes this deterioration, you can protect metal trays by lining them with waxed paper.

• **Disinfecting** — To disinfect the cage, use a bleach and water solution of twenty parts water to one part bleach. Even with all the fancy disinfecting products on the market, bleach is still the best, cheapest, and easiest to use. The problem with bleach is that the odor and fumes are unsafe. Never use it around your pets, and when you use it, be sure it is thoroughly rinsed off.

Bleach will also ruin some surfaces, especially upholstery, so it cannot be used on everything you may need to disinfect. Chlorasan, sold under the name Nolvasan, is an effective disinfectant that is less odorous and can be used safely on most surfaces (always test in a less obvious spot before using). If you use Nolvasan, mix one ounce to one gallon of water. You can get Nolvasan at your veterinarian's office. Never mix disinfectants, and never mix them with other cleaning solutions.

The easiest way to get the solution in all the corners and each crack is to put it in a spray bottle and spray it on. Let the bleach solution set on the cage for a couple of minutes. Be absolutely sure to rinse thoroughly; this is very important. The cage must not have residue of bleach solution left on it. Rinse three times as long as you took to get the cage wet in the first place. Then rinse again.

• **Cleaning a Large Cage Indoors** — A large cage that cannot be taken outdoors to clean because of the weather or other reason can be cleaned inside your home; however, the task is more difficult. You will just have to be careful and realize it will take a bit longer.

Place a plastic drop cloth under the cage to protect the floor from overflow. Use a bucket of hot water and a large sponge to wet the cage. Let it soak. Scrub with a stiff-bristled brush. It is difficult to remove sudsy residue with a sponge bath, so you may not want to use a soap product. Rinse by gently squeezing a trickle of water and wiping it away with the sponge. The trick is not to use so much water that you make a mess; use only enough to do the job.

Disinfect the cage by using the bleach solution in a spray bottle. If you spray too much bleach solution, it will puddle under the cage, so use caution and don't go overboard. Let it soak a couple of minutes.

The biggest, most difficult part of cleaning indoors is the rinsing. You must get all bleach residue off the cage. Use a few buckets of water, being sure to rinse out your sponge thoroughly. Wipe, rinse, wipe,

rinse. This is not the time to get lazy.

Let the cage dry completely before you put your pet back. Your animal may get a chill from a cage that is still damp. Rabbits don't like to have their feet resting on damp floors, so they are especially sensitive about this.

Cleaning Perches

Bird cage perches take extra consideration. They have to be scrubbed vigorously. Birds use their perches as a napkin, wiping their beaks and feet after eating. Because of their porous texture, perches get permeated with food and feces, providing a rich environment for bacteria and mold. Using a wire-bristled brush makes the job easier. Use the same bleach solution as you do for the rest of the cage to disinfect the perch. It is critical that the perches be completely rinsed.

Perches take longer to dry than the cage. A damp perch is not healthy for your bird's feet. Having extra perches is convenient. While the perches you just washed are drying, you can use the other set. Alternating the perches in this manner helps you get the cage back together quicker without jeopardizing the health of your bird's feet. An added benefit is that using different shapes and sizes of wood keeps your bird's feet exercised and healthier.

If the perches are small and you want to speed dry them, place them in a 400-degree oven until they are dry.

Perches need day-to-day cleaning as well. Having a perch scraper on hand makes frequent cleaning less burdensome. Even if your bird's perch is larger than any perch scraper you can find, use the pointed ends to scrape off the mess. You can also use a strong putty knife, butter knife reserved for this purpose, or sandpaper. Use sandpaper while the bird is out of the cage, or she may inhale the dust. Wipe the perch with a wet cloth after using sandpaper.

Cleaning Toys and Dishes

Clean your companion's toys at the same time you deep clean the cage. Plastic and acrylic toys are the easiest to keep clean and can be run through the dishwasher. The hot water and heat from the dishwasher cycle sterilize them. Wooden toys may be cleaned and scrubbed but will have to dry thoroughly before being returned to the cage. Speed dry them in the same manner as the perches.

The problem with wood, rope, and other natural fiber toys is that they are difficult to get completely clean. Getting them wet may actually encourage bacteria and mold growth. Toys made from rawhide and leather should be tossed if they get wet. Clean these toys by scraping them, but when they become very dirty or if you have already scraped them a few times, replace them. Rope and cloth toys can often be washed in the washing machine, depending on what other goodies are attached.

While cleaning the cage, soak the dishes in bleach solution for disinfecting. Also soak, scrub, and disinfect the rabbit litter box. Since you already have the bleach solution mixed, clean the kitty litter box.

Tips on Keeping a Bird Cage Clean

Spraying a light coat of cooking spray on the grate of your bird's cage saves some scrubbing. Coat the grate with an organic or natural spray when the bird is out of her cage.

Many birds are territorial and protect their cage. Others can be so mischievous — stealing the paper, pulling your hair, dropping items as you are working — that they make the job take longer than it needs to. While completing your daily cleaning, you may find it is best to have your animal on her play stand.

When you do your vacuuming around the cage, also vacuum the tray of the cage. Seeds, seed hulls, food, and feathers accumulate in the tray quite quickly. If this mess becomes wet, either by water from the water dish or feces, it can rapidly grow mold or bacteria. I've even heard of seeds sprouting in disgustingly dirty cages. The buildup will also ruin the tray, rusting and pitting it.

Skirts around the bottom of bird cages have been a great help to bird caretakers everywhere. These skirts, or aprons, flare out from the bottom of the cage and collect debris that falls from above. Many cages come equipped with, or offer as an option, an apron. You can also purchase one to fit your current cage. They are usually made of metal or Plexiglas.

Your bird will still make a mess. I can find food as far as six feet away from my macaw's cage even though it has an apron. I've seen her scoop a claw full of seed and toss it out of the cage; it ended up all over the room.

SMALL EFFORTS THAT MAKE A BIG DIFFERENCE

A couple of times a year, you'll need to perform a disinfecting extravaganza. Floors and twelve to eighteen inches of surrounding walls around the feeding area will need to be cleaned and disinfected. Crates, waste containers, and scooping equipment will need to be disinfected. Dog runs or cat enclosures need to be done regularly. Use a bacteria/enzyme product on runs and "toileting" areas. Pet bedding can be washed and dried in a hot dryer every week.

Keeping mud and dirt out of your home is best accomplished through prevention. Any outside area that your pet has access to is a potential dirty spot and should be cleaned. Mud and dirt should be cleared from sidewalks. Bark, a favorite at my house, needs frequent sweeping. Grease and oil should be cleaned off driveways and garage floors. If there are bare spots in the grass, your pet will track in dirt or mud. Fill these spaces by growing grass or cover in another way. If water spigots are a problem, pour concrete under them or place gravel or rocks there.

When your pet comes to the door to come in, have her wait to be brushed off or towel her off in wet weather. She can learn to be patient and cooperative while you do this.

The best way to prevent dirt and mud from being tracked in is to put high-quality mats inside and outside of every entrance. These mats should have stiff, solid pile and a rubber backing. These mats used at businesses are the best for catching messes from dirty feet.

If your pet brings in mud, let it dry before attempting to clean it up. Loosen it gently and then vacuum. Use a cleaner, such as dish soap or an all-purpose cleaner mixed with water, and blot the area. Let it soak five to ten minutes, then rinse with water and blot dry.

KEEPING THE HOUSE CLEAN

So you've organized all the animal chores and have a great care plan that makes them easy and quick to accomplish, but the rest of your home is still suffering from neglect. The methods in this chapter apply to everything you do, but there are some additional tips for housecleaning that can make a big difference.

Clean up as you make messes. After you make lunch, clean up the dishes, utensils, food, and counters. This only makes sense, but this sense is commonly discarded. "The dishes can wait." No they can't; do them now. It will only take a second and then it's done. You won't have to look at them or face their mess again later. If you (or your animal friend more than likely) knock a plant over, vacuum now, not later. Later you have to do other things. Pick up as you go. Your mom told you so, and she was right. This is the secret of those who are very busy but have a clean, tidy home.

Speed clean fifteen to twenty minutes daily and do one major chore, one big cleaning job, every day. If you go to brush your teeth and you notice dirty sinks, take fifteen minutes and clean them. Have the cleaner and cleaning equipment by the sink. It is a waste if you have to spend five minutes looking for the cleaning equipment before you clean. Dust the furniture when you notice it is dusty. Doing these small chores and duties keeps your house remarkably presentable.

Loosen your concept of "clean." Your house is not going to look like the Cleavers'. It will look like the best representation of yours. So what if there are lick marks on the back door window? So what if the birds dropped five toys on the floor? It's okay. Chances are no one will notice but you. If you keep your home tidy and concentrate your efforts where most needed, your home will be a welcome, inviting place. Keep smells down by diligently cleaning cages, grooming, and cleaning animal messes as soon as they occur; and keep hair, feathers, and debris down by vacuuming daily. Your house will hardly be recognized as an "animal house."

People are always amazed how many animal companions I have because my house is so clean. To me it could be cleaner, but I've learned what messes make the house "feel" dirty and animal-like. Those take precedence. The rest I take care of as I can. But I've had to learn to live with walls that aren't scrubbed weekly, bathrooms that get rugs moved into ruffly piles for doggie beds, muddy footprints in sinks and tubs, and wet messes around water dishes. This is just a sampling.

The companionship of my animal friends is far more important than a sparkly house. I like it this way much better, and I'm sure you will too; just relax and accept the less than perfect.

DAILY RESPONSIBILITIES

The health of your creatures depends on how responsible you are to their care. This level of responsibility also determines how clean your home is kept. Just because you have more than one pet does not mean your home has to smell repugnant.

It is possible to keep your home in good order even when sharing your living space with many animals. Even one dog or one cat can dramatically influence the cleanliness of your home. A dirty, smelly home becomes a reality only if you allow it. The quality of cleanliness does not have to change even with five pets if you keep your standards high and keep on top of the work.

Some cleaning responsibilities will be done daily. These chores are what makes keeping a multi-animal household so time-consuming. The secret to success is performing these duties in an organized and consistent manner.

Cleaning Food Dishes

You must wash your pet's dishes everyday. The easiest, most efficient way to keep your pets supplied with clean dishes is to have two sets of dishes for each animal. Use a clean bowl to feed your pets and remove the dirty bowl for cleaning.

A run through a dishwasher is a good sterilizing technique but not always possible. If you can't put the dishes through a dishwasher, wash the bowls thoroughly and pour boiling water in them and let them soak for a couple of minutes to sterilize them. Rinse and then these bowls will be ready for the next day.

When you finish washing the dishes, don't dry them with the dish towel you have hanging in the kitchen. Dry the bowls with a paper towel. I don't advocate adding waste to our overcrowded dumps, but the easy spread of contaminants is risky. It is much safer to use a clean towel or paper towel.

Some people do not see the value of washing dog and cat bowls as they might for bird and rabbit bowls, but it is just as important. Pests come to clean out the remains of the bowls, spreading disease. Dirty bowls and ones left with food in them attract mice, roaches, and a number of other undesirables. Water bowls get filmy, especially if you have a slobbery dog.

Food falls from the animal's mouth into the water bowl. In warm climates, algae and mold can form. If your pet uses a water bottle, it also needs to be scrubbed every other day and disinfected weekly.

All of these conditions are prime breeding grounds of trouble. Keep these bowls washed. To keep the area surrounding the water bowl as dry as possible, use a tray a few inches bigger than the water bowl to catch most dribbles and splashes.

Vacuuming

During shedding season, you may find that vacuuming once a day doesn't seem like enough. I can vacuum from one end of the house to the other and by the time I'm done, I feel like I need to vacuum the first area again. It is an endless chore.

The area around your bird's cage needs to be vacuumed every day (not that you will necessarily be able to vacuum every day). Even with the skirts that are designed for cages, like those mentioned earlier, there will be a scattering of offerings on the floor. A hand-held vacuum close to the cage area is convenient. Have one charging nearby so you do not have to drag out a full-sized vacuum every time you need to pick up food debris. This hand-held vacuum, if it has a rotating brush, can also be used to pick up hair that accumulates around sleeping and resting areas of your other animals.

Cage Liners

The newspaper on the bottom of a bird cage needs to be changed at least once a day. I change the paper twice a day — once in the morning when I feed the birds and then after the birds have eaten their soft food. The morning paper has been collecting feces since the afternoon the day before and they usually drop quite a bit of food and make a big mess by afternoon. The second change of paper is especially important in the summer where the warmer temperatures can rot food quickly.

If your rabbit generally uses her litter box, you may not have to change the paper liner every day. This will, of course, depend on how messy your rabbit is with her food and urine overspills. Some rabbits are very reliable in using their litter box to urinate. You best know your rabbit and can change the paper as often as necessary.

Your rabbit's litter box will have to be changed daily. Rabbits will sit in their litter box and just "hang out." It may seem unhygienic to us, but they don't find it so terrible. Keep the box as clean as possible by changing the litter often.

Daily Cage Cleaning

You'll be cleaning cages often. Your animal companions view their cages as a sanctuary, and they should be as comfortable as possible. Feces, food, dust, and urine-coated cages are not the best living environment for your beloved animals. Because the mess is concentrated in a small space, diligence is necessary.

Line the bottom of the cage with absorbent material to catch droppings and discarded food. You have many choices; some are quite fancy and expensive. Crushed corn cob, wood shavings, walnut and peanut shells, and special papers are all available. All liners, except for paper, should be avoided. The potential harm in using other liners is not worth the extra effort or money. These products increase the possibility of bacteria and mold invading your creature's home. They also contain too much dust. Dust is a carrier of the bacteria streptococcus, which can be harmful. The best cage liner is still newspaper.

On a day-to-day basis, a warm rag can be used to wipe up any major messes. Wipe down the bars of the cage, concentrating on the areas around food and water bowls and the areas where your pet eliminates. Don't forget the aprons or skirts.

This daily cage wiping takes only an extra minute or two of your time. Simply use a squirt bottle with water to spray the dirtiest areas. Let this set for a few minutes, then use a warm rag to wipe up the mess. Keeping up with messes like these makes it easier when you do an all-out cleaning job, and it is healthier for your animal friend.

The area that requires your most concentrated effort is the bottom grate. Rabbits will have no choice but to walk and lay in their feces if you aren't constant in your duties. Dirty rabbit homes are the source of hutch burn, a nasty irritation on the genital area of our long-eared friend, caused by urine and feces.

Hockburn, the same sort of burning irritation on their feet, can also occur. The cage doesn't have to be very dirty to induce either condition.

Kitty Litter Box

Your cat needs a litter box, even if she is allowed outdoors. The litter box must be scooped daily. If you have more than one cat, you may have to clean the box a few times a day. Keeping the box in a room with a linoleum floor makes cleaning the mess easier. If it must be kept in a carpeted area, protect the floor under the box. You can use ideas mentioned earlier to protect floors under cages or use a large drip pan that catches oil from leaky cars.

Cats can be very wild with their litter while using their box. Litter gets all over the floor and once it has been ground in, it's not easy to get it out of carpet fibers. Linoleum is easier; you can just sweep it up. Your cat will still carry litter around in her furry little paws. Place a litter trap outside of the box to catch litter off her toes when she is done. A simple idea is to place a bath rug or other small rug in front of the box. Shake the rug out every couple of days.

Keeping the litter box in the bathroom makes it convenient to check the box and scoop it clean each time you use the bathroom. Some people flush clumpable litter, but it must be a brand that states it is flushable on the label. If you flush nonflushable litter, you may have to call a sewer maintenance company. For convenience, you can keep a small garbage receptacle with a lid by the box for the scoops. A large jar with a lid works well to keep the odors down. You can paint it or cover it in another decorative manner so you and your guests don't see the contents. Put a layer of baking soda on the bottom of the can or jar to absorb odors. Dump the receptacle every couple of days. The cleaner you keep the litter box, the more your cat will faithfully use it.

Keeping the litter box in a laundry room or other room that isn't frequented by guests works well. People who don't appreciate your pets won't enjoy maneuvering around a litter box full of cat deposits when they use the bathroom. You too would probably appreciate being spared the view.

Keeping Dogs Out of the Litter Box

If you have a dog and cat, you may have to consider how to keep your canine from exploring the feline toileting area. This is an annoying habit because they tend to eat what they find.

• **Dog-Free Room** — Find a room that you want your cat to use but allows you to keep the dog out. In my home, the laundry room doubles as the cat room. Keeping my dogs out of the cat box was simple. I installed an eyelet on the doorframe laterally across (even with) the door handle. A piece of light rope is strung from the eyelet and looped over the door handle to allow a four-inch-wide opening that only my cats can use. When I go into the room, I just undo the rope and hook it when I leave.

Another common solution is to set aside a room for the litter box and then put a gate your cats can jump over in the doorway. It also serves as a place of reprieve from dog enthusiasm.

I also feed my cats in this room, at the opposite end from the litter box, so that they can eat in peace. When you have a dog that likes to get involved in the cats' daily life, you need to give your cats a place to escape, play, rest, and eat where they know they are free from the enthusiasm of a playmate that may weigh eighteen times more than they do.

Installing a pet door to your special cat room is effective. This would work if the dog is larger than the cat and you want something more permanent. If your dog is the same size as your cat, then it will be harder to keep your dog out of a designated room while allowing your cat free access. A key-lock pet door may be the answer. These doors only open when an animal with the special magnetic key, placed on her collar attempts to pass through the door.

• **Barrier Methods** — Some people put the litter box in the bathtub, but this makes a terrible mess. If you want to take a shower or bath, you have to do some cleaning first because you cannot just let the litter wash down the drain. Place the litter box in a large container or on an oil drip pan and lift the entire mess out at once to bathe or shower. Regardless, some mess will escape your most dedicated efforts, and most dogs can still get in to the litter box.

You can put the same idea to use by placing the litter box in a bigger, taller box that your dog will be unable to get into. Place the entire setup in a different room. The box must be solid and stable, and it has to be large enough for the cat to move around in comfortably and for the litter box to fit. The box should be tall enough that the dog cannot get in but short enough for the cat to feel secure when jumping into it. The skinny sides of a thin cardboard box would probably make the cat feel too insecure to jump in. A large plastic tub would be a better solution.

A number of fascinating contraptions designed to hide litter boxes are on the market. Cabinets with doors on the front are used for the box, and the back of these cabinets have a small opening so that the cat can get in and do her duty. If this cabinet is close to the wall, curious canine noses won't be able to fit, but slinky cat bodies can. Just open the front doors to clean.

I've seen advertisements for cat boxes "hidden" in planter boxes. Plant your favorite, safe houseplant and your kitty uses the compartment below for a litter box. If you have an older cat with bladder control problems and she needs several boxes around the house, these would make ideal solutions.

If you use these creative suggestions, make certain that your cat understands where her box is and how to gain access to it.

Dog Messes

Another chore that should be done daily is picking up dog feces. Your neighbors will surely appreciate you. There is nothing worse than stepping outside to enjoy your garden and having your whole yard permeated by the stink of your neighbor's dog deposits.

If you are consistent about picking up after your dog, the chore can be a simple, quick affair. Putting it off for two weeks will turn it into an hour-long ordeal.

• **Convenience Is Paramount** — Make it as easy on yourself as possible. Have the garbage can on the same side of the house as your dog's favorite spot. Keep the tools you need close to each other and close to the yard. Have a special shovel or scoop just for the poop and keep it right by the garbage. A scoop specially made for this purpose is ideal, because it was designed for ease and convenience.

Eliminating the hassle of searching through the yard for dog poop is easy — just train your dog to go in a specific spot. This spot can be a particular part of the yard, a corner, or a little-used area. You can even design a special "dog toilet."

This spot need only be three by three feet. Concrete the area or use gravel. You can get fancy and design a drainage system with a hole in the middle of the area capped with a drain. Slant the concrete toward the drain but not so much that your dog doesn't have comfortable footing, or you can place a draining area on one side. Surround the area on three sides with low bushes or flowers to hide the view. You will need a spigot close by to hose off the area when you pick up feces.

When searching for the best place to put such a convenience, keep a few things in mind. First, you don't want it too close to your house. If it is backed up against the window of your bedroom, you may get an unpleasant smell during a nice spring breeze. If you are going to retrain your dog, you want the area to be relatively close. If you choose a spot at the far end of your yard, you may give up. Leash your dog and walk her out to the toileting area every time she needs to go out. You will have to be diligent in your training — no laziness even during rain, heat, snow, or hail. It's a good idea to do the training when the weather is pleasant. If you work, begin training when you have a long weekend or vacation time.

This system is so convenient that you will wonder how you ever lived without it. Scoop up the poop twice a day if you can. It is so simple that you will hardly notice this frequent cleaning. Your dog won't use such a small spot if it isn't kept clean. Every month or so use a bacteria/enzyme product on the concrete or gravel.

• **What Do You Do with It Now?** — In some cities depositing dog feces in the garbage is not allowed. When you can't get rid of the waste in your regular garbage pickup, you can bury it or use a digester. A digester is a small canister that is buried in the ground with just the lid exposed. A digesting product is put in the canister along with a specified amount of water. The feces are broken down and then released into the ground. Although relatively safe, you want to place the digester away from a water source and your veggie garden. Numerous designs are available. Generally, a large digester accommodates two to four dogs and cats.

Using a digester is easy, keeps odors and pests under control, and is not as messy as other methods. It isn't expensive either. Place it by the designated toileting area and have a poop scoop handy to make the job easier.

Elimination and Other Accidents

There will be times when your pets have accidents in your home. You need to clean these up as soon as possible; the longer they sit, the more they become a permanent fixture in your carpet and furniture. If you are renting, you need to be increasingly diligent in cleaning up after your pets.

Carpet and upholstery absorb odors quickly and stubbornly. A house designed with pets in mind would have hardwood floors and predominantly wood furniture, but that hardly fits the description of most homes. Most people prefer carpet and have to learn how to clean up messes.

• **Urine Messes** — Clean up dog or cat urine immediately by soaking it up with paper or cloth towels. Step on it, blotting the carpet until all wetness is soaked up. The area then needs to be cleaned.

Wet the spot with water and a cleaner. You can use dish soap, an all-purpose cleaner, or a deodorizer/cleaner made for pet messes. Let the cleaner soak in for five to ten minutes. Never scrub a carpet; it will ruin the fibers and spread the spot. To pick up any soap scum, rinse the area with white vinegar or plain club soda. You can dilute the vinegar 25:75 or 50:50 with water. Spray the vinegar on the spot using a spray bottle. Blot this with more paper or cloth towels after allowing it to soak for a couple of minutes.

You may want to follow up your cleaning with a bacteria/enzyme product that neutralizes odor. If you have a puppy, you may as well have one bottle with water and soap and one with water and vinegar made up and ready for accidents.

If you find an old urine spot, saturate the carpet longer with deodorizer/cleaner. Then use the enzyme/bacteria product, letting it soak. You may have to repeat this process a couple of times.

• **Old Accidents** — If you come across a urine accident that has dried, wet it again and then start from the beginning. Prevent your animal from returning to the same spot by making it as awful as possible until she learns her manners. Use two-sided tape to tape down foil, waxed paper, or plastic wrap over the spot.

• **Accidents** — If your dog or cat has a bowel movement on the carpet, pick it up using a dust pan and something flat and stiff like a piece of cardboard or a squeegee reserved for this purpose. Use the process described above for urine to clean the remaining mess. If there are any stains, you can clean the carpet with carpet cleaner. If the stain is near a rabbit or bird cage, remove the bird or rabbit before you clean up the mess. Don't return your animal to the cage for at least an hour. Air out the room during this time.

• **Vomit** — If your pet has vomited, you should follow the same process beginning with soaking up as much as possible. Then use the bacteria/enzyme product and stain remover if necessary.

• **Why Did Your Pet Have an Accident?** — No scolding or clapping — your animal did not have an accident to be mean or bad. There is probably a reason.

If your cat suddenly has an accident after being box trained, call your veterinarian immediately. Usually if a cat has an accident, there is a physical cause. If your adult dog has an accident and the reason isn't immediately apparent (such as you left her in the house for eight hours straight) or if she repeatedly has an accident, she needs to see your veterinarian. If

a puppy is having difficulty eliminating outside, take her in also. She may have a medical cause for her lack of skill.

A male cat may spray if not neutered, but a female cat may also spray if she is in love or if there has been an upheaval in her life. The addition of a new family member, animal or otherwise, can instigate a show of dominance.

• **Special Rabbit Concerns** — Rabbit urine is surprisingly easy to clean. Even accidents heavily tainted with vegetable juice have never stained my white carpet or walls. Simply blot the accident with a wet rag and it comes right up. If the stain is stubborn and has an odor, you can clean it with a deodorizer/cleaner or carpet cleaner.

Rabbit feces are small firm pellets that are easily picked up. Rabbits seem to have less control over these pellets, and even the most dedicated litter box user leaves a couple of pellets about. Your rabbit also marks territory by leaving pellets for any intruders, and these can be vacuumed or swept up with ease.

• **Special Bird Concerns** — If your bird eliminates on linoleum, simply wipe it up as soon as possible. If your bird has an accident on your clothes, it washes out in the washer.

Bird feces on the carpet is best left to dry. An attempt to clean up fresh feces tends to spread and rub it in. If you wait for it to dry, you can scrape it a bit and vacuum it up with no residue. Even on my white carpet, this works perfectly and requires no chemicals. Other animals or children may be too nosy so you can cover the feces with an upside-down plastic bowl. You can then place a book or something heavy on it to keep curious noses from turning it over.

One interesting problem often experienced in a multi-animal household is your bird eliminating on your furry creatures. It happens often in my house. Wipe it off right away so that the animal does not lick it off. It may smear a bit so use a wet rag. You can then comb or brush the hair to finish the cleaning.

Grooming

• • • • • • • • •

Grooming is not only necessary for the physical condition of your pet but it is also beneficial for the emotional well-being of your beloved animal friend. Daily grooming sessions help your pets stay accustomed to the grooming routine. The more often you groom your pet, the quicker and easier it becomes.

BENEFITS OF DAILY GROOMING

Your daily grooming sessions will save you work in the long run. If you keep the physical care of your pet, especially a longhaired one, on a schedule, you won't have to perform the once-a-month miracle. When grooming is combined with a high-quality diet and good exercise, your animal's hair and skin will be in such good condition that a quick daily grooming session takes only minutes. You save yourself the hassle of having to repair any damage that has been done since the last time you brushed or combed your furry friend.

Preventative Opportunities

The added benefit of checking your animal from head to tail daily is that you will be able to spot any problems before they become unmanageable. Fleas will be spotted before they have a chance to reproduce into the millions, and you can immediately begin your flea abatement program.

Other than catching grooming problems early such as mats and skin conditions, you will be given the chance to locate other physical problems before they have a chance to get worse. Lumps, bumps, sores, and other abnormal physical characteristics will readily be noticed when you are grooming your pet. Earlier in this chapter, you read information on performing your weekly observation session and keeping notes in your record book. The daily grooming session will be a quick, less intense version that focuses on a condition check and keeps the coat healthy.

Daily grooming sessions keep down the amount of animal hair spread throughout your house. Grooming also stimulates the skin to produce beneficial oils and distribute them through the hair and on the skin. This increases the health of your pet's coat and makes her less susceptible to pests.

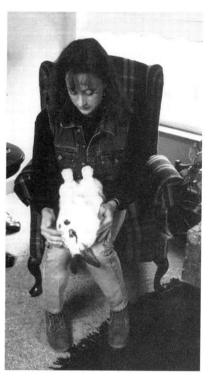

This rabbit has been "hypnotized" by stroking her nose and is in the perfect position for a thorough grooming job, including a nail trim.

Bonding

One of the greatest and often most secret benefits to a daily grooming session is your animal's exposure to your physical contact on a daily basis. Yes, maybe you pet your dog on the head frequently, play games, and train her. Maybe your cat gets her chin rubbed and her back stroked plenty. Maybe your rabbit gets nuzzled and pet throughout the day. Grooming is altogether something different. The animal gets the physical contact on each part of her body. She must remain relaxed with your touch and be reminded of the comfort of the brush and comb against her body.

This one-on-one attention, combined with your soothing voice and gentle touch, is especially helpful with adopted, previously abused, shy, fearful, sick, or old pets. It is a time for bonding, a time to deepen your relationship with your companion. It is an expression of your commitment to the physical and mental health of your pets.

TIME COMMITMENT

With practice, you will get your daily grooming sessions down to manageable chunks of time. Even a longhaired cat will only take five to ten minutes. Of course, the more pets you have, the more minutes it will take. You do not have to groom each animal daily, but keep in mind the incredible benefits when planning your schedule.

My first suggestion is not to get more animals than you can groom in a day. If that doesn't work, my second suggestion is to create a rotating schedule. This schedule can include half your pets one day and the other half the next day, and then begin again. This way you are still grooming each pet every other day. This is frequent enough to get the benefits but is not ideal. If you have so many pets that they can't get their own five to ten minutes every other day, maybe you have too many pets or a poorly executed care schedule.

Evaluating advice

Because you are an animal lover, you are often in the company of other animal lovers. They are everywhere — in the pet store, feed store, veterinarian office, and obedience training courses. They help you when you are searching for a veterinarian, boarding kennel, or pet sitter, or if you just want advice on a good motel to stay at with your dog when you go away next month.

This kind of interaction can be helpful, but it can also be frustrating. Some people give advice you don't find useful at all. Some advice can be outright disastrous.

Most of the time unsolicited knowledge is offered from the genuine caring and kindness of the person. Sometimes it is offered only as an example of the person's supposed expertise and assumed animal education. Be cautious and do your own research. Only through your ability to understand your pet and interpret different points of view will you be able to make an informed choice about which advice is beneficial to you and your animal companions.

Differing Philosophies

Some people are only perpetuating unnecessary and harmful means of pet care that have been passed on to them from other uneducated sources. These people may be resistant to training methods or care procedures that are different from what they have been exposed to. You can try to educate them, but don't waste too much of your time and don't hold it against them. You can simply say, "Thank you, but I'm going to try it this way."

Stick to your own philosophy, without letting yourself become coerced, even if your opinion contradicts "conventional wisdom." Know that you are right to use safe, humane, and loving animal-raising methods with your animals. You may try different techniques to find what works best for your pet, but whatever you try will have a foundation that fits your view of nonaggressive, respectful interactions. Reading many different books on training and behavior gives you a well-rounded education. If you have to seek advice from professionals, you will understand what they are doing and saying. By being an informed caretaker, you can make the best decision regarding your animals.

Seeking Assistance

If a problem arises and you are confused about how to deal with it, seek the guidance of a professional. You may consult a veterinarian, a behaviorist, or a trainer. In order to eliminate any physical reason behind trouble, a veterinarian should be your first stop. Provide your veterinarian with as many details as possible using the records in your observation book for reference.

When did the behavior start? Under what circumstances does it present itself? What changes have been made in your pet's environment? If there is no physical reason behind your pet's misbehavior, then your veterinarian may try to manipulate your pet through drugs. Before trying this method or in conjunction with it, search out a behaviorist or trainer who specializes in your species of animal companion.

HOW TO HANDLE ANGER TOWARD YOUR PET

I get so angry sometimes. What do I do if I find myself just wanting to hit my pet?

First of all, know that it is perfectly normal to get angry with your animal companions — even angry enough to want to strike them. But don't! Hitting an animal does not teach her anything but to be afraid of you. Yes, maybe she will avoid the behavior in the future but only out of an association with fear. Is this the kind of companion you want? Or would you rather have a pet who understands the acceptable limits of behavior and complies out of respect for your leadership?

When you are this angry with your pet, you must take steps to avoid the release of your frustration through violence. Here are some suggestions that will help.

- Don't take it personally. Your animal friend is not punishing you or getting even. There is nothing vengeful in your pet; she is simply engaging in a behavior that at this time seems more appropriate and rewarding than the alternate behavior you would rather she pursue. It is your responsibility to show her what is expected.
- Then again, don't feel guilty about your pet's bad behavior. Guilt is a demotivating emotion and will get you no closer to curing the problem. Guilt also keeps you from correcting the problem because it makes you feel as though you can do nothing to fix it. Your situation is not hopeless.
- Remain as calm as you possibly can. This may seem paradoxical and impossible, but if you think "calm," it will help you deal with the situation.
- Use the old standby anger-reducing method of counting to ten before you do anything. When your anger boils, ready to explode from your hand to your pet — stop, and slowly count to ten. These seconds may be enough time for you to get your emotions under control.
- Take deep breaths: deep, slow inhales, followed by slow, even exhales. Breathing often calms even the greatest temper. If you sing, you have to breathe, so try a song. It may make you feel better just by distraction.
- Detach yourself from the situation. Close your eyes as you take a couple of deep breaths. Concentrate on your emotions coming back into your body, squeezing them tight into your midsection. Think of your weight heavy on the ground, sinking through your feet. (I know, that weird stuff again. It's not though. This is a technique you unconsciously do when you get control of your emotions. I am giving you the visualization so that you can make yourself do it when you need to.) This is often called "grounding" and will make you concentrate more on the physical sensation of the ground or floor and less on the nontangible emotions of anger, giving you control of the situation once again.

If your anger does not immediately dissipate, retreat. A retreat is not a surrender. If you cannot deal with your companion or your anger, leave the company of your pet. Take time away and you will feel better, and most importantly, you will have refrained from using violence on your precious friend.

It Is Not Personal

The most important thing to remember about animal companion misbehavior is not to take it personally. They are not "bad" or "getting even," and they are not mad or upset with you. When your animals have a lapse of good behavior, release feelings of guilt over the situation. Take a deep breath and deal with it. Only with this attitude will you be able to alter bad behavior.

Correcting behavioral problems takes time; there are no miracles. Your understanding and patience are essential, and your commitment is vital.

CREATE A RELATIONSHIP BUILT ON MUTUAL RESPECT

Mutual respect is the cornerstone of any relationship, and this is especially true with the human/animal relationship. Creating a bond with your animals is only possible with mutual respect. Even animals that seem to react to every whim of their caretaker may only be doing so from fear or coercion. If you want to live peacefully with an animal and include this creature in a home with other animals, you must create a relationship where your pet will willingly and respectfully accept your place as leader of the family.

This requires training your pet in a manner that facilitates understanding and eagerness to please. It also means recognizing the needs of your pets and your desire to meet these needs. If your companion needs time alone, you must fulfill this need. The need for food, water, shelter, and veterinary care is obvious, but you must be able to interpret psychological and emotional needs as well.

Again and again, you must remember that your animal companions are individuals. They have received some genetic material that determines a part of their personality, but in the big picture they are each unique. An appreciation of their distinctive souls will help your acceptance and perception of your animal friends. This is the beginning of building mutual respect.

If you see each pet as a valuable being, capable of trusting and honoring, she will view you as worthy of respect. This is part of what makes the animal/human bond a team project. Willingness from all involved is what makes the relationship a wonderful and special one.

TRAINERS

It has been conventional wisdom that training was the answer to correcting many behavior problems. While this may be true for some behavioral

A POSITIVE ATTITUDE

What does your attitude have to do with the animal/human relationship?

A positive perspective on your world and the people and animals in your life affects the harmony of your home. Intelligent animals learn about their world through the important beings in their life. Initially, it is their mother and then their human caretakers. If the people in your home taunt each other or harbor hostile feelings, either repressed or expressed, your animal companions will demonstrate the same negative temperament. You cannot hide your resentment at your spouse. You cannot conceal your mistrust of strangers or your disinterest or lack of enthusiasm. You witness these traits manifesting in your pets. Problem behaviors may reflect what is happening in your own life. You must learn to take a long hard look at yourself when seeking answers to your animal friend's misconduct. A positive change in your attitude may make all the difference.

problems, it depends on the misbehavior, your pet's species and breed, the underlying cause of the misbehavior, the animal's present level of training, and the emotional and psychological condition of both creature and caretaker.

Training and discipline require creativity. Animal behavior and individual personalities are diverse and complicated. Although people have tried to establish a "do-A-and-B-will-follow" methodology for raising and living with creatures, the fact is that it won't work. Your pets are not cookie-cutter creations that respond with predictable patterns; they are spirited, intense, and vivacious. Search out a trainer who is flexible and imaginative with a repertoire of techniques for molding animal behavior.

Cats

Most people don't bother attempting to modify their cat's behavior, but a cat can be trained if she wants to be. However, cats cannot be trained with punishment because they do not understand correction or discipline. The best way to control a cat's misbehavior is to make it easy for her to do the right thing and difficult to do the wrong thing. You can motivate her with treats and praise.

The first step in training a cat is to alter her environment so that inappropriate behaviors never have a chance to develop. Boredom is a major cause of misbehavior, so decrease boredom from the beginning.

Providing a good scratching post and keeping nails trimmed will protect furniture and curtains. Planted grass available for nibbling will help deter kitty from chewing on your houseplants. Providing healthy food in adequate quantities, removing temptations from the counters and tables, and cleaning up when you're done eating will keep your cat from jumping on counters and tables to get to your food. Supplying a clean and attractive (from the cat's view) litter box will alleviate elimination problems. Of course, spaying and neutering reduces many unruly and inappropriate behaviors. Providing toys and permitting no roughhousing will teach your cat to play in an appropriate manner. Protect your cat from household dangers in order to eliminate emergency situations.

Rabbits

A rabbit can be trained. For example, training her to use a litter box is usually easy. Initiate training to discourage chewing, digging, and other destructive activities by telling her "no" when you catch her in the act. Your long-eared friend will be able to understand the word "no"; however, like a cat, she will follow her own whims when you are not present to stop her. As with cats, your best method of training is prevention.

Parrots

Parrots are highly intelligent creatures with the capacity to learn and understand what you teach them. You will have to make an effort to learn as much as possible about how to influence your parrot's behavior.

You have learned basic guidelines in the care of dogs and cats through your experiences. Few people have grown up with birds, especially parrots, and so have absorbed little information. This is a curable condition, requiring only curiosity and devotion. Read books and magazines, and talk to many people who will share their time and wisdom on bird care and behavior in order to understand what you may expect from your feathered friend and how to develop her inherited ability to coexist in your household.

You will find many conflicting opinions and advice in your education. Apply the knowledge you acquire to your own situation and your own feathered friend.

I cannot overemphasize the benefit you will experience by reading the magazine *Pet Bird Report* (Sally Blanchard, editor). The information on bird behavior is invaluable. Although more is being written about the emotional and psychological makeup of these feathered jewels, this magazine is the best source for invaluable information.

Parrots are wild creatures that have not been genetically programmed to please humans; they are not submissive. If your parrot begins to have behavioral problems, do not take her to a bird trainer. Learning tricks is fun and can be a wonderful experience, if done in an atmosphere of love and patience, but it will not eliminate bad behavior on its own. Consult your veterinarian first and then seek the advice of a respected behaviorist.

Dogs

The advice given to many dog companions regarding their pet's behavioral problems is to enroll in obedience training. This is true to an extent. If you exercise your dog's brain with basic obedience lessons, her comprehension of your control and need to follow your requests will develop. A good, reliable down-stay can be a saving grace in many situations.

Although these things are positive and important, they are not the solution to all behavioral problems. Every dog should be obedience trained, but what if your dog does the best sit-stay and recall of any dog in your obedience class and yet still chews the couch? Find the underlying cause of your pet's destruction. By better understanding where the behavior is originating, you can modify the activity. For this kind of help, seek an animal behaviorist.

• **Finding a Trainer** — Anyone can become a dog trainer. You do not have to be licensed, and most states have no requirements. If you can run an ad in the newspaper or have flyers printed up, you can become a dog trainer. Find a dog trainer who has more to offer than sales savvy.

What kind of activity do you want to pursue with your pet? Do you simply want an obedient companion? Are you interested in obedience trials? Are you interested in a specialty sport? If you have an area of interest, check it out. Find a trainer who participates in the activity. If you don't have a competitive yearning for organized dog sports, that's fine; your dog should have basic obedience training regardless. If she will do nothing but warm your lap and step outside to do her duty, she should be obedience trained.

Find an individual who has had extensive experience handling dogs. This experience can come from training guide dogs, therapy dogs, or dogs for military or police work. It could be hands-on experience with obedience trials or other dog sports competitions. They may have years of experience working at a boarding kennel, groomer, or veterinarian hospital. As long as the individual has interacted with hundreds of dogs, you can hope that he or she would possess a solid understanding of canine behavior and communication.

Get references from the trainer and make phone calls. It is useless to get references if you are not going to call and see how the former clients felt about the training. A competent trainer will be glad to offer you references, so don't be afraid to ask.

• **Things to Look For** — Attend a trainer's class. What is the overall feeling you get from the instructor, the handlers, and dogs in the class? Is the class being taught in an upbeat, encouraging atmosphere? The dogs should look interested, not bored; they should look enthusiastic, not frightened. Trainers usually bring their own dog to use for demonstrating the lessons. Is the trainer's dog well behaved and obedient? Don't expect robot precision (even dogs have bad days), but get a good feel for willingness to obey.

Does the instructor guide the people with respect and kindness? The instructor should be encouraging, not derogatory or patronizing, to the people in the class. In group instruction, the distractions are many and dogs learn little in the class itself. The purpose of a group class is to train the people to train the dogs in the quiet, controlled environment of their own home. Does the instructor give the people the confidence necessary to follow this advice and train their pet when they leave?

The cost of the training course is not a measure of quality. Many good trainers who have been training dogs successfully for many years teach classes just for the fun of it and because they love it so much. Their fees may be small compared to the trainer who is in it only for the money and has little regard for the dogs or their handlers. Some communities may offer dog training classes at no charge as a service to its dog owning citizens.

• **Training Methods** — Different breeds of dogs have different learning styles and rates. Each dog is an individual with a different set of life circumstances and her own personal characteristics. Does the instructor take these differences into consideration? There should be evidence of flexibility and a knowledge of different approaches to the same lesson. If the instructor only offers one method to teach a command and attempts to make each dog adhere to this method, find someone who is more caring and better educated.

Attending an obedience class where punishment is the training method of choice can do more damage than good. Even if all is going well except for one brief loss of temper or if any method of physical roughness is used, leave. These training tools and methods have no place in a respectable obedience class. They only cause harm and mask problems. You want your dog to work with you as a team. Your pet can learn better through mutual respect and will be more obedient at all times rather than just when the collar is around her neck.

If you sign up for an obedience class and have a bad experience, don't give up. Many caring instructors are available whose main goal is to provide you with the tools to shape your dog into a wonderful companion. Search these instructors out; they are worth the effort.

ANIMAL BEHAVIORISTS

Forget the notion of your pet lying on a couch while a Freudian-type human questions her on her babyhood. Behaviorists are people who know animals well and have a deep understanding of their nature, mind, and roots of behavior. They use positive reinforcement to shape the actions of pets with behavioral problems.

Finding a Behaviorist

There are no licensing bureaus for animal behaviorists, so rely on word of mouth and your own intuition to choose a behaviorist you can trust with the mental health of your pet.

Ask your veterinarian, friends, organizations, and clubs for names of behaviorists. Check the credibility and experience of the behaviorist. Is the person fresh from college with a degree in microbiology? Is this the kind of qualification you are looking for? Has the person been relating with your species of pet for many years, meeting hundreds of animals, and helping shape their behavior? If he is somewhat new, does he have a mentor who he can rely on for further advice if needed? Do you also respect this person?

Get references and check them. Hear from the people who have been helped by the behaviorist and get a feeling for what they liked and disliked about the advice and the outcome.

Practicalities

Ask the behaviorist how you are expected to pay for the advice. For a telephone consultation, you may have to pay in advance. Are you paying for a one-time consultation or are you paying for consultation until the problem is resolved? Do you pay it all up-front or as you go? Are you paying the behaviorist an hourly fee or a flat fee regardless of how much time you will need?

Guarantees and Quick Fixes

How reliable is the advice? If the behaviorist is offering you a guarantee of success, be suspicious. There are no guarantees when it comes to correcting behavioral problems. The dynamics of the problem include two or more social, sensitive creatures attempting to understand one another's language and trying to create an enjoyable relationship.

Be cautious of quick fixes. Quick fixes to behavioral problems don't exist; they simply don't work or work only temporarily. Quick fixes tend to use coercion or punishment, both of which can do more damage to your animal's psyche in the long run. Treat the underlying cause, not just the symptoms. A quick fix treats only the symptoms.

Communication

The behaviorist must also be a "people person." You should feel as if you are considered an important part of the solution. The behaviorist should listen to a full explanation of the problem and should ask you questions, listening completely to your answers. You should never be made to feel silly or inadequate. You deserve to be treated like the caring animal lover you are; you should be offered encouragement.

When the behaviorist gives you advice on what to do for your pet, make sure that you fully comprehend the techniques and suggested actions. Do you have a full understanding of the cause of the misbehavior? Have all the requirements been explained?

The Behaviorist's Philosophy

When analyzing the advice you have been given, first be sure it betters the relationship with your pet. Any punishment or treatments that seem harsh or unnecessary should alert you to a possible conflict with the behaviorist. The relationship between you and your animal companion should become stronger as a result of your actions. You don't just want control — you want mutual respect and a bonded relationship.

Any actions or advice that threaten the sense of security of your animal should be avoided. If you threaten the security of your bird or rabbit, you may never be able to rebuild your relationship or at least not without considerable effort. Animals are sensitive and vulnerable; choose your actions wisely.

Is the advice based on generalizations and misconceptions? Does it seem outdated and in conflict with what your intuition is telling you? If the behaviorist is just rehashing the same old information, you'll just have the same old problems — not that only new information is good. Instead of placing the mental health of your pet in the hands of someone who can only reiterate overused advice, you want a behaviorist who takes your individual animal and your life situation into account, giving you relevant advice for your situation.

If there is something you completely disagree with, then you will have to decide if you will take any advice from the behaviorist. A few small discrepancies are tolerable; however, if the behaviorist presents an opinion with which you totally disagree, you should find another behaviorist whom you can fully trust.

Your Contribution

You will get the best advice only by being honest with the behaviorist. Don't make excuses; just share the information about your situation. Do what the behaviorist suggests, all of it, every detail. If you don't follow the advice exactly, you cannot expect results.

Remember that any behavior modification takes time — do not expect miracles. If one method doesn't work, try another if it's humane and does not compromise the security and trust of your pet. Understanding and patience are essential to behavior modification therapy.

These two dogs are beautiful as well as behaved and emotionally sound, but sometimes loving caretakers need the advice of professional animal trainers or behaviorists to better understand their pets and modify undesirable behaviors. Remember that caring for animals is a constant educational adventure. Don't hesitate to ask for help if you need it.

If you don't have this level of understanding, you may unintentionally recreate the problem.

Evaluate the behaviorist to see if his or her animal ethics mesh with yours. Finding someone who believes that animals should be treated with the same respect and concern that you do is paramount to success. Listen for expressions of affection and respect for your species of pet.

76

GET EDUCATED!

Curiosity about the true essence of your animal companions leads you to enlightening adventures. The search for information directs you to interesting people, fascinating facts, and inspiring speculation. Education reveals the secrets of animal behavior, and you discover the veiled identity of your companions. Your appreciation increases as your knowledge expands. By learning, you experience the life of your pet more fully.

Curious caretakers want to learn as much as possible about animals. You become a collector of knowledge and advice by observing the pets in your home and absorbing information from other sources. Many animal lovers have extensive libraries on all aspects concerning creatures. Television, videos, and computers are additional sources of facts, nonfacts, truths, and half-truths. It is up to you to sort the information and decide what you believe is worthy.

Saving as much information as possible for future reference is invaluable. Keep folders, boxes, and records on the articles you collect. Read books and create a library. Talk to anyone who has pets; communicate with the "experts" and the "not-so-expert." People who have experiences with animals are great information sources. They have lived the advice they share. Whether what they have to offer is valid or not, you may find a crumb of inspiration in a sentence. Even if you end up discounting most of the advice, at least enjoy the "pet talk."

Education is more than reading about a subject. Spending time with your animal companions, learning about what they like to do and how they like to be cared for, will be a big part of your education. Enjoy it! The more you learn, the more you'll love them.

*The highlight
of interplay
between
humans
and animals
is mutual
adoration.*

Having fun

Now that the nuts and bolts of daily life in a multi-animal home have been discussed, let's concentrate on the fun part. The highlight of interplay between humans and animals is mutual adoration. Spending time with the animals that fill your existence with unrelenting wonder, participating in their unique lives, and being fortunate enough to catch glimpses into the "hidden" kingdom of nature remind you of the integral belonging you have with all creation. Sharing play and affection through fun, respect, and love expands your view of the universe and yet humbles and brings you closer to appreciating each moment.

The joy in being the guardian of a multi-animal household is interacting with species who seem to have a finely tuned understanding of the value of living life completely by experiencing it in the purest sense. This chapter is meant to give you some practical ways to increase your participation in the lives of your animal companions.

You, your pets, and this playground called life

Play is an important part of an animal's life. Through play, animals learn the skills necessary to survive and the manners required to be a member of their community. When you bring animals into your home, you make them a part of the human community and ask them to conform to your social standards. Training is a necessary tool for them to understand their roles, boundaries, and duties. Play is another tool. In the hands of the best trainers, training and play are one in the same.

EMOTIONAL BENEFITS OF PLAY

Play helps animals and their caretakers learn to relate to each other and better understand the other's personality and spirit. Playing with your animal companions strengthens your bond with them and increases their ability to synchronize with your moods and emotions, which are essential for a peaceful, happy coexistence. Whether the play is a game, a physically healthy romp outdoors, a relaxing engagement, or just

clowning around, being together is good for you and your pets and develops trust between you.

Play is important to prevent boredom, which is the cause of many behavioral problems. Parrots can develop a myriad of neuroses if left alone in a cage devoid of toys and your interaction. Dogs can become destructive without an outlet for their playful energy. In order to alleviate boredom, it is important for you to encourage play and provide toys.

PLAY PROMOTES HEALTH

Play promotes activity and therefore increases physical fitness. Activity stimulates the metabolic and circulatory systems, helping the body to remove wastes more efficiently. Play does all the wonderful things for animals that it does for humans, such as staying younger longer and lessening the risk of many diseases and illnesses.

Unfortunately, many pets live the same physically inactive lives people do, and like people, they can become obese and be at risk of dangers related to obesity and inactivity.

Play is an opportunity for health observations. Playing with your pet each day gives you an opportunity to observe the creature in action. Through encouragement of physical activity, you will know when your companion is feeling stiff, sore, or lethargic; experiencing loss of coordination; or just doesn't "feel" right.

JUST FOR THE FUN OF IT

As if you needed another reason to encourage play, it is a wonderful personality booster. Personalities emerge and blossom as your animals express themselves through play. Rabbits, which are often cast off as not having much personality, are truly one of these animals. Anyone with a rabbit that is secure and confident and given fun toys knows that a rabbit is a comedian, a gymnast, and a tease. Cats become frisky and lively after luring them in a chase game. I get a great chuckle out of watching my macaw beat up her plastic man, and I know she must be pretending it's her rival, my husband.

Play just for the joy of it is also important in an animal's life. Animals play to express their happiness, comfort, spunkiness, contentment, and thrill to be alive. Animals love to play, and they appreciate their human friend joining in for a good adventure.

Encouraging Play

Believe it or not, some animals simply don't know how to play. If you rescue an animal, you may experience this lack of impulse for fun because pets that come from deprived backgrounds often did not get the chance to play. Other pets may be shy and insecure. But you can show them how to engage in play and have fun.

PLAYING BY EXAMPLE

Imagine that someone comes to your yard and puts up a wading pool. You have never seen a wading pool before and have absolutely no idea what it is or what to do with it. If you are really brave or extremely curious, you may walk over and investigate. More than likely, you would simply ignore and avoid the pool. If someone came into your yard and began splashing about in the pool, you would watch curiously; if you are outgoing, you may join in the fun. If you're shy, you may wait until no one was watching and cautiously try it out yourself.

Now imagine a dog encountering this scenario. He will need some sort of orientation to help him understand and accept the new situation. If you introduce something new to your animals, whether it is a game or a toy, demonstrate what it is all about. Show them how much fun it can be. Play with the toy on your own where he can see you, and then coax the animal to join you.

Based on his personality, this could take just a moment, or it may take several days for him to catch on and be impelled to try it out for himself. If your pet is the shy type (many parrots fall into this category), be quite animated as you demonstrate how fun the toy can be. As you play with the toy, exclaim, "Wow! This is fun! What a fun toy!" (Caution: Use this technique only when you are sure no one is around watching or hearing you. Let go and have fun!)

WHAT IF YOUR PET ISN'T INTERESTED IN PLAY?

Your animal is still not interested in the toy? There is nothing wrong with him; he just may be a bit more reserved than others. My Bouvier, Retta, thinks she is far too sophisticated to play with toys. I've tried to get her interested in many different kinds but to no avail. She is extremely smart, so intelligence isn't the roadblock. I also know she loves to have fun. When we work on the agility equipment, she has a ball. She loves to play with people and other dogs in quite a puppylike manner.

If you have an animal friend like this, relax and don't worry. Continue to introduce new toys, and you may suddenly find one that he finds irresistible. If he is not destroying your furniture out of boredom and seems content, just give him plenty of other stimulation, attention, and love. Count your blessings; if he were a toy fanatic, you would, in a year, be spending a month's wages on toys (those of us who care for these pets can relate to this statement).

Choosing toys for your animal friends

Use your imagination when choosing toys and games. You don't have to spend enormous amounts of money on store-bought toys. Look around your home and open your mind to opportunities. In the following sections, suggestions for each pet include toys that are common household items.

The key to finding things around your home for your pets to play with is to think safety and fun. As you would with young children, keep small toys away from big mouths. Birds, especially, can break apart almost anything. A beak that can break a brazil nut like a toothpick can easily turn a plastic toy into confetti. This can be dangerous if the bird swallows a piece. The same bit of advice that comes up again and again in a multi-animal household is appropriate here as well — always be observant and cautious.

To keep excitement high and boredom low, alternate the toys you give to your pets. The "newness" of an old toy reintroduced keeps your animal entertained longer than if it were left out indefinitely.

Toys that collect bacteria must be thrown out after awhile. Bones will only be good for a couple of weeks at most. Rope toys that have been dunked in water or pooped on should be thrown away. Any toy that becomes frayed or cracked, loses parts, or in any way becomes dangerous to your pet should be tossed and replaced.

HAVING A SENSE OF HUMOR

The people who see humor in their animals' personality are the blessed ones. Like people, animals have a sense of humor; some have more than others. Without it, you miss out on some of the most memorable moments of living in an animal household. Graced with this attribute, you are more likely to survive the trying times with a smile and retain your appreciation for your animal companions.

The luckiest animal lovers are those who experience a childlike wonderment and enjoyment in the antics of their pets. Animals are amusing — your pets do funny and delightful things. If you offer them a comfortable, safe existence, your pets will entertain you. If you are open and willing to experience their joy, you will be delighted and revel in their fun.

Dogs

• • • •

Taking thirty minutes a day and devoting it to playing with your dog increases his emotional and physical well-being. Dogs love excitement and play is the vehicle to adventure. The more adventures they have, the happier they are at home. New smells, sights, and experiences are important for a high-quality life.

TOYS FOR DOGS

So many toys are available for your dog that you can find a suitable toy in most pet shops and feed stores. Hard rubber toys are quite popular. The Kong toy is a good, tough toy for active mouths.

Dogs love fake lambskin shaped in teddy bears and other creatures. If you have children, avoid the stuffed animals for dogs; your dog may think that all stuffed animals are okay to chew on. The same goes for shoes. Give your dog an old shoe to chew and he may think all shoes are okay.

Rope toys are commonly found in stores and come in many designs. Don't play tug of war, though, which is discussed later in this chapter.

Tennis balls and racquet balls are fun, but watch for breakage. A hard plastic ball, which is practically indestructible, is also available and comes in a few different sizes. They are great for "soccer" games of kicking and chasing. Other balls made of soft plastic require your supervision while your dog is playing with them because they are easily torn and the pieces can be hazardous.

Your hand is never a toy; no part of your body is meant to be a plaything for your dog. Teach your dog to respect human flesh. Discourage this kind of play the day you bring the pup home.

For a dog that is left alone for long periods of time, adding an apple to his water dish keeps him entertained for awhile. Bobbing for the apple is great fun and when your dog is successful, he is rewarded with a good treat. You can also give your dog a carrot to chew on. Food toys give your pet two benefits, fun and nutrition, but they do create a mess. However, alleviating boredom is worth the mess.

Rawhides are a bit controversial. Pressed rawhide can fall apart under the tenacious jaws of your canine, creating a choking hazard or an impaction further in the digestive process.

Manufacturers of rawhide chews must use harsh, dangerous chemicals in the tanning process. If hides are tanned properly, there is no reason to worry because all chemical residue is absent from the finished product. Because the United States has such strict regulations involving the use and disposal of these chemicals, prices for tanned hides are expensive.

Most companies buy from overseas to save on cost, and these countries have more lenient regulations involving chemicals and their use.

Unfortunately, animal caretakers have no way of knowing if the chews they offer their pets are safe or not. Giving your dog Nylabones is a better idea. Gumabones are a bit softer, and some dogs enjoy them more. Another favorite is a sterilized bone with a piece of cheese stuffed inside.

NOT-SO-GOOD GAMES

Some games people commonly play with their dogs can have negative consequences; many can cause bad habits or behavioral problems.

Some people believe that tug of war curbs a dog's aggression, but the opposite is usually true. Tug of war teaches the dog to fight for what he wants, to be tenacious, and to be forceful and strong with his caretaker. If he wins often, he begins to see himself as top dog, and this can make for a bossy dog that is not afraid to use his mouth to get his way.

A gentle game of tug of war where the dog doesn't win could be a part of play, but both human and canine are often unable to stop the game soon enough. If you decide to let tug of war be a part of your dog's play, stop every one or two minutes and ask for a sit-stay or a down-stay to keep control of the game and reinforce a consistent "drop" command.

Some advanced training requires a strong mouth hold, and professional trainers may use tug of war as a component to training, but for the pet caretaker who wants to share life with a well-behaved, obedient canine companion, tugging games should not be part of the play repertoire.

Chase games can also be detrimental. You will be unsuccessful at teaching your dog a trustworthy recall if you are always chasing him in play. If he chases you, then you can be in trouble. Many times the excitement of the chase will get the dog overstimulated, and a playful game becomes a very serious game where someone may get hurt. Don't encourage any pet in a multi-animal home to chase a moving thing. Cats and other animals are at a disadvantage if your dog is a chaser.

Wrestling is also a big no-no because it can create problems for all the reasons mentioned above,

Running with your dog is an efficient way to exercise his mind as well as his body. If you work outside of your home, exercising in the morning before you leave will help your companion use some excess energy and allow him to be calmer while you are away.

and your dog thinks he can use his mouth, teeth, paws, and body to get his way. It may be fun to wrestle with a little ball of fur, but remember that ball of fur is going to grow up. It isn't fun to have a dog in the house who wrestles you to the ground and pins you down. It can be dangerous if this dog has aspirations of being in charge and is willing to use physical force to prove it.

DOG ACTIVITIES AND SPORTS

A vast array of sporting opportunities are available for you and your dog. Obedience trials, lure coursing, field trials, Schutzhund, sledding, and disc catching are some of the organized activities you can do. Research some that seem interesting by talking to people who participate in them. Plan to attend a competition as a spectator before you commit training time and expense.

You want to have fun, so choose something that you and your dog can enjoy and that matches your personalities. Some sports are more competitive than others, and some may be too intense for a laid-back canine. Other activities may not offer enough intensity if you and your dog are competitive.

Experiment with different adventures. You may already have a hobby that you want to include your dog in, or you may be looking for something for yourself as well. Bringing your buddy with you while you participate in your favorite activity makes it incredibly rewarding and loads of fun.

If you have a dog that requires a high level of physical exercise, you can choose from a variety of ways to make sure he gets what he needs; in the meantime, you may get a little exercise too. If you have a toy dog, a very large dog, or a dog with a pushed-in face, a walk may be the most vigorous form of exercise you should do because of their sensitive respiratory system. A dog that is in his senior years, sick, or recovering from an injury will also have to be a walker. A few fun activities that you and your dog can participate in include walking, jogging, biking, mountain biking, swimming, skating, canoeing, camping, hiking, horseback riding, cart pulling, skiing, skijoring, and search and rescue.

THERAPY ANIMALS

You can also spend quality time with your furry friend and help others by having him become a therapy dog. Any healthy dog that has the right attitude can become a therapy dog, and other animals in your care can also become therapy animals. A therapy dog, or other pet, may visit children's hospitals, veterans' hospitals, rest homes, convalescent hospitals, and rehabilitation centers. Your dog must be well behaved and needs to understand basic obedience. Many therapy dogs know tricks or are able to show off special traits to entertain the people they visit. Sled dogs have been known to pull patients in their wheelchairs gently down the hall.

The Best Therapy Dog

Your dog must have the right temperament to be a therapy dog. A gentle, affectionate animal who loves people and has the intuitive understanding of the weaknesses and vulnerabilities of humans is important. He must also be friendly and outgoing. He will be meeting many people, sometimes in large groups, so crowds should not rattle him. Other dogs or animals may be visiting the facility, so you want to make sure that your dog is tolerant of many creatures. Your dog should not be frightened by the equipment and machines he will be exposed to while in hospitals.

To be a therapy dog, he must be healthy, up-to-date on his vaccinations, and parasite-free. Behind every appreciated therapy dog is a dedicated caretaker who is diligent when it comes to grooming. The dogs are often invited by the patients to sit or lie on their beds or on the furniture. They will have close contact with many people, some whose health may be currently unstable. Your dog will be enthusiastically welcomed if he is squeaky-clean and good-natured. Bathing often and brushing thoroughly before visits assure your pet a place in the therapy program.

Becoming a Therapy Team

You and your dog do not have to be registered to be a therapy dog team, but it is highly recommended. It gives your team credibility and provides you with contacts and information about getting into therapy dog work. Several organizations certify therapy dogs. Some require the Canine Good Citizen test, and some don't. Ask around and find out what registration organization is active in your area.

If you want to get into therapy work, contact your local volunteer service organization. You may contact various centers directly and ask if they have a current program initiated. If they do, this is a good opportunity to observe the teams. If they don't have a therapy dog program, offer your services and set up a meeting with the person in charge. He or she may or may not want to see your dog at this interview. Remember that you are representing yourself and your dog, so treat it like any interview and be clean and tidy for your visit.

Therapy work is very rewarding. The joy that your pet brings to the people you visit is immeasurable. They look forward to your visit, so you must be consistent and committed. The patients may form strong emotional bonds with your pet, and your animal friend may develop special attachments to his "favorites." Be prepared to make a difference if you decide to do therapy visits.

DOG PLAY

Dogs playing with other dogs is one of the best forms of exercise for your canine buddy. It is good for the dogs physically as well as psychologically to let them socialize with others of their kind.

They will chase each other and have mock fights. Watch the fun and games to be sure it is not getting too rough or becoming aggressive. If one dog becomes frightened, you must separate them. Often an older or bigger dog gets rough with the other, but depending on the personalities of the animals, it can also be the opposite.

Read the section on introducing dogs before introducing a new playmate to your companion.

OBEDIENCE

Basic obedience training should be fun. Keeping your sessions short and your dog's interest high keeps both of you motivated. Integrate obedience lessons into your play sessions by asking your dog to perform a command that you have been working on. When he obeys, praise him and return to playing.

For example, you can include a down-stay in a fetch game: make your dog down-stay, then throw the toy and don't release your pet right away. After a couple of seconds, or however long you are working on, release him to fetch the toy. Return to playing and make it fun and games again.

This discipline associated with play teaches your dog to obey you even when he is excited. He wants to play the game again, so he will be quick to listen to you and follow your commands. Always end your training session on a positive note. Finish by performing a skill that you know your dog can do so you can praise him lavishly before ending the session.

Cats

· · · ·

You may have a sophisticated cat that would rather lounge around on the back of the couch all day than move a muscle. I know the type; I share my couch with one. In order for your couch cat to get exercise and put his hunting instinct to work, you will have to initiate games and encourage activity with stimulating toys.

A single cat in the household will be bored. Without another cat to play these games with, you will be the lucky play companion. Getting your cat to move, especially if he is an indoor cat, is necessary for his health. It's also fun.

TOYS FOR CATS

You can find all types of cat toys at a pet store or order them from a catalog. However, many items in your home make great cat toys. When choosing a toy for your cat, don't choose something too heavy or hard. Ping-pong balls are an all-time favorite, but tennis balls are also enjoyed. Newspaper or other paper crinkled in a ball is just as good.

Another way to play with paper is to lay it out flat on the floor and let the cats scoot the paper around and scuttle about on it. I had to finally tape down the newspaper on the bottom of the bird play gym. The cats in the house kept taking it off and playing with it on the linoleum. I instead offer them their own paper once in awhile.

Foil balls and bottle caps are okay to play with for a short time, but make sure you pick them up when your cat is finished. Small, indigestible pieces of the foil might be swallowed, and bottle caps can hurt your feet.

Empty toilet paper and paper towel cardboard rolls are fun to roll around on the floor. Other toys for batting and chasing are seashells and walnut shells. Notice which items your cat seems to like best. This gives you clues as to his favorite games. Then let your imagination run wild.

Items you should not let your cats play with include string, yarn, rubber bands, or anything so small that they could swallow it. Cats cannot spit things out, so they could require a trip to the vet if these things are ingested. If you are unsure whether the toy is safe, check over the list of household hazards in chapter 7 and use your best judgment, erring on the side of caution.

You'll want to keep an eye on other animals or small children in your household when there are cat toys. If swallowed, small toys can become lodged in the throat or cause problems further in the digestive track. Dogs and birds have strong mouths and can break cat toys and swallow pieces. However, cat toys are generally safe for rabbits, so you shouldn't have any problem letting your rabbit and cat share a toy supply.

CATNIP

Catnip is a traditional favorite. Catnip is a nonaddictive inebriating herb and does seem to have an influence on the behavior of two-thirds of the feline population. The smell produces a "high" lasting five to twenty minutes. Each individual cat is affected differently. The most common reaction is a burst of craziness, but your cat could also become mellow and quite sedate. Know your cat and use this to your advantage. If your cat gets mellow, then you can offer catnip during stressful periods. If your cat gets a burst of energy, catnip may be offered in conjunction with your playtime. Wait until your cat is six months old before offering him catnip.

You can either purchase dried catnip or have catnip planted in pots and allow your cat to chew on it. If yours is an indoor cat, he will appreciate it. Catnip can be valuable in coaxing your cat to use his designated scratching post instead of the couch. If you offer fresh catnip, give it two or three times a week; if you use dried catnip, it can be offered more often. Do not use catnip too often or your cat will become immune to its intoxicating effects.

HUNTING GAMES

Cats at play are very entertaining. Watching your domestic tabby in a game can make you feel like you're on the African landscape watching a lion expertly hunt his prey. Cats like to play hunt games, and you can get your feline to "hunt" a ball of crinkled paper with the same intensity and cleverness that his wild cousin would hunt food.

A cat wants to play these hunting games, so devise games that use your cat's natural hunting skills.

The Hunt Is On

Something moving out of the corner of your cat's eyes attracts his attention. Usually, it's something small and quick. He slyly sneaks up on the unsus-

pecting "victim" and pounces. A stalking cat is a wonder to watch.

Next, the cat catches the victim and attacks it with intensity. My cat, Fiera, is quite the attacker. She finds something on the linoleum floor of the kitchen and goes at it with fervor. She hits it with her paws, shooting it across the floor, and then pounces, holding it with her front feet while she wildly kicks it with her back feet. Then, pow, she bats it again, hitting it across the floor.

She'll also throw the victim over her shoulder, turn around, and quickly chase it as it slides across the floor; then she pounces on it again. I have learned quite a bit about cat play from watching this wonderful "hunter" in the wilds of my kitchen.

Think like a cat when devising ways to play. What kind of skills are necessary during the hunt? Attacking and defending are part of hunting. Many cats will be playing and then suddenly dart out of the room at full speed. The cat is, no doubt, fleeing as if being chased. These are skills easily adaptable to toys around your home.

Act like Prey

To get your pet interested in a toy, have it "act" like real prey. A mouse would never come in front of a cat and run quickly back and forth in front of the cat's face. A mouse would be busy in the corner of the room peaking out around the corner and then darting back into the shadows. A mouse would run past a cat, running away from him, not toward him.

Quickly roll a ball a couple of inches past the cat. Throw a feather or toy gently in the air about a foot or so away from him. Pretend you don't even notice that your cat is in the room while you toss a toy across the floor a couple of times. Something in a cat's personality makes him especially interested in things that aren't interested in him.

It Just Seems So Vicious

If you have a problem with all of this hunting talk, don't despair. As a vegetarian who is not at all interested in hearing hunting stories, I found this natural instinct of the cat disturbing at first. I refused to own a cat for fear it would kill a bird at my bird feeder. Not wanting to be deprived of feline companionship, I found that keeping a cat indoors is not only acceptable but is actually better in many ways. Now I don't have to walk outside to find one of the precious finches left as a present on the step.

There is no way to curb such an instinctual part of a cat; if you could, it would take away many of the endearing qualities that make people want to share their lives with cats in the first place. Supply your cat with many hunting games that you can be a part of and you help satisfy his needs and have a good time.

ENCOURAGING YOUR CAT TO PLAY

If your cat is not showing an immediate interest in the toys or games, you may have to do a little persuading, especially if he is one of those couch-potato types mentioned earlier.

Time of Day

You may notice that your cats get frisky at a certain time of the day — usually in the evening. The opportune time to initiate a game is when your cat is looking for something to do and has the energy to expend. Let a napping cat sleep. You'll just get a dirty look and a cold back turned in your direction if you attempt to disturb feline beauty rest. You'll be ignored for awhile as payment for your intrusion. Use your cat's natural energy cycle to your advantage.

Getting Rough

Cats can become rough in play. This kind of roughness, if allowed to continue, can become an annoying habit that escalates into dangerous behavior. Never use your body to roughhouse with your cat; your hand or other body part is not a toy.

If you allow your kitten to "play" attack while interacting with you, he may scratch and bite other people and children when he matures. This kind of response to the friendly overtures of a human can get your feline in trouble. And it hurts!

If your cat gets rough and grabs your hand, relax toward him. If you pull your hand away, the cat instinctually grabs tighter and you can get a nasty scratch or bite. If you move toward your cat and gently release your hand, you lessen the chance of getting scratched. No yelling is necessary; give a stern, serious "no" and then ignore him for while.

A cat that has been overstimulated by play, cuddling, or stroking may suddenly attack. Learn the signs your cat exhibits when he is almost over the edge and about to lose control. Stop before he gets this far. You and your hands are a source of affection, not something to be attacked. Keep the games gentle, and give your cat time to relax when overstimulated.

Birds

· · · · ·

Play is important to a bird's psychological well-being. Consequently, a bird deprived of play develops many neurotic behaviors. Screaming and self-mutilation are two common, frustrating problems that can develop in a bored, unstimulated bird. A bare bird cage is the equivalent of "bird hell."

Parrots are wonderful at accepting a life with humans. They are happy, healthy, and vigorous in their love for people when provided the right environment. Because they are complex creatures, you are confronted with the significant, but not impossible, task of providing them with a satisfying life. Play is an important component of this challenge.

Parrots are highly social, intelligent, and emotional, and they require dedicated interaction with humans. Without this interaction, they suffer endlessly. The reality of captive life is that companion birds must spend time alone. But in the wild, a parrot would rarely be completely alone because a mate or companion would always be nearby. Even if you are fortunate enough to be home most of the day to keep your bird company, you would hardly be able to carry a parrot around with you every minute. Your feathered friends must learn to entertain themselves.

The good news is that if you provide your bird with enough physical and mental stimulation, he can learn to spend time in his cage and enjoy it. You will, of course, have to provide for the emotional needs of your bird in addition to toys and games.

Parrots live to be destructive. In the wild, they can do so much damage to crops, homes, fences, and trees that they suffer the consequences of "population control." For instance, in many parts of Australia, flocks of cockatoos are destroyed after they invade a property. In your home, birds are just as destructive. If left with nothing else to destroy, they will chew your furniture, window sills, and books, or if denied access to these things, their own bodies.

TOYS FOR BIRDS

Bird toy manufacturers are wising up; many wonderful toys are now available. Parrot caretakers have designed, manufactured, and distributed many entertaining bird toys. When the new breed of toy designers are at work, they are taking into consideration the parrot's personality. The curious, destructive, and always hungry characteristics of these animals are being used to design innovative toys.

An adult bird needs at least one new toy each month. You can rotate the toys, taking one out and replacing it with another, but always have several toys available. Baby birds need even more toys, so offer several new ones weekly.

What You Will Probably Find in a Pet Store

Oftentimes you may find only the small weighted toys, small mirrors with bells, or plastic toys in pet supply stores. These are all meant for small birds. The weights used in many of these toys are often made of lead. If a bird with a strong beak were to break open one of these, he may swallow the lead piece and become poisoned. Some bells may have lead clappers. If the clappers are not lead, they are still easily removed and dangerous if swallowed. These toys may be safe for cockatiels and budgies (you'll have to observe your bird to be certain), but for birds that have stronger beaks, you may have to look a little harder to find adequate toys.

What You Might Find in a Pet Store if You're Lucky

If you are fortunate enough to live in a city that has a store exclusively for bird lovers, you will find an array of fun toys. Caretakers of birds demand to have more specialized products made available to them, and more of these stores are opening all across the country.

In an extensive toy collection, you may find toys made of wood, rope, beads, acrylic, and indestructible plastic. Seashells, cactus wood, rawhide, and leather are also frequently used for bird toys. Many of these are offered in the tiniest version for small birds and up to a large version for the biggest parrots. Swings, ladders, and rings are offered in many different sizes and materials. If you choose to buy a ring toy for your bird, make sure the rings are either large enough for the bird's entire body to fit through or too small for even his head to fit through.

Indestructible plastic and acrylic toys with many parts that clank and dangle are regularly thrashed about by an enthusiastic psittacine. Some toys have music boxes in them that the bird can learn to activate for his entertainment.

Mind-challenging toys are welcomed by inquisitive and mischievous birds. Metal toys with wing nuts that have to be undone to get the toy apart are challenging. Some even have treats hidden in them as a reward for your parrot's hard work.

Miniature cages made of wood with nuts rattling inside are a great way to make your parrot work for a treat. It's a good toy to give when you are away for a length of time because it keeps your feathered friend occupied.

Glance through a magazine catering to bird caretakers and you will see many exciting bird toys advertised. If the store near you doesn't have a well-stocked supply, request that more toys be added to their stock. Oftentimes, ordering directly from the toy company may be the only way to acquire these toys. If you have a very large bird, such as my macaw, finding toys of appropriate size in a store is next to impossible.

DESTRUCTIBLE TOYS FOR ACTIVE BEAKS

Your bird lives to chew, so you must provide him with plenty of destructible toys. Watch closely to be certain that he is not swallowing pieces of it. Some birds swallow pieces of toys and create blocks in their digestive system. Make sure that yours isn't one that does this.

Wood

Provide an endless supply of chewing opportunities by using chunks of milled wood. The toxicity of wood is predominantly caused by the sap, and milling removes the bark that holds the sap. Avoid any wood that has been chemically treated such as pressure-treated lumber, particle board, or plywood. Do not use wood that has been painted or varnished. When shopping at your local lumber store, look for pine, maple, oak, ash, and walnut lumber to make your bird's toys from.

You can hang chunks of wood from the top of the cage, screw them to the sides of the cage, or use them as hand-held toys. You can drill holes through the wood for interest and texture.

Assorted shapes of wooden toys are available through magazines or a good bird supply store. You can even cut some fun shapes on your own. I personally tend to go for "cute" so I like to buy manufactured wooden toys for my birds. My macaw can make splinters of an expensive wood toy in less than a few weeks. So I provide her with several chunks of raw wood to destroy and, to satisfy my need for cuteness, I buy her some toys from a toy company every couple of months. Also, nontoxic wooden toys intended for children can be given to your bird.

Visiting a good craft store can be a creativity-igniting adventure. Many of the precut wood shapes used by crafters can be used to make toys for your bird. The wood should be one of the safe varieties previously mentioned and should not be painted, glued, or treated with any chemicals. You can also buy craft sticks, small wooden thread spools, corks, and other inexpensive, bulk craft supplies.

Attaching Wood to the Cage

If you hang a toy from the cage, be careful about the type of attachment you use. Parrots are notorious for getting into unpredictable trouble. Key ring–type attachments are dangerous; they can get stuck on beaks and toes. Link chains also get stuck on body parts. You can screw an eye hook into one end of a chunk of wood. Tightly clamp the open end down or use a sealed hook, and then you can attach a series of "C" clamps. The clamps can be purchased at hardware stores and they come in many different sizes. They are the safest clamps to use with birds, and the birds have fun undoing them. Another way to attach the chunk of wood to the side of the cage is to drill a hole through the wood and then use a shoelace to tie it to the cage bars. Birds love to chew on shoelaces.

Branches

Branches are another destructible toy readily available for no cost. Generally, branches from citrus and apple trees are safe for birds to chew. Other favorites are willow, eucalyptus, maple, and manzanita.

To avoid any risk of poisoning, you must be certain the trees have not been treated with pesticides. Avoid collecting branches lining a busy road because the exhaust pollution is absorbed by the trees and the branches are tainted with dangerous chemicals.

Wash the branches with a bleach and water solution, half and half, and rinse well. The branches should be completely dry before you offer them to your bird. You can let them dry on their own for a few days or weeks, or you can speed dry them using the oven set at 400 degrees.

Your parrot will delight in stripping the branches of their bark. This is healthy, entertaining, and time-consuming. Perfect for a busy parrot.

More Ideas

Many birds love to shred the newspaper on the bottom of their cages. Even if you have a grate separating the bird from the tray, the bird may get hold of a corner and pull the paper through to destroy it. Weave newspaper or junk mail through the bars of the cage. You can also weave a nutritious leaf lettuce through the bars for snack power, which is a sneaky way to get veggies down a resistant bird.

Many household objects can be given to your parrot to destroy. Empty, unscented toilet paper and paper towel cardboard rolls seem to be a favorite. If your bird isn't interested, stick some paper towels in the ends. Birds love to make confetti from paper. Cardboard boxes and empty egg cartons will be welcome and enthusiastically torn to bits.

Your pet also needs indestructible toys. A toy that your parrot can beat up and not destroy is necessary for his fun as well as your pocketbook. Very large or very destructive birds need to have several of these toys as well as chew toys.

Metal spoons are indestructible and have the advantage of being "hand-held." Hand-held toys, hanging toys, and those attached to the bars of the cage are important for diversity and entertainment value.

Many birds enjoy baby and children's toys. My macaw has a baby activity center that she bangs around. Other commonly appreciated toys are rattles and stacking toys.

Whenever choosing toys for any pet, make sure that the toy is safe. If you are at all unsure about the safety of an item, don't use it.

FOOD AS TOYS AND NUTRITION

Food can also be a great toy. Whole nuts are favorites; however, if your pet tends to get fatty tumors or be obese, you should limit the amount of nuts. A pet that doesn't have the ability to open the nut would appreciate your cracking it slightly to give him the advantage.

Filling a bowl with fruits and vegetables is not only a great way to provide nutrition but also a way to provide activity for your parrot.

For food that offers entertainment, try crunchable delights such as uncooked pasta, cinnamon sticks, dog biscuits, and monkey biscuits.

TRICK TRAINING

Games and toys that require your bird to use his brain are important, but another mind-stimulating activity that birds enjoy is learning tricks.

Be discriminate when reading trick training advice. Some trainers may advise food deprivation as part of training based on the theory that if you withhold food, your bird will learn faster in order to receive the food reward. This is cruel and unnecessary. Food is extremely important to birds, and you should never deprive your pet of food. You destroy the trust he has in you and make him anxious. If a training method advocates food deprivation as a means to teaching your bird a behavior, discard the entire advice.

You can teach a bird to be a classic show-off.

The author's bird Casper has made good use of her traveling basket. She has an instant perch that is easily carried into any room of the house.

Begin by choosing tricks that incorporate his natural abilities or habits. These can include hopping, playing dead, fetching, or playing "eagle." Start with simple activities and take your time; your intelligent pet will learn. You can also purchase ready-made props for all sorts of tricks. The secret to training a parrot is to never bore him. Stop the lesson before he's ready to quit participating.

BATHING A BIRD

A fun activity for both you and your bird, which also is healthy for him, is a bath. I give my birds turns with me in the shower. They fluff up, spread their wings, and dunk under the water, shaking and splashing. They transform a mundane shower into a party.

Casper, the rose-breasted cockatoo, sits on the shower door and patiently waits for her turn. Not so with Salsa, the macaw; she gets excited and talks and yells. I had to learn a different way with her because she got into everything — she tried to chew the shower to pieces, kept hopping to the hanging plants, and jumped to the bottom of the shower where she reappeared looking like a drowned rat. I bring her perch into the bathroom, where she anxiously talks to and yells at me; she stretches in my direction and dilates her eyes. When I'm ready to give her a shower, I bring her in and then return her to the perch when she's done.

Showering with Your Bird

If you want to join the ranks of partners-in-showers, you are in for quite a treat. Make sure that the water is not too hot. Once the water gets to your bird, it will have cooled down a bit, so you don't want it to be too cold either. A comfortable temperature for everyone is too subjective, so it is difficult to recommend an exact temperature. Remember that moderation always works.

I hold my birds out away from the water and let the water bounce off of my body first. Salsa sometimes forces her way under the direct flow, but this would be too forceful for dainty Casper. You will quickly be able to tell what your bird enjoys most.

Showers with your bird are great because they give you time together. If your bird is not enthusiastic about taking a bath, having you in the shower and demonstrating the fun of it may help him to be braver, or at least more curious. If this doesn't sound like it would work for you, then you can try the following suggestions.

Misting Your Bird

Misting your pet with a squirt bottle works for many birds. Have the bottle twelve inches from your bird and spray from beneath the level of the bird upward so that the mist falls down. You can also place him in the sink, shower, or tub and use a nozzle or hand-held shower head on low pressure. Spray it the same way that you would with the spray bottle.

A Bathing Pool

Some birds prefer to bathe in a pool of water. You can supply your parrot with a tub of water each morning and then clean his cage when he is finished so that you remove the wet paper. Vacuuming stimulates many birds to bathe, so this may be a good time to offer a tub of water.

Getting Your Bird Accustomed to a Bath

If your bird shows any reluctance to bathing, back off and move more slowly. It is worth the effort that you put into showing him the joy of bathing; it keeps his feathers in good condition, and he'll discover what fun it is. At first he may make you think that you are killing him, but talk soothingly and be gentle. Don't overdo it, but to get a really good bath your bird must be quite wet. A light sprinkling of dewlike mist won't do. Starting off with just a light dusting of water may be best while your bird is learning to enjoy his bath.

Getting Dry

Morning is the best time to give your bird a bath. This gives him time to completely dry by nightfall. If the weather is particularly chilly, you need to help your pet dry. A blow-dryer on a low, warm setting may be tolerated. Make sure you move the dryer around without concentrating on one area for too long. If you have a diffuser, you may want to use it.

Although some birds love the dryer as much or more than their shower, if your bird won't tolerate it, place a small heater in the bathroom or near the cage until most of the wetness is gone from his feathers. Never leave one of these heaters running if you are not there to supervise. If you dry your pet too quickly with too much heat, you will dry the needed humidity out of the feathers. Dry your feathered friend until he is somewhat dry and safe from getting a chill.

If the weather is warm, just let your bird dry on his own. He will then spend quite a bit of time grooming his beautiful feathers to perfection. This keeps your bird occupied for a good length of time.

PHYSICAL EXERCISE

Parrots also need physical exercise. In captivity they do not get the opportunity to fly and often they don't have much of a chance to climb about. In the wild, they are constantly doing both.

Birds need flying exercise. They need to keep their muscles strong as well as their heart and respiratory system healthy. Since you cannot let them be fully flighted in your dangerous world, provide alternatives.

Play with your bird in an open area over a soft

place such as a bed, sofa, or carpeted floor. Gently swing your bird as he holds on to a length of rope. Hold the rope close to the ground in case he falls. Start slowly and only do this a short time. Let the bird become accustomed to the game and increase his fitness level over time. Most parrots love this activity.

You want to encourage as much wing flapping as possible. A caged bird often flaps his wings vigorously when let out for playtime. Encourage this behavior by telling your bird what a good job he is doing and how wonderful his wings look (birds are vain and respond to compliments on their appearance).

Your pet should be provided with an interesting climbing area. A play gym or play stand with lots of climbing toys and swings is mandatory. Make sure there are many different levels and that the stand is covered with toys. The play stand should be away from the cage area, although a cage with a play stand on top is fine for occasional recreation. Birds in the wild visit many foraging areas during the day. Duplicate this as much as possible by providing more than one play area.

Rabbits

. . . .

Encouraging play in rabbits is not a difficult venture and one that will reward you greatly. Play brings out the personality of your long-eared friend and is important for his psychological well-being. Rabbits love to play if they are provided with the correct prerequisites.

Your rabbit must be secure and comfortable and trust you deeply. If you have developed a relationship built on mutual respect, your rabbit will feel little stress and be able to spend more time having fun and less time worrying about his future.

For a rabbit to emerge into his happy-go-lucky self, toys must be offered. You will find that your rabbit enjoys an array of toys. I had always enjoyed giving my birds toys, and I never thought another animal had that kind of effect on the human soul until I got my first rabbit. Oh, what happiness she found in the toys I offered! It is a good feeling to be able to supply such fun, and it is a joy to watch the action.

TOYS FOR RABBITS

If you go searching the pet stores for toys designed with your rabbit's enjoyment in mind, you will quickly be discouraged. Even large stores in populated areas have little to choose from. Don't give up though; most bird and cat toys are harmless to your rabbit.

Safety considerations are the same as for all animals. Make sure no small parts can become dislodged and cause a choking hazard. Avoid long strings or ribbons because your rabbit can become entangled. Also avoid giving your rabbit soft rubber that he could chew up into small pieces.

Expose your rabbit to many activities and toys. The more his mind is stimulated, the more his world expands — and the more interactive he can become. Your rabbit also needs entertainment. It is not only easy but incredibly rewarding to provide your rabbit with the tools to fill his life with amusement.

Digging and Chewing

What are your rabbit's favorite activities? This will give you an idea about the toys he would appreciate most. Rabbits have a strong need to chew and dig, and you can incorporate these activities into the choices of toys.

If you have a bird, many of the same toys you supply to him can be shared with your rabbit, such as branches and wood pieces. Read the section on bird toys to find out which woods and branches are harmless. As discussed previously, more and more manufacturers are developing toys for birds, so take advantage of this trend by purchasing chewable bird toys for your furry friend too.

Wicker baskets and grass mats make wonderful chew toys, and your rabbit will have fun playing on, in, and with these objects. Grass mats are also good for getting some of your rabbit's digging energy expended. Also, empty toilet paper rolls (unscented) and paper towel rolls stuffed with paper towels are good for nudging, rolling, carrying, and chewing.

Being burrowing animals, rabbits love to hide and play inside of things, so provide paper bags and cardboard boxes for hiding and chewing. Give your rabbit objects to chew on;

otherwise, he may decide to chew on less favorable items such as your couch leg or speaker wires.

Noise and Ruckus Making

Rabbits like to play with toys that make noise, so toys with rattles and bells can be especially fun. Balls that make noise are also greatly appreciated. Rabbits like to push and roll balls, but they also like to pick them up with their teeth, so offer a ball that he can really get hold of.

Baby toys, especially rattles, have always been favorites with my rabbits. They really enjoy picking things up and tossing them — sometimes from one side of their cage to the other. I've watched my rabbit pick up a toy in her mouth and shake it for a moment and then toss it. Then she hops over to get it again. There is nothing cuter than watching a rabbit play.

I find that my rabbits like to play with their bowls. Often the bowls are dumped before the food is gone so that it can be played with. My rabbit Amelia loves to stack and restack her bowls. Some days I can witness a different bowl arrangement every thirty minutes. She has such fun thrashing them about and rolling them around, even though I offer her many toys at all times.

Another toy that my rabbits enjoy is a stuffed animal. Make sure that there are no loose parts that can fall or be pulled off. Rabbits cuddle up to their stuffed animal to sleep, as well as play with it; they bash it around like they do their other toys.

FREE TIME

It is paramount that you allow your rabbit free time out of his cage. This has been previously discussed, but it is relevant to play because your rabbit must have an opportunity to jump, run, exercise, and just act silly — and silly he will be!

An excited rabbit outside of his cage is a very happy, acrobatic, and crazy creature. You can get a reluctant rabbit interested in physical play by talking to him in the silliest voice you can muster. If you act goofy, he will probably let his guard down and act goofy also. Get down on the floor and be silly in an effort to promote craziness in your long-eared animal.

Once you get your rabbit roused, you'll witness midair 180-degree turns. Your acrobatic rabbit's repertoire of moves will include arches, dives, sudden takeoffs, running backward, jumping straight up with a side turn, and jumping with a swift kick of the hind legs in midair. Watching a rabbit relish life in such a manner is one of the most delightful occasions in an animal home.

Spending time with your pets

The companionship, affection, entertainment, and unconditional acceptance that your pets offer you are the primary motivating experiences you seek when keeping animal companions. Your animals are a part of your life because you want to interact with a part of nature. The sacrifices you make to care for them do not seem like sacrifices at all when you consider the rewards.

Is this reality? It should be. In addition to investing many hours and much money in the physical care of your pets, you must take time just to enjoy them. But often, many people have difficulty finding time to spend with their pets.

The human world is high pressured and fast paced. You are expected to do more, achieve more, and have more — and do it all in less time. To counteract this pace, pets can calm your life, yet they are often the first to suffer from your time constraints. It is possible to have an animal friend, even a number of them, still be as successful as you desire, and have time to properly care for and spend with your animal companions. To reduce your stress level, take pleasure in emotionally connecting with the animals, spend special time together, and allow yourself to be soothed by their presence.

If your pet suddenly develops a bad habit or misbehavior, a trip to the veterinarian may be in order to rule out physical problems. However, you may find that many difficulties arise when your pet feels that his place in your heart and home is questionable. Reassure your pet by spending time with him; let him know he is still important to you. Build his self-confidence and the undesirable behaviors may disappear.

Make your animal companions a part of your life. They are not a separate entity from the other responsibilities in your daily routine. They share your existence on the most basic, significant realm — in your heart. Make them participants in your everyday activities such as washing the car, getting mail, scrubbing cages, picking your kids up, writing letters, paying bills, and mowing the lawn.

INDIVIDUAL TIME

If someone is home most of the day, you may think that the animals are getting enough attention. A closer look at how the day is spent may be in order to determine the validity of this statement. If there are too many pets, the individual creatures may lack sufficient, one-on-one "quality" time with their beloved human. A full schedule dictates making a conscious effort to guarantee that your creatures are getting enough affection.

Each of your animal companions needs his own individual attention, and depending on the number of pets you share your home with, this could become quite difficult. This is why I implore you to carefully consider every possible problem when thinking of adding another pet to your kingdom. You will know in your heart whether you have time for another pet.

Time alone with you away from the other animals keeps your pets emotionally stable and content. This doesn't mean that every day you have to take each animal out by himself for an ice cream cone; it simply means that every once in awhile, you need to spend some one-on-one time together.

Your animals are capable of learning to take turns. If you want to take your dog on an errand but don't because you don't want the others to be jealous, everyone loses. Take one this time, and do something special with another one later. It is also fun to take a couple of animals once in awhile. Give your pets credit for the ability to share. If you are sensitive and observant, you will soon be able to feel when they need you before their behavior gets out of control.

JEALOUSY

In a multi-animal household, attention and affection will be regarded by your pets as increasingly valuable. Unfulfilled attention needs can create mixed messages and confusion, which can ruin relationships with you and the other animals of the household. Try to balance your attention equally among your pets.

This equalization of attention does not mean that each pet needs exactly thirty minutes of your affection daily. The amount that each animal needs to be content and emotionally healthy depends on the individual and differs greatly from animal to animal, even those of the same species. Your job as caretaker is to understand how much each animal requires and then fulfill this requirement.

If I talk lovingly to any one of my pets in an audible voice, I can be assured that at least two other animals in the house will come to check out what favors are being granted. It is a pleasure to know that all my animal companions want my time and attention. I rely on my intuition and observation to tell me if every one of the creatures has had enough affection and who may be in need. You too can develop this ability to perceive your animals' needs. When you do, you will find that giving your pets enough emotional attention is less of a challenge.

HOW MUCH TIME?

This is a difficult question that cannot be answered with absolutes. Some individual animals demand more attention than others. Some more aloof creatures will not even tolerate as much attention as other pets demand with exuberance.

Some species require much more interaction than others. While a couple of cats can be company enough for each other even for a day or two, a bird without your attention for too many hours suffers greatly.

If you have not yet adopted another pet and are curious about what kind of time you will have to spend with your new charge, just remember to plan high and be sensitive, especially in the beginning, to the animal's needs.

The same animal you have had for many years continually varies his need for affection. Just like people, sometimes animals need more attention when they are sick, anxious, or depressed, and there may be other times when they want less of your affection.

Lonely animals are pathetic and miserable. They

are more susceptible to illness and may develop irritating and irrational behaviors such as barking, depression, digging, chewing, self-mutilation, unreliable elimination habits, excitability, and unexplainable fears. These pets become withdrawn, and eventually it is difficult for them to relate to people on any level.

Be a friend and companion to your pets, and they won't be lonely.

DOGS

Dogs require different levels of interaction. Some dogs are very people oriented and want to be with you every minute. They follow you around throughout the house, never leaving your side. Some dogs find a good spot to nap and spend most of their day there. However, most dogs are somewhere in between these two extremes.

Difference among Breeds

You have to consider the breed of dog; some breeds have been developed to work all day. These are demanding animals with endless energy and devotion to their caretaker. If you have a dog like this, you have a pet that wants to be with you continuously and prefers to be doing something exciting. Do you have the time and energy?

Other breeds of dogs would rather not do anything at all and have to be persuaded to get their exercise. These dogs lounge around and accept your attention as you bring it to them. They are less likely to follow you around all day wanting their head scratched. Although these more laid-back breeds may not jump all over you all day, they are still attached to their people and need their affection and attention.

The best way for you to find out what kind of attention your pet may require before you adopt is to look into the breed information. If the breed is highly motivated by its desire to please its owner, it will be very sensitive to your energies. Some breeds of dogs were developed with an independent nature necessary to perform their job. These dogs would be less likely to suffer if you were limited on time to spend with them.

Also talk to breeders and get their opinions on the amount of attention their breed requires. Talk to as many caretakers as you can. When you are at dog shows or other dog events, talk to people who have the kind of dog that you are considering.

All dogs have the need to be with their "pack," but some breeds have highly developed pack instincts. These dogs need to be with others, and they suffer if left alone. However, this does not necessarily mean that they need constant hands-on affection. Some dogs prefer to be with you but don't need your petting and cuddling. Other dog breeds were developed with their job being that of pet and therefore seek loads of physical contact.

Each dog is an individual with a unique personality and needs. Even though every other mastiff owner I have ever talked to laughs at their dog's laziness, I live with a 190-pound, three-year-old puppy. Contrary to what I expected, my mastiff bounds through the house with endless energy, so you can always be in for surprises. You must be willing to adapt.

Spending Time Together

Some of the most memorable times in your relationship will be during exercise. Playing is great fun for the both of you. Each of your dogs needs thirty minutes of exercise a day, and this exercise can take the form of a romp outdoors playing fetch games. A multi-dog caretaker can exercise all the dogs together if the playtime is equal. This exercise time can also mean a jog or other more formal exercise.

Grooming is also time spent together. Some caretakers believe that a grooming session should be serious business and be done in an orderly, speedy manner. This belief has its merits. Sometimes you need to groom your pet when time is in short supply, and the last thing you want is a dog that thinks it's playtime.

Grooming is a necessary part of life that must be accomplished no matter how limited your time, so getting it done quickly and efficiently is important. Also, you may not be the only one who does the grooming. You may think that your pet's rolling on his back and pawing your brush hand mean pause for a quick belly rub, but a professional groomer or your cousin who is watching your household for the weekend may find this behavior unacceptable. Their sudden reprimands for such behavior may be bewildering for your dog, so you will have to decide if you want to make grooming time also fun time.

When You Work

If you work outside of the home during the day, you should spend some time with your dog in the evening. Spend this time playing with him and letting him use up some of his energy. He has been home all day alone and bored. Show him you care about his well-being.

Mornings are generally most hectic, with more caretaker responsibilities, but if you have no energy yourself when you get home after work or if you are leaving for an especially long day and know you will be tired when you get home, get up a bit earlier in the morning and play with your dog then.

Competing for Your Attention

What about one-on-one cuddle time? Each dog deserves his daily moment of your undivided attention. As mentioned previously, the amount depends on the individual dog. At least fifteen minutes a day of reminding your canine how important he is in your life is a necessity.

Keep competition to a minimum; this can become quite a problem if not monitored carefully. If your dogs come to you fighting for your attention, do not reward their behavior by giving them the attention they desire. To lonely dogs, even negative attention is valuable and they may misbehave to get it. Direct them to leave by giving them the command "go." Later, after they have calmed down, take the dogs out for a friendly game of fetch or some other activity in which they can participate together in a friendly manner.

Emphasize through your actions that you accept their cooperation with each other but will not tolerate their lack of acceptance. Expect them to get along in a peaceful manner, and then be prepared to enforce your ideal.

CATS

Cats are curious creatures who have differing attention demands. They usually want your affection only when they feel the need. In other words, unlike dogs that accept your affection any time you offer, cats seem to prefer things on their own terms.

Cats Need Attention

Although cats can tend to act aloof, this does not mean that they don't want attention. Some breeds and individuals are quite demanding; they'll sit on your paper while you are trying to read, rub on your legs as you dust the living room, nudge and rub on your hands as you put on your makeup, and jump on your lap the second you sink into the couch. You can count on your feline friend to be honest and direct in expressing his desires. What this characteristic implies is that you will have to rearrange your schedule somewhat to accommodate your cat because your cat will not rearrange his to fit your lifestyle.

This is a generalization, and like all generalizations in life, there are exceptions. Life is greatly enhanced by the companionship of cats, and they also benefit from acceptance and affection. So just because your cat doesn't seem to need you, he does require your attention and companionship.

Variation in Attention Needs

As mentioned previously, some individuals are more demanding of your attention, and some breeds are relentless in their quest for your special nurturing. Others are more aloof and easygoing. My Himalayan rarely asks me for attention, although he doesn't dislike human contact. I pet him and love him in short bursts of affection throughout the day. I can hug him and cuddle him, and he purrs like crazy when he's brushed, but he just doesn't need physical affection as strongly as the other cats in my life. Mendy craves attention; she loves to hug, nuzzle, and knead my neck and shoulders. She is very demanding and needs loads of affection or else she becomes bratty and sullen. My other cat follows me around quite a bit, wanting a stroke of my hand, but that's it.

These are three different examples of the feline affection requirement and you can see the variation.

Feline Entertainment

Cats that have other buddies keep each other pretty much entertained. Cats that have access to the great outdoors are busy roaming their territory, chasing off intruders, running after small animals, and running from larger ones. Indoor cats require more of your time when it comes to exercise and stimulation. You will have great fun initiating games as described earlier in this chapter.

Respect a cat's need for independence. If he doesn't want to be touched, don't demand his cooperation. If he wants to leave while you are petting him, let him go.

Seeking Your Attention

Although some cats let you know in obvious ways that they need your love and attention, it's easy to let the independent cats get neglected. Even if they don't openly seek your affection, you should spend time with each cat daily. Cats seem to be more lovable at night, so just before turning in for the night, give your felines some nurturing. This is also a good time to brush your furry friend. This is an opportunity for you to make your daily physical check and make sure that everything is okay.

Cats may hiss and scratch at each other, fighting for your attention. Being in the middle of a cat battle is no fun. Usually one cat is the more submissive and while he may hiss to show his displeasure, he may get up and leave so the more dominant cat can take over your lap. Permitting this kind of hierarchy demonstration with your affections will be understood as permission. Reject any cat that fights for your petting. Send him away and enjoy yourself with another pet.

Grooming time can be caring time. Make the grooming session gentle and compassionate, and your feline may not be able to separate grooming from cuddling. Grooming is an expression of your devotion.

BIRDS

Of all the animals mentioned in this book, parrots are the most demanding. They require large amounts of attention and time. Because of the unintentional lack of knowledge in their human caretakers, they have suffered endless portions of their lives in solitary confinement and cramped in cages too small for efficient exercise. We know better now, but many people are still confused about the needs of their bird friends.

The Need for Attention

Birds are highly intelligent and thrive on interaction with their people. They should not be regulated to a life as an ornament and an addition to one's home decorating scheme. I once had a friend ask me to help her find a Moluccan cockatoo because the salmon color matched her couch perfectly. Of course I talked her out of adopting a bird.

You can enjoy a fulfilling relationship that extends beyond simple pet "ownership" with these remarkable creatures. How does a parrot become an affectionate, emotional creature rather than a screaming, fearful bird in a cage? Through attention, affection, and guidance.

One-on-One Affection

Parrots need physical contact each day. Your feathered animal needs you to scratch, pet, preen, and cuddle him every single day. This must be time separate from any other distractions — no television, no reading, and no talking on the phone. He knows if he has your undivided attention and demands it if you don't oblige.

This one-on-one session does not need to be a love marathon. Ten to fifteen minutes a day is usually satisfying. If you are in an incredible rush, you may get by with five minutes of this intense affection, but if you do this for a couple of days in a row, you will be reminded.

My macaw lets me know if I have let her time alone with me diminish by getting feisty, nippy, and reverting to acting like a baby bird. I know this means an emergency cuddle session and a reorganization of my schedule to include more time with her.

Side-by-Side Activity

The one-on-one session is not the only interaction that you need to have with your bird. Parrots are not solitary creatures; they require the presence of a companion. They flourish with side-by-side activity, so include your bird in your daily routine.

Mattie Sue Athan, in *Guide to a Well-Behaved Bird,* suggests using a basket as a mobile perch. I have tried this suggestion and found it to be a wonderful way to include my birds in my daily activities. Choose a basket with a comfortably sized handle to act as a perch. Wrap the handle in jute rope for more gripping power. With the larger, heavier birds, you may need a weight of some sort to keep the basket upright. A thick chunk of chewable wood can serve as both a weight and chewing activity.

Your bird will delight in helping you fold clothes (or should I say unfold?). Remember your sense of humor. Your bird can join you at your desk while you pay bills and busy himself shredding your junk mail. Take your bird with you from room to room as you make beds. Side-by-side activities also include showering, which I highly recommend.

When Not to Include Your Bird

Having your bird with you is not a good idea during some activities. Going outside is one. It makes me a nervous wreck to see people walk around in public places with their bird on their shoulder. Even a bird with clipped wings can become frightened and catch enough of a breeze to make it to the highest tree in the neighborhood. Keep your bird with you, safe in the house, and use a crate or cage when outside.

Another risky venture is when you are using any chemicals, sprays, powders, or cleaners. When sprays or powders are used, your bird should be removed from the room. His delicate respiratory system will not be able to handle this onslaught.

Cooking is another time to beware. Open pots of hot food, knives and other sharp utensils, carbon monoxide poisoning from gas flames, hot burners, cups and pots of water or other liquids, and nonstick cookware are all potential dangers.

Fitting a Bird into Your Lifestyle

Even if you have a tight schedule, you can fit your birds into your lifestyle nicely if you plan and make being with your pet a priority. Unlike animals who are not caged, a bird cannot come and find you if you happen to be so busy you forgot about him. Then again, some are great escape artists and will get out and find you. Others remind you with loud shrieks. Before you have a screaming problem, make sure that you are spending adequate time with your companion bird.

As mentioned before, you can include your feathered friend in your shower and morning time. You can also eat breakfast with your pet. Before leaving for work in the morning and returning your bird to his cage, give him intense cuddling. Make this a relaxing, comforting occasion — the last moment of calm before you start head-on into your busy day. You both deserve it.

When evening comes, you can spend more side-by-side time with your pet by including him in some of your chores or by holding him in your lap while you watch your favorite television show. This petting is different than your intense cuddling session. You can also make evening a playtime by including a short romp on the floor or on your bed before bedtime.

"The" Social Event

Being a part of your life is what is most important to your bird, and eating is the most significant social event in the life of a bird. Your birds should have a place close to your dinner table in order to be a part of this affair. Before you yell, "Yuck, I won't have a bird walking through my spaghetti!" you must realize that this does not mean he must physically share your plate, although it isn't uncommon and can be rewarding for those of the right temperament. Have a perch close enough to the table for your comfort and for his ability to interact with the activity. You can fill the cups of the perch with some of your dinner or a birdie snack, or you can hand your pet portions of your meal as you eat.

If you are a very busy person but you still want to have a bird as a pet, sharing your meals is the most crucial time-sharing period of the day. Including your feathered pet in your mealtime can lessen his stress, increase his confidence, alleviate bad behavior, and strengthen your bond.

HOW TO PET A BIRD

If your bird enjoys physical contact, petting is the obvious choice of expressing affection. Most birds prefer "skirtches" rather than full body strokes. With your finger contacting the skin under the feathers, gently make side-to-side movements or slight movements against the feather growth.

Watch your bird to get an idea of what he likes best. If your animal is enjoying your petting, he closes his eyes and fluffs up, and if he makes faint noises, he really likes it. If he doesn't seem to be taking pleasure in your efforts, switch to a better spot. Move around to avoid irritating a particular area. Some birds are sensitive and prefer you pet them in the direction of feather growth.

Most birds appreciate your petting attention focused on the facial area, especially around the beak and gently around the eyes. Other body locations to try are his neck, under the crest of cockatoos, the top of his tail (this may instigate sexual excitement if it is that time of the year so be in tune to this cycle), or under his wings.

You can also preen your bird, strengthening your bond in the process. The newly formed feather shafts are prickly and irritating. He cannot reach the ones on his head and neck. You can help him rid the growing feathers of their encasement in these hard-to-reach spots much like his mate would do.

These new feathers can be tender and if you pinch the blood area, your bird will let you know it hurts. To be safe, preen the feather shafts that are already working off on their own. I only help out on the ones where the top of the feather has broken through. The others are too sensitive.

Gently break the shaft loose by squeezing with your fingernails beyond the blood supply and then work it off rubbing it between your fingertips. Most birds will be like putty in your hands with this attention.

For birds that do not tolerate physical handling or for those family members who are too intimidated to handle the bird, there are other ways to make friends. Talking, singing, giving mist baths, and feeding treats by hand are good methods to try. If you feed your bird a treat, offer something that he does not have in his food dish, is easy to feed, and is well appreciated.

Sleep is important to your bird. Don't keep your bird up too late because he may get cranky in the late evening. Parrots are emotional creatures, and they have good moods and bad moods. If your bird seems feisty, he probably is, so leaving him alone may be a good idea.

RABBITS

Of all the creatures mentioned in this book, I believe rabbits suffer the most from benign neglect. Rabbits endure their fate in silence. A rabbit that is captive in his cage with no interaction can do little to improve his condition. He does not scream for attention or develop neurotic behaviors like birds. He does not have the ability to beg, whine, run away, or be such a bother that you can't help but notice like dogs and cats. He is silent, cage bound, and doesn't "appear" to be suffering. He will pine away from loneliness and usually dies an early death of sadness.

Most people do not realize the affection and companionship that a rabbit can show his people. Rabbits are a yet undiscovered marvelous pet, and those that are nurtured, loved, and have bonded with their caretaker are expressive and fascinating. Their personalities emerge, and they will amaze you with their complex and kindly nature. If they trust you, they will let you share their captivating world.

Free Time

As mentioned again and again, rabbits should have time outside of their cage. This is the most important responsibility you perform. In a house full of animals, this can sometimes require juggling and an increase in attentiveness. A rabbit being chased by a dog, even a friendly one not bent on catching him, can die of fright. You should take whatever measures necessary to guarantee that your rabbit has some safe, stress-free romp time.

My favorite time to include my long-eared friend Amelia is when I am in my office working on my computer. I can shut the door completely and let her have the run of the office. Depending on the mood of the family dogs, there may be quite a bit of whimpering on the other side of the door. A child's gate cures the problem — the rabbit is protected from

chasing, but the dogs and cats can see me.

It is great fun to have the rabbit in the office with me. Being circled by a rabbit is an expression of affection, and I am the recipient of such a demonstration. Constant tugs at my pant legs or shoes reminds me it is time for a quick head-petting break. A box or bag is provided for hiding games. Chew toys and balls for play and a litter box for the obvious important duties should be provided.

Safe Excursions

Rabbits need exercise, so this freedom out of the cage is necessary. Your rabbit should have as much time outside of his cage as possible. You can use a gate and secure him in one room where he has access to his cage with a ramp or other method and a litter box. At a minimum, allow him to roam free for at least one hour of the day.

Even though there is a gate separating dogs from rabbits, as this picture shows, the curiosity never dims.

An older rabbit with consistent elimination habits and an ability to curb his need to dig and chew on wires should be allowed to spend most or all of his time outside of his cage. If possible, cages should be used only for nighttime security. The happiest rabbit and the best companion is one that is allowed free range of your home. It also builds a level of trust between you and your rabbit friend.

This is not always possible in a multi-species household. My dog is trained not to chase the rabbit, but I would never allow them to be alone together. The predatory instincts of dogs toward rabbits is just too strong for me to be comfortable with this arrangement. My rabbits can run about the house when the dog is outside, or they can be secure in a room where the dog does not have access. During uninterrupted time with my rabbits, I also train my dog to become accustomed to being around the rabbits without chasing them.

If you are not the only person in your home, you must make sure that others know where the animals are at all times. You may put the dog out to let the rabbit out of his cage, but your spouse or child may let the dog in without knowing the rabbit is free. As a precaution, devise a system. You can use signs or

RABBITS ARE INDOOR PETS

Pet rabbits should live inside your home, not outdoors. Although rabbits will benefit from time in the sunshine and fresh air, they should only be allowed freedom outside in a protected environment.

Backyards are dangerous, even for a caged rabbit. As a prey animal, your pet will be at risk from predators and, even in the middle of suburbia, your pet is not safe. Dogs, cats, raccoons, skunks, owls, possums, and hawks are likely predators. The risk for your rabbit is higher at night, but attacks can also happen during the day. If your rabbit senses the presence of a predator and he feels as though he is in danger, even if the predator is in your neighbor's yard, he can injure himself in panic or die of shock. Some of the more dexterous of predators, such as raccoons, can even open a hutch to get at your pet.

If allowed to run free in your yard, your rabbit could ingest poisonous or moldy plants as well as fertilizers and pesticides that could be toxic and life-threatening. Even if you are careful in your gardening habits, your neighbor may not be, and your rabbit may accidentally be poisoned by the far-reaching effects of chemicals used on the other side of the fence. Your rabbit will also be subjected to bacteria and the spread of diseases that are contained in the dirt and spread by flies and mosquitoes.

Your furry friend will be, even with your most conscientious care, exposed to the effects of sun, heat, wind, and rain. Although rabbits can tolerate the cold pretty well, a day of heat above 100 degrees will kill him.

The saddest part of life for an outside rabbit is the denial of interaction with his family. Living alone in a cage outside is stressful for such a sensitive creature. Developing a relationship with your rabbit is a magical experience that enriches your life as well as the life of an expressive animal, but only if you share your daily life with him, which you can't do if he lives outside.

locks or something that works with the adults and all ages of children in your home.

Cuddling with Your Rabbit

Most rabbits don't like to be held, although some like it very much. My five-year-old neighbor has a rabbit, Bingo, who she carries around like a baby doll. She can wrap Bingo in a blanket, put him in a stroller, and take him for walks. She can carry the rabbit over her shoulder for hours — Bingo truly enjoys all this attention. He shows no signs of stress (heavy breathing, quick nose twitching, or bulging eyes) and has lived with this kind of intense loving for years. This rabbit shows an extreme level of acceptance.

You may not get to carry your rabbit around, but you can spend some wonderful time with your pet. You are the one who will have to make it comfortable for the animal, and this means getting down on the floor at his level. While your rabbit is out of his cage, sit or lie on the floor. It won't take your pet long before he is rushing over to get some attention. Rabbits are very curious creatures, and they will not be able to help themselves. If you have already developed a relationship with your rabbit, he will come over right away for some cuddles.

Your rabbit may hop into your lap and sit contently while you watch television and pet him, or he may hop in and out for quick rubs while he is playing. If you lie down on your stomach, your rabbit will probably hop on your back or over you, play in your hair, and circle you again and again.

Creating a Bond

If you just adopted a rabbit or, after reading this, you realize you have missed out on some wonderful rabbit affection, you can build a relationship with your friend and create a bond between you by demonstrating your trustability.

Let your rabbit loose in a safe, quiet, and enclosed room, preferably one that doesn't contain a bed or couch he can hide under. Offer him treats without forcing yourself on him. He will have a good time checking you out.

One fun way to bond with your rabbit, especially an older adopted one, will have your friends

and relatives believing you have finally gone over the edge. Place the cage and litter box in a room that can be closed off. Sleep on the floor that night with your rabbit loose in the room. Down at rabbit level, you will be approachable and your rabbit will be more confident exploring you.

If you want a less dramatic showing of your ability to be trusted, sleep on the floor by the rabbit cage for a night or two. Animals that sleep together demonstrate a level of trust and belonging; it is a statement of friendship that any animal, especially a sensitive rabbit, can understand.

You are there to communicate with your pet, show and receive expressions of affection, and be a playmate. The expression of your rabbit's personality is directly influenced by the bond you develop. Love your rabbit and encourage his demonstration of affection; you will have an incredible companion.

Bonding with your animal companions

The ability to bond is what makes the relationship between humans and animals special. Some people can create lasting bonds with another living being without recognizing the actions, thoughts, and emotions invested in the formation of the relationship. Others are never aware they have failed to create this bond. Understanding some of the facets that lead to this rewarding emotional possibility can further the process of bonding and assist in developing strong and lasting friendships.

A number of things stand out as necessary for a true bond to occur. The connection is complex, so narrowing the process to essential components helps simplify, but fails to define, the dynamics.

SHARED TIME TOGETHER

In order for a relationship between animal and caretaker to develop, you must spend shared time with each other. Only through interaction will you come to understand the nuances of your animal friend, and he will begin to relate to you. Just being together is healthy for emotional security. An "outside" pet misses the opportunity to spend time with his caretaker and vice versa.

Human couples who have been together for a long time begin to "know" when the other person is tired, hungry, bored, or whatever without the benefit of verbal communication. Like people who have been married for years, the time animals and humans spend together increases the intuitive comprehension of personality and emotion.

INTUITIVE SENSITIVITY

Part of learning and understanding comes from the caretaker's intuitive sensitivity. The ability to "feel" the emotions of your animal companions and relate to them on this level is paramount to bonding. Intuitive sensitivity allows you the freedom and joy of relating to your animal friends on an emotional level. Humans and animals share many of the same emotions — happiness, fear, anger, sadness, and jealousy. Your pets need to experience emotions from you. Their relationships are meaningless without an emotional connection. If you fail to offer positive emotions, they will actively seek demonstration of any emotion, even anger.

Animals relate to their world on this emotional, instinctive level. They respond to their environment by what they feel. Unlike humans, they do not stop to consider, ponder, or contemplate the situation and the consequences before they act. They respond by what they feel in their bones.

"WILD MIND"

When you relate to your animal companions, you too must acknowledge and act on your feelings and emotions. The ability to follow through on raw perspective is intuition. The secret to relating to your creatures is developing your own animal intuition — understanding the animals and communicating with them using your "wild" instincts. These instincts include positive, helpful, gentle, and respectful behaviors, but do not give leeway to aggressive, fear-inducing, or hurtful behaviors.

Natalie Goldberg discusses the insight of "wild mind" in her book with the same title. Although she uses this idea to spark the creativity of writers, the concept also works when relating to animals. Wild mind is the realm of consciousness that reacts on an emotional level. It is not a "thinking" state but a "feeling" state — where you meet your creatures on the most equal domain.

Because of overly analytical brain processes, people miss opportunities to learn and experience. While you are sorting thoughts, establishing patterns, computing past and future relations, and attempting to create a blueprint of actions and reactions, you miss the lessons offered by your companions. You miss the opportunity to mold and develop an impressionable mind.

LEARNING FROM YOUR ANIMAL COMPANION

In order to fully enjoy the "wildness" of your animal companions, you must humbly admit your need to learn from them. Humans sometimes believe that because they can create movies, build space shuttles, or start a fire, they are smarter than the creatures. You must realize that on an emotional, feeling level — the stuff that makes everything worthwhile — animals and humans are relatively equal.

Intuitive understanding can be developed. Trusting your instincts teaches you to listen and respond with more sensitivity and accuracy. In the beginning, you may make some mistakes, but you can only fine-tune your intuition with practice. Acute observation, accurate recordkeeping, and an overwhelming willingness to learn are the means. The rewards spill over into every facet of your life. This is one reason why I believe animal people relate easily to other animal people — they sense the spark, awareness, and sensitivity.

YOUR PETS ALSO HAVE MOODS

Allowing your pets to have their own moods is the key to understanding their emotions. The animals you keep in your home are complex, unique individuals. Just like you, they have good and bad moods, and social and solitary moods. An animal's emotions are influenced by the same factors that influence peoples' moods: illness, weather, energy level, nutrition, and feelings of success and failure. It is your job as caretaker to respect these moods.

THE VALUE OF TOUCH

Touch is important for all living animals, and it is an excellent means of creating a bond with your animal companions. This physical contact must be regular, often, and gentle. Enjoyable for both animal and caretaker, touch can be petting and massage, including special and rewarding methods such as "TTouch" designed by Linda Tellington-Jones. Each animal, as an individual or as a species, desires different approaches to touch. Learn to read the signs of appreciation in your pets and adjust your contact accordingly.

Remember some animals don't appreciate physical contact, such as abused, fearful, or shy animals or those that just haven't learned to enjoy it. They will learn to accept touching to differing degrees; some may be more comfortable than others and only allow particular kinds of physical contact. For example, some wild-caught birds will tolerate physical contact most readily on their cheek area or under their wings. Many cats do not tolerate touch on their belly. You will find a mutually agreeable connection through your interaction.

THE EMOTIONAL CONNECTION

Animal caretakers must be able to give love freely in order to bond with those in their care. Animals love unconditionally. They do not understand the withholding of your affection, and you only confuse them when you are unable to give of yourself. If you are able to love and express this love openly without hesitation, your animal friends can flourish in your companionship and a bond will be created.

It often helps if you envision your animal companions as having chosen to live with you. If you believe this, you see their friendship as a gift and are less likely to take them for granted. This resulting appreciation is healthy for a mutually respectful relationship. If you view yourself as omnipotent in the life of your animal companions, the ability to keep a strong and balanced relationship is diminished. Believing they could live with anyone but want to live with you frees you to create an attachment.

Let go of the thought that without you your animal friends would fade in the void of emotional and physical deprivation. Releasing the idea of dependency (whether you on your pet or your pet on you) and mutually enjoying your interactions enable a bond to occur naturally.

Also realize that your animals will appreciate you no matter what. You do not have to be the richest or prettiest or offer the fanciest care accessories for your pets to be happy. They will take whatever you have to offer if you are giving of yourself and share a strong bond.

LACK OF UNDERSTANDING

Although there is much a caretaker can do to strengthen a bond, there are also actions that present stumbling blocks to the formation of a solid relationship. The most common is a lack of understanding on the caretaker's part. Not being able to interpret what your animals are trying to communicate to you makes it difficult to relate to one another.

This does not mean that you must always know everything about your pet; this is a learning experience — for life. You will constantly be discovering things about your animal companions and increasing your sensitivity to their communication. Sometimes you will be right, sometimes wrong. The most aware caretakers will find their friendship with their pets to be strong and delightful.

AGGRAVATION

Aggravation is a looming deterrent to a healthy bond. It is difficult to avoid because the frustration level of living with animals can be high. When your dog chews a hole in your new couch, your parrot screams every time you are on the phone, your rabbit digs up a corner of your carpet, or your cat stops using the litter box, you can become frustrated. However, these are repairable problem behaviors. You can take measures to prevent them or correct them once they occur, but in the meantime there is irritation. If a caretaker lets the irritation become the predominant emotion when interacting with the animals, a bond will not be developed, and any bond that was established can be tainted.

When you first bring an animal into your home, you will most likely experience these kinds of undesirable conduct. The lack of understanding combined with the animal's exploration of acceptable behaviors create a period of needing increased tolerance. This may be when many relationships between pets and their humans never recover.

Could this be why it is so seemingly easy for people to part with their pets at a later date? Possibly. If a strong bond is restricted from forming at this early stage in the relationship, it may be impossible to recover without much work. If these same caretakers do not even comprehend the lack of bond or are not willing to put the effort into creating one, then parting with the creature and beginning anew with a different one would seem the only choice. This is not a true choice because the same mistakes will clearly be made again unless the caretaker becomes educated.

Your aggravation influences your pet's emotions, your attitude, your relationship, and the strength of your commitment to the animal. Of course you will be aggravated at times; the key is to acknowledge this, release it by accepting your contribution to the problem, and move beyond this feeling by concentrating on the positive.

NEGATIVE ASSOCIATIONS

This same theme continues when discussing one of the most influential stumbling blocks to a healthy bond — negative associations. Every time you strike, yell, discipline, or interact with your pet in a negative manner, he will associate you and the place with the bad feelings. The more negative associations your pet has with you, the less likely you will have a strong bond.

Remember this when you are training your pet. If you are positive in your training approach, your animal friends will learn with more commitment and dedication. Your pet will respect your authority because you have always been fair. Mutual respect is the catalyst for a cherished friendship. With a strong relationship encompassing positive associations, your pets will be bonded to you for life.

OVERLY ATTACHED CARETAKERS

Some caretakers form extremely strong, unhealthy relationships with their animals, commonly referred to as "displaced attachment." The creatures they share their life with become their children, their parents, their spouse, or their only friend. A pet may be the only stable, unconditional love that the person experiences. This kind of attachment can be smothering and may make the animal neurotic. It also puts the animal in charge of the life of the family, which is far too much responsibility. Animals are animals; placing the burden of being human on them is confusing. They offer so much natural love and happiness that it is unjust to ask for more.

Caretakers acknowledge that their pet is a significant part of their existence, and maybe the animal is the most important connection with life they have, but the creature cannot take the place of a human. An animal lover, no matter how great, must associate with people to be well balanced.

Remember that each animal is an individual with his own personality. When you respect or value those characteristics, it makes your friendship stronger. On the other hand, you may have difficulty accepting other personality quirks, thus making your enjoyment of the individual more challenging. Appreciating him for all his quirks is part of your responsibility.

Getting to know your animals and seeing what extraordinary individuals they are strengthen your acceptance and build strong bonds of friendship.

CREATING A BOND

The Keys to Creating a Bond

THE ESSENTIAL COMPONENTS
- Spending shared time together
- Touch
- Intuitive sensitivity

THE STUMBLING BLOCKS
- Negative associations
- Aggravation
- Lack of understanding

BONDING AND THE AGE OF THE ANIMAL

Why are so many adolescent pets sacrificed to shelters or abandoned? This is a complex question, but I believe one reason is that the people who care for these animals have not properly bonded with them. The reasons for this lack of bonding are varied and perplexing. A contributing factor may be a lack of understanding of the different stages of a pet's mental development.

A baby animal needs much patience and understanding. In the current world, there is little of both these commodities. High-pressured, stressful, and complicated lives leave little time or effort for the tolerance of baby behavior. Often the caretaker assumes a personal affront when the animal makes messes or mistakes. "Why does he vomit all over the rug?" "Won't he ever be housebroken?" "He never listens to me!" "I'm tired of chewed baseboards!" These are all normal behaviors, but they are difficult to handle. Just the fact that many caretakers are currently pressed to the limits of emotional stability by life itself makes handling these common difficulties near impossible.

A bond between animal and human usually occurs within the first two months of their time together. If during this initial period of acceptance the caretaker is constantly frustrated and perpetually aggravated, this bond is not likely to occur. The pet may be cute, and the caretaker may like him, but an actual bond for life is nonexistent. When adolescence comes into full force and the problems escalate, there is little to hold the relationship together.

If your life is this frantic, you should question whether another animal companion fits into your schedule. If you decide that you can give a pet all that he needs but know that babyhood will make it difficult to completely enjoy your companion, then look for an adult pet. There are many great adult animals for adoption at shelters and from breeders, rescue organizations, and individuals.

Knowing the history of the adult animal you are considering for adoption is the key to the easiest adaptation to your life. If the animal has had a good life and has an upbeat, curious attitude, he should accommodate the change without undue trauma. Some animals will have unknown histories or scant information on past experiences at best, so it is difficult to predict the ease of transition. They may require special handling in the beginning to adjust to your home. All animals of different ages and backgrounds can make great companions with your understanding and assistance.

Planning and knowing the sensitivity of your pets will help changes and challenges occur with the least amount of stress and the greatest amount of growth.

Changes and challenges

Stress. All living creatures are, at times, victims of this predicament. No one is immune to periods of disturbing, energy-draining anxiety, including your pets. It is nearly impossible to live without occasionally confronting fear or nervousness.

Your responsibility as caretaker is to lessen the amount of stress that your animal companions encounter. When your pets are gripped by the claws of apprehension, you need to be sensitive to their needs.

Stress can interrupt normal organ function, disrupt sleeping and eating habits, alter immune system responses, and consequently make your animal companion susceptible to illness. Stress can also create behavioral problems and psychological distress.

If your pet is anxious or experiencing stress, she may exhibit minor symptoms of illness. She may manifest her discomfort by scratching, licking, vomiting, increasing vocalization, staying very close to you, whimpering, or doing other unusual actions. Be alert to variations in your pet's normal daily patterns so you can take measures to reassure her.

Overcompensation

If you overreact to your pet's sudden personality changes, you will be rewarding this new behavior and encouraging its continuation. Instead of lavishing attention, give your animal good overall physical and emotional support. Overcompensation may only make the problem worse. Because your animal companions look to you for guidance, if you act as if there is something to be worried about, they believe it.

Looking for a scapegoat

When under stress, human nature sometimes makes us seek a scapegoat for our frustration, and we often take out the built-up anxiety on innocent bystanders. Too often, these innocent victims are animal companions. Keep your energy gentle and calming. When you feel yourself being unfair, such as reprimanding or ignoring, pause, take a deep breath, and find the comfort and reassurance in the furry or feathered creature of your life.

Disruptions in a peaceful life

The changes that cause turmoil in your life are even more disturbing to your pets. You have the advantage of understanding what is happening (although this is not always true), and you can make choices.

Many things can cause worry in your pets — change of home, change in the caretaker's job and work schedule, loss or addition of a family member, or a drastic change in sleeping, eating, or cleaning schedules. If there are many small changes to your pet's environment or an increase of psychological conflict, she can become anxious and nervous. It will be up to you, the caring guardian, to eliminate the unnecessary stresses and minimize the unavoidable.

This chapter deals with many changes and challenges that confront your orderly life and add a twist of excitement and anxiety. Planning and knowing the sensitivity of your pets will help changes and challenges occur with the least amount of stress and the greatest amount of growth.

Moving

Aside from death and divorce, moving is the most stressful event people experience. If moving is this stressful to people, you know your pets are feeling the same but with increased intensity and confusion.

Routine is comforting to animals, and changing environments isn't easy. Depending on their personality, some accept a new home quite readily while others have greater difficulty adjusting.

PLANNING AHEAD

An investigation into a new city to obtain important information that can impact your life with animals is crucial. Contact the city clerk of your future town and ask for local pet ordinances. Leash laws are common and will probably be in effect in every city. Some cities do not allow dogs out of your yard within the city limits, including walking your dog down the street! This sounds far-fetched but happens in cities all over the country. It only takes a couple of irresponsible dog owners to ruin a city for all dog lovers. Check into any of these ordinances before you finalize your moving plans. If the laws are strict, you may decide on a different area.

Read the section on landlords and zoning requirements in the first chapter. These are laws that are going to influence your life, and you should know them before it is too late in the planning stages of your move.

Veterinary Information

If you are moving to a different state, contact that state's veterinarian's office or the Department of Agriculture to find out if there are any state pet entry laws and regulations. You will almost always need proof of a rabies vaccination, and often a tag is not enough. Make sure your pet's vaccinations are current and have records from your veterinarian supporting this fact in writing.

Ask your current veterinarian to recommend one in your new location. If possible, introduce yourself to the veterinarian before you make the move. Don't forget to get copies of your previous veterinary records. If you share your life with an exotic animal such as a bird or rabbit that requires special care, you may have to find a veterinarian who is far away. It may take a bit more research, so plan ahead.

Precautionary Cleaning

Before moving into your new home or at least before bringing your pets in, you'll need to perform some precautionary cleaning. Your main concern will be the elimination of insect infestations. If you discover an infestation, you may want to use bug bombs or a professional exterminator. Do this at least three days in advance, and air your new home completely before moving in. Also do the yard.

Have all carpets properly and deeply steam cleaned. Scrub the house from corner to corner. This is a usual practice during relocation, but with pets you need to be even more diligent. The smell of previous animal inhabitants may encourage your pets to claim the territory as their own. To avoid this messy affair, you will have to rid the home of any remaining odors from the previous animals. Wipe down at least the bottom eighteen inches of the walls with white

vinegar. You can also paint the walls, but do it before you move in to avoid exposing your pets to the fumes. Wash all window coverings. Replace all the filters in the air conditioners or heating units.

The Problems with a Newly Constructed Home

If your home is newly constructed, you may have to deal with the problem of toxic fumes released during the building process. These fumes become trapped in your house, taking as much as five years to dissipate. A common problem is formaldehyde and is accompanied by an array of toxins. If you are building your own home or moving into a new home, research some of these problems and adjust your plans. New homes can be built with care for your health, but you must be educated to know what steps to take.

Renting

If you are renting your home, you will want to protect yourself by making a complete record of the condition of the house. Make a list of any existing damage and take photos if necessary. This record must be signed by you and your landlord. If your landlord tries to hold you and your pets responsible for previous damage when you move out, you will have a record to support your claim. Of course, you should be willing to promptly fix any damage your animals caused. Being a responsible renter furthers the possibility of more landlords opening their doors for animal lovers.

Pre-Move Visit

If you are moving a short distance away, taking your dog to the new house to explore a couple of times before you actually make the move can do wonders to ease his mind. A well-adjusted bird would also benefit from these pre-move explorations. Take the bird in a crate or travel cage to the new home and then play "real estate agent" by taking her from room to room, explaining how much fun the two of you will have in this wonderful new house. Other more sensitive animals that do not handle change as easily will do better and be less stressed if you wait until you are completely moved to show them their new home.

SAFE ROOM

Your animal companions will be anxious and nervous with all the excitement surrounding packing and moving. Begin packing early, doing so methodically and without the hectic rushing that can overwhelm them. Moving your pets at the last moment and in the interim helping them feel as secure as possible will make it easier.

When moving day arrives, place your pets in a safe room, or a couple of rooms if necessary, where they can get a sense of security and are away from the hub of frantic activity. Clear the room of boxes and furniture so there is no reason for any of the moving help to enter.

Once the room is emptied, you can make it comfortable for your animal friends by setting up their bed, dishes, and toys. Caged animals should have their cage, with everything just the way it has been, moved into the room. If you have animals who are uncomfortable with each other, you most certainly do not want to confine them together. If this is the case in your household, you will have to find two rooms where you can safely leave your pets.

Before any help arrives and after the animals are comfortable in the room, hang a sign on the door that reads "Do Not Open." This prevents someone from inadvertently letting your pets out. With your animals safely behind closed doors, you can now begin moving.

While your animals are in their room, you will be busy packing boxes and loading trucks, but don't forget that your pets need reassurance. Be calm, take a deep breath, and relax. Carefully open the door to the room and spend a couple of minutes talking to and petting your animals, letting them know that they have not been abandoned. Let your animals spend some time outside if this is part of their normal routine.

KEEPING YOUR PETS OUT OF HARM'S WAY

If you are hiring professional movers, your dog may see them as threats and want to protect you and your possessions. You must make sure that your dog does not have access to the movers. This is a good time to use a crate. Place the crate in the safe room. Your dog may bark when she hears all the excitement on the other side of the door, so pets that are more sensitive to barking should be kept in another room.

If you are enlisting the help of friends and family, keep your friendly dog locked in a safe room. She may get underfoot, causing someone to drop something heavy or injure someone. She may also take the opportunity of your distraction to be naughty or escape. If the crate is an impossibility and your dog is one that barks and gets upset when many people are in her house, then it may be less stressful to take her to a friend's or family member's. You can also board her at a kennel for the day.

LONG-DISTANCE MOVING

Moving to a close location makes the actual move of your animals easier. You can load up the car like you are going for a fun drive, and your animal companions will be more willing and reassured.

However, if you are moving to a farther location, you must make some decisions on how best to move your pets. Being separated from you may make them nervous, so they will appreciate traveling with you to the new home.

If you only have a couple of pets to move, taking them in the car, even if it will be a couple of day's ride, is the best solution. You must carefully plan ahead if you are driving a long distance. Remember, both you and your pets will be stressed, so be sensitive in dealing with their emotions, reassuring them throughout the drive without being overly sympathetic. You can alert them to trouble by babying them too much. Just keep a positive, encouraging attitude, and share it with your animal friends. Read the section on traveling, presented later in this chapter, for a discussion on car travel.

If you have a number of pets or if some cannot handle the stress of a few days on the road, then you will have to make other arrangements to get them to their new home. You may have to ship them by airplane or if you are flying, they may be able to ride with you in the cabin. Again, read the section on traveling to get more information.

Bring your pet to the airport a couple of hours before the flight and be there immediately after the plane lands to pick her up. If you are not flying on the same airplane, you need to have someone reliable on each end of the flight — preferably you on the receiving end and a friend or family member on the sending end. If this is not possible, hire a professional to take care of the details. Some boarding kennels take care of shipping your pet for a fee.

ARRIVAL DAY

Once you have arrived at your new house, there will be much confusion and activity. The first thing to do is to put your animal companions in a secure, closed-off room. Arrange it the same as you did when you were packing up to move.

Set up the animal's area or cage as soon as possible after reaching your destination. Bring water from your previous home if it is different than water in the new home. Gradually accustom your companions to the new water by adding more new water to the old every day.

The first day in a new house is notoriously chaotic. You may be tempted to load up the family and head out for dinner. If you suddenly leave your pets in a strange environment after the hectic moving day, they will feel abandoned and be quite upset. Order dinner and have it delivered.

INTRODUCING YOUR ANIMAL COMPANIONS TO THEIR NEW HOME

Let your animals have access to the new house portions at a time if they appear overly anxious or fearful. This process of getting your pets out and about in the house may only take a couple of hours or it may take a couple of days. The level of commotion and the sensitivity of your animals will determine how quickly they will be able to calmly explore their unfamiliar environment.

Once your companions feel secure in their immediate surroundings, they will be ready to expand their horizons to other areas. Let each animal set her own pace. Reassure your pets and tell them how wonderful their new home is. Your pets should know

where everything important can be found. Beds, crates, litter boxes, toys, and eating area should be presented. Offer the same toys and dishes. This will give your animal companions a sense of security. Now is not the time to buy your dog that new wicker basket for a bed. Stay with the familiar at such a stressful time.

If your cat is allowed outdoors, keep her inside for a week or two until she is comfortable with the new house.

Many animals have house training lapses after a move. Some, like male dogs or cats, want to mark their new territory; others may just be stressed and become forgetful. A new environment makes sensitive creatures feel insecure, and this would be the worst time to reprimand them. Treat them lovingly by simply cleaning the mess without drama or comment. Remember, babying an animal when she is stressed will not help alleviate her anxiety — it will only perpetuate and reward it. Just be understanding and sympathetic.

Moving is hard on you and your animal companions. It is even more difficult on highly sensitive, sick, or old pets. Keeping yourself calm and keeping things as normal as possible make the transition smoother. Be perceptive to their emotions and treat their uncertainty with tender reassurance.

Vacation time

Vacation time! Just what you needed. You deserve one. You begin making plans. A week, just the two of you, on a beach in Jamaica. Maybe it's a few days skiing the snow-powdered mountaintops in Colorado.

Oh no! The animals! Who is going to watch the pets while you're away? Dare you go? Can they handle your absence? "Maybe, maybe not." You wonder — what can you do?

You plan well in advance and use your creativity. This section will help you devise a plan so that you can get away from it all while your animals are well cared for and content. You have a number of options, and it will be up to you and your pets to make the best of vacation time.

You have two basic choices when deciding what you can do with your pets at vacation time. You may either leave them at home or you can take them with you. If you have many animals, you may find that a mixture of different solutions works best for you and your household. Having them at different locations is often confusing and hectic. Your goal is to find the best plan that allows your animals to maintain the most normal routine and keeps them healthy and happy.

If you have just added another animal to your home or have a very sick, old, or young pet, this may not be the time to take a vacation. There will be more opportunities in the future. Your responsibility to your animals means occasionally making sacrifices, and a vacation may be the sacrifice when your pets need a secure, stable home life.

HOME ALONE

If you leave your animal companions at home, you must make arrangements for someone else to take care of them while you are away. Under no circumstances should you leave them home alone with no one checking on them at least twice a day. The dangers exposed to unsupervised pets are great, even if they are left for only a couple of days.

Natural disasters, fires, and other emergencies are the most obvious concerns. Consider also accidents in the yard and home. If no one is at least checking on them twice a day, they could suffer greatly. A bird with her foot caught in a toy will be in terrible shape by the time you return. You won't know if your dog can get the rabbit cage open until she does. The cats may go crazy from lack of supervision and tear up the new curtains in the living room. What if your dog gets her head caught in the dryer vent? (It has happened at my house.) If no one is there to observe illness manifestations, they may have progressed so far that your veterinarian can do little by the time you return.

Some accidents may be only an inconvenience when you return; some may be fatal. You're taking a risk leaving your pets alone while you are away. Even if someone just comes over for a quick check once a day, it would be better but still not comforting.

You also need to think of their emotional well-being. An animal that is accustomed to the presence and affection of her people will be devastated to find herself alone. The anxiety these animals face is overwhelming and definitely not a condition in which an animal lover would leave his or her precious pets.

FRIENDS AND FAMILY

The most ideal situation for your animal companions would be to stay at their own home with the least amount of disruption in their schedule. Being cared for by someone they know eases their distress in your absence. If you have a family member or a good friend who is willing to care for your pets, you are fortunate. If he or she can stay at your home while you are away, you are extremely fortunate!

Having friends or relatives care for your pets is the easiest solution for old, very young, sensitive, or fearful animals. It is the least stressful alternative for an already anxious creature. Your leaving is a disruption, and making it as easy as possible on your companions is the nicest thing you can do for them. Even your pets that are great adventurers will appreciate getting to stay home with a good friend.

This perfect solution is not always possible, so if you have been blessed with a caring person who takes care of your pets for you, you should express your thanks enthusiastically. Never assume that your friend or brother (or whoever) feels appreciated. The unfortunate flip side is that your friends or relatives may feel they are doing you a favor and you should pay them back in excess. They are, however, probably worth it.

Are Your Animals Comfortable with the Sitter?

If your sitter is a regular visitor to your home, you will not have to worry about whether your companions appreciate his or her company. If a trusting friend has volunteered to help out but hasn't met your animal family, you need to make introductions.

Planning ahead is an advantage because you can have the sitter come over several times. This gives you an opportunity to eliminate any question about how the animals and sitter will get along in your absence. This is especially true if you have territorial dogs. It would be your worst nightmare if your sitter were unable to enter the house because your dog did not trust him or her. The entire time you were gone, your pets would have no care or your sitter would beckon you home. So make sure relationships are developing smoothly before you leave.

What You Can Do to Help

Assist your sitter by making his or her time caring for your creatures as easy and as trouble-free as possible. If you created a schedule as mentioned earlier, your pets and sitter will benefit. Your sitter will know exactly what to do and will not forget or overlook any important activity that needs to be performed. Your animals will be less stressed because their normal routine will not be altered greatly.

You can also make it easier on your sitter if you divide the food up by animals and days and put each serving in a plastic bag or container. Clearly mark each bag (who gets what and when). This is especially helpful if your animals are on varied or special diets, if there is a lot of mixing, or you have quite a few pets to feed. It helps guarantee that each pet gets her food when she is supposed to. It's quicker for your sitter, and the animals benefit from more play time and attention.

Preparing food in advance for your pet sitter will make it easier on him or her and will assure that all animals get the food they are accustomed to. The bags are lableled with the pets' name and the date.

All of your supplies should be easily available and well stocked. Your observation/record book should be left in a convenient place so that your sitter can refer to it or make notes as needed. Your observation book documents any idiosyncrasies, and this can at times reassure your sitter. It will also have the important phone numbers he or she may need in an emergency.

Explain everything clearly and demonstrate how to use the information you have provided. The first time your sitter helps you out, it would be beneficial to walk together through the entire caregiving routine at least once.

Leave the sitter with emergency cash in case he or she runs out of a necessary care item or an emergency presents itself. Leave written instructions about where you will be, complete with phone numbers. Leave phone numbers for close friends or family who are available in an emergency. Make sure you talk to these backup people before you leave. Let them know you are going to be gone and who would be calling if help is needed.

Letting Others Know Your Plans

Notify your veterinarian that you will be out of town and who will be caring for your animals. Give permission for the sitter to bring your pets to the clinic, and you can often leave an imprinted credit card slip or set up a plan where you pay for services rendered when you return. Ask your veterinarian for assistance.

If you have a good relationship with your neighbors, let them know that someone will be taking care of your house and animals. Alert neighbors may call the police department if they see a stranger going in your home — only to place your sitter in an embarrassing situation.

Diversions for Your Animal Companions

If your sitter won't be staying at your house, your pets may become lonely, so arrange diversions to keep them entertained. A wonderful and easy idea is to place toys and treats in paper bags marked with the animal's name and the date. As the sitter leaves each day, he or she gives a bag to each animal, and they have a new adventure, for awhile anyway. Most animals have fun ripping the bag apart to get their special boredom-busters.

Slumber Parties

It may work better for your pet to stay at your friend's house. An animal that is not overly sensitive and has been socialized to accept change enjoys a slumber party. If your friend has other animals, you should reassure yourself that all are healthy. If your pet has visited before, you will find the visit to be simple and fun. Bring your animal's favorite bedding, toys, and food. Also bring the information in your pet's observation book and a schedule.

PROFESSIONAL SITTERS

Professional pet sitting is a new and expanding business area catering to the needs of many animal guardians. These people are generally caring animal lovers who give your pets attention and care while you are away. As in every aspect of pet care, you want to give your pets only the best, so choose carefully when hiring a sitter.

Because this profession is growing rapidly, some people are taking advantage of the business opportunity and are interested primarily in financial gain. While professional pet sitters deserve to earn a good living, you want to avoid those who wish to make a quick buck. These companies are less valuable to your pet's emotional well-being than a sitter who truly cares about animals. You are looking for someone you can trust with your precious animal family, someone you can trust in your home, and someone who offers quality care and attention to your pets.

Finding a Pet Sitter

To find a professional pet sitter, start with your veterinarian. Sometimes assistants and technicians at veterinary clinics also pet sit for clients. This is quite comforting when you know that your sitter has some knowledge of health care and can readily reach a veterinarian if necessary. You can also ask friends for recommendations, as well as fellow members of any animal clubs or organizations. You can look in the yellow pages but you would have better luck calling

the Pet Sitters International Referral Network at (800) 268-SITS(7487). You can also check bulletin boards at pet supply stores and ask the personnel there.

Interviewing the Sitter

Once you have gotten a couple of names and phone numbers, begin making calls. You should interview the sitter on the phone first, get references, and check them out. If the sitter does not readily offer phone numbers of people who have used his or her services, then skip the company and find another. Is one of the references a veterinarian? Great! When you call the references, ask what they liked and disliked and if they had any problems and, if so, what were they and how were they resolved. It is also a good idea to check with the Better Business Bureau to inquire whether any complaints have been made against the company or the individual.

If you like what you hear, a more in-depth interview conducted at your house is in order. The sitter will meet your animals, and you can assess his or her interaction with them. Do your animals seem to like the sitter? Does the sitter talk to them in a gentle, caring tone? If you have a shy, nervous, or reserved animal, you may want the sitter to return a number of times to play with and get to know the animal before you leave.

If you feel comfortable with the sitter and so do your animals, then use the sitter for a short vacation when you will be close to home. As your relationship develops and your trust is justified, then you can leave for longer periods and go farther away. A trustworthy pet sitter can become an important component in your pet care support network.

Further Considerations

When you ask a stranger to come into your house when you are away, you should be willing to pay for any emergencies that occur. You should also have good homeowner's insurance. Reputable professional sitters will probably have insurance of their own, but make sure your insurance is adequate.

Ask your chosen sitter if he or she has a backup person in case of emergency or illness. If so, you should also meet this person and make sure your animals are accepting. You may want to appoint your own back-up. If this is what you decide works best, give your sitter the name and phone number of the substitute. Make sure you discuss your plans with the chosen alternate caretaker.

Again, let your trusting neighbors know of your absence and who will be caring for your home and pets. The neighbors may also be able to confirm that your sitter came to your home as scheduled. It would be devastating to find out the sitter only showed up part of the time.

Helping Out

Follow the previously mentioned advice on sitters. Leaving the same kind of information for the professional sitter as you would for your friend or family member helps them tremendously. They can refer to your observation/record book and will have all the information, including phone numbers, they need. The professional sitter will have forms for you to fill out and will ask you for quite a bit of information. You can give him or her a copy of your pet information ahead of time and they can ask you any questions when you meet at your home.

Although a professional sitter may cost you part of your vacation money, the peace of mind is worth it. Plan well enough ahead and budget the sitter's fees into your savings plan. If you have no friends or relatives who can help you, a professional sitter is a great way to keep your pets happy while you are away.

BOARDING

If you cannot find a sitter or are uncomfortable with someone coming to your home, you can make arrangements for your pets to stay at a boarding facility. Even though most people are aware that there are dog and cat kennels to board furry friends at, you can also board more exotic animals at some veterinarian hospitals and other specialty boarding facilities. As more of these animals find their ways into homes as companions, there will be more businesses catering to their special needs.

Many boarding establishments are comfortable, well run, and offer plush facilities. If you can find one that caters to the needs of your pet and is run by people who truly care for the physical and emotional well-being of the animals, then the stay will be enjoyable. If her schedule is altered, her playmates and people are gone, or the new people taking care of her are less attentive, then she may become increasingly stressed. For a pet in a sensitive condition, such as a sick, very young, or very old animal, a stay at a boarding facility can be detrimental. You will have to use your best judgment.

Finding a Good Boarding Facility

Ask your veterinarian, fellow pet enthusiasts at club or organization meetings, and friends who have boarded their pets for recommendations. The rest is up to you, your intuition, and research.

Visit as many facilities as you can. Have a list of questions that you ask each business. Meet the staff and see where your animal will be spending her time. How does it feel? Are you comfortable? Are the staff members friendly, helpful, and knowledgeable? Observe how the staff interact with the animals.

How are the animals housed? Do they stay in crates? If your pet is not accustomed to this, the time to practice is before you leave. Do they have adequate shelter from the elements? Where do the animals sleep? How often are they allowed to play? Is there grooming available? Does each creature get her own space? Are different species separated? Are the animals kept so close that they can injure each other through cages and fencing? A tall, solid wall between unfamiliar animals is important to subdue fence-fighting. Your pet deserves her own space where she does not have to deal with the added anxiety of interacting with unknown animals.

The boarding facility you choose should uphold the same strict standards you keep for cleanliness, feeding regime, and consideration of the animals and their emotions. Check whether the facility is a member of the American Boarding Kennel Association, and ask if a veterinarian is on call. A good boarding facility will keep written records of your animal's stay, so ask that they do and tell them you will want a copy.

Will someone be there twenty-four hours a day? Often there is not around-the-clock staffing. If not, ask about fire and theft alarms. Is there someone who will check on the pets during the night? In intense weather conditions, you want to know that the temperature will be regulated and there will be some way for staff to be alerted if the temperature fluctuates greatly, such as if the heater breaks down during a January snowstorm.

If you feel good about everything that you have seen and like the people, then ask for references. References are no good if you don't use them, so call and talk to the people who have previously boarded their pets at the facility.

Boarding Birds

If you are boarding a bird, you will want to be sure that the staff members wash their hands between caring for each bird. If you are boarding at a veterinarian clinic or pet store, ask if the ventilation for the boarded birds is separate from the other birds. Airborne diseases are easily transmitted in these types of environments.

Veterinary Care

Notify your veterinarian that you will be leaving town and leave written permission for the facility to get your pet emergency medical care. Make sure you are adamant about the boarding facility getting your pet veterinary attention at any sign of trouble. The staff should understand that you are willing to pay for false alarms and want them to take no chances with the health of your animal companion. You will be required by reputable facilities to furnish proof of current vaccinations, and some may require a health certificate or note from your veterinarian.

Bringing Your Pet to the Facility

Bring your pet to the boarding facility before your scheduled departure and allow her to become somewhat familiar with the strange surroundings. It would be beneficial to leave her for a couple of hours as a test run before your trip. This helps your pet become accustomed to the strange sights, sounds, and smells. If you become uneasy about the facility after this brief stay, this also gives you time to find other accommodations.

Arrange your vacation plans so that you can drop off your pet in the morning. This gives her time to adjust to her new surroundings before nighttime. Bring a familiar item to serve as a security blanket. When you leave your animal at a boarding facility, be nonchalant as you part company. If you make a big deal out of your leaving, you will stress your pet. She will think something very terrible is happening if you are crying and apologizing to your baby for leaving her behind. Be matter-of-fact; you will see her soon.

The traveling animal companion

Traveling with your pet can be a very rewarding experience. With careful planning and an open mind, taking your animal friend or friends on vacation can be wonderful! Many more people are doing just that. With a rise in the number of people who take their pets on vacations, hotels, restaurants, and other hospitality-oriented businesses are becoming more flexible and accommodating than ever before. Some hotels and other businesses use their acceptance of pets as promotion.

This change in attitude makes it easier on those who want to travel with animals, but remember that you will still need to plan accordingly.

CONSIDERATIONS

Some animals travel better than others; consequently, making generalizations about species is difficult because it always depends on the individual's personality. If your pets are accustomed to change and would rather be with you than anywhere else, then they are good candidates for traveling. You must also think about yourself. Is the animal one that is easy for you to be around constantly? You may greatly appreciate your bouncy, hyper dog, but the thought of a six-hour car ride with her jumping around doesn't sound fun. You should admit this to yourself and find other arrangements for her.

Your vacation will have to be one that accommodates animals. You may have to adjust your activities to conform to the needs of your animal companion. Are you willing to design your vacation around her requirements? A trip to the mountains, camping by the lake, or a week at the beach would be heaven for your pet. If you plan on a busy trip of shopping and sightseeing, your animal may not have as much fun. You will not be able to leave her in the motel room for an extended length of time, so your excursions to places where pets aren't welcome will be limited. A day of shopping is too long to leave your animal unattended in a strange room. In some places, you would not be allowed to leave your pet in the room. If you were looking forward to a bustling schedule, staying out late, getting up early, and going all day, you may not have enough time to show your pet any affection. She may be happier with a sitter.

If you are bringing your dog along, you must make sure that she will be able to get enough exercise. Will you be able to stop frequently enough to walk her throughout the trip? If you are strained for time, extra stops will leave you feeling frustrated and frantic. You must stop every one to two hours for at least ten minutes. If you can't take your time and go by the whims of your animal, then she would benefit more by staying in the comfort of her own home.

This same kind of flexibility is also needed if your animal becomes car sick. Will you be able to stay calm and avoid getting annoyed? What if your pet seems ill; will you take the time and spend the money to take her to a veterinarian — even if it means missing that great tour you were dying to go on?

You will also need to spend time cuddling and interacting with her. This is actually the good part of taking your pet on vacation with you — neither of you will suffer any cuddle withdrawals. At the end of a busy day, some cuddling and playtime are welcome diversions that aid in a better night's sleep for all. This time spent interacting with your pet should not seem like a chore but like the icing on the cake. It is what makes traveling with your pet worth the extra effort.

YOUR ANIMAL'S PERSONALITY

Your pet must be confident and nonsensitive to change. She must also be trustworthy around strangers. A stable temperament is a must for traveling pets. Worrying whether your dog will bite the hand of the waitress in an outdoor restaurant will make your vacation a venture in apprehension. If your bird is likely to become fearful and start screaming at car lights shining through the motel window at night, waking everyone in the motel, you will find it difficult to deal with such behavior, as will the other guests and the motel manager.

Your pet should be accepting of new and strange environments, exploring them with curiosity and not trembling in fear at every new stop. Only you know your companion's personality well enough to give vacationing with her a chance. Then, in the end, only experience will tell you whether her temperament is one compatible with traveling.

The Personality of a Traveling Canine

Your traveling canine must be well trained, know basic obedience, and be reliable in her responses. When your pet meets people along your trip, you want the encounter to be positive. A dog jumping on someone and knocking them down at the beach is not fun for anyone involved. If your dog does not accept your direction and authority, you will have a hard time convincing her that you are in charge of the trip. If you are recognized as the one in charge, your pet will be less likely to become nervous during the vacation. She trusts your judgment and understands that you will not put her in any harm.

Your Animal's Physical Condition

Is your pet old or sickly? You should consider whether the trip will put her at risk. She may be physically or psychologically more comfortable in her own home with a sitter. On the other hand, if your pet is still a baby, this is not a good time for a long vacation. Short trips can be a learning situation, but long trips may become too trying for babies. Of course, you should never travel with a pet so young that she is not housebroken or is in danger because she has not had her vaccinations.

How Will You Be Traveling?

The final deciding factor on whether you should bring your pet along with you on vacation is how you will be traveling. If you are traveling by car, it is relatively easy to bring your pet along. You must plan

VISITING FRIENDS AND FAMILY WITH YOUR DOG—AND HAVING A GREAT TIME!

You're planning a visit to Cousin Emily's, and you decide a week at her beachside residence would be a fun adventure for your canine buddy. You know better than to just show up at her door with Spot in tow, so you call her on the phone. Even if she says, "Sure, no problem," it is important that she means it. Pay special attention to her voice. She may be cringing at the thought — perhaps preferring a root canal to a week with a hairy, drooling flea bag (her thoughts).

If she is receptive and supportive, a few details will make your trip more enjoyable for everyone. Ask what rules you and your dog need to adhere to. No pets on the couch? No begging pooches allowed? If your dog chases Cousin Emily's feline royalty, you may have to move to a motel. If cat chasing is a popular pastime for your canine, maybe bringing your dog isn't a good idea. Respect these requests, even if you do things differently. You are a guest — a guest who wants to get invited back.

The best way to impress your cousin, earn a reputation as a responsible dog person throughout your family, and hear "come back soon" as you pull out of the driveway is to have a well-mannered, obedient dog. If you haven't stressed compliance to good behavior, now is the time to brush up on the training. A dog who is crate trained is an asset in this situation. When you are visiting or exploring and you don't have the level of attention needed to keep an eye on your pooch, a crate is a great break. Also, before you leave on your trip, de-flea and bathe your dog. A clean, sweet-smelling dog is a welcome dog.

Plan to arrive at Cousin Emily's as early in the day as possible. This gives everyone, especially Spot, the opportunity to settle in and relax by bedtime. This also gives you a chance to introduce your dog to Cousin Emily's dog, if she has one. Do this in neutral territory.

When you arrive at your destination, leave your belongings in the car until everyone feels comfortable in their new surroundings. Walk your dog around outside on a leash. Keep the leash on and give your canine a tour of the house. It is a wise idea to keep your dog on a leash for the first day. In a strange environment, a loose dog may have unpredictable or excitable behavior.

When you leave, you want your host's house to be just as it was when you arrived. Clean up after yourself and your dog the entire time you are visiting. Vacuum up any hair left behind. Pick up all dog deposits from the yard. Don't let you or your canine buddy be a nuisance of any kind.

Once during a family dinner, with thirty in attendance, I used a fork to scoop canned dog food and left it on the counter. It didn't bother me; I didn't even think about it. The uproar over the "gross" fork alienated a couple of relatives, and they quickly acquired a distaste for my adorable, well-behaved puppy. What a shame. Be diligent when you visit in someone else's home.

This example spotlights your dog, but you can use the same planning ideas and thoughtfulness if you wish to visit with any of your animal friends. Be cautious regarding communicable illnesses if your friends and family have the same species as your pet. If you follow these guidelines you will greatly increase the probability of being invited to return. Yeah! Next summer at Cousin Emily's!

well in advance and make reservations for hotels early in your planning stage. You have to be sure that you have the space and are willing to make some adjustments in your traveling style. Other means of travel may not be worth the hassle, expense, or risk. Read on to see the possibilities.

TRAVELING BY CAR OR MOTORHOME

Your creature should be accustomed to riding in the car before you leave on vacation. If she has not been in a moving car, help her get used to the unusual sights and motion. Take short rides with your pet, letting her adjust to car travel slowly. Take your companion with you when you run errands or stop by a friend's for a short visit. You can accustom her to being left alone for short times by leaving her in the car when you run into the post office or bank. Then reward your pet for her patience and good behavior with a treat when you return. The reason to accustom your pet to these short stays in the car is for situations that may arise on your trip, dictating that you leave her unattended a few moments.

Be very aware of temperature when you leave any living creature in a car. Brief departures should occur only in cool temperatures. Even 85-degree outdoor temperatures will heat your car to 100 degrees in ten minutes and 120 degrees in thirty minutes.

If you find that your pet gets car sick, you can help her by withholding food (from your cat for six hours or dog for three hours) before your scheduled time to leave. Feed your pet the night before and then when you reach the day's destination but not during the trip or right before you leave. Exercise your animal, initiating fun games of a physical nature before loading up to leave.

Paperwork

If you are traveling over state lines or over the border, you need to ask your veterinarian what paperwork is needed. You should, no matter where you are planning to travel, have a copy of a current health certificate, immunization records, and a copy of your pet's rabies certificate. Rabies tags are not always enough proof. Some motels will even request this information to stay at their establishment, so ask when making reservations.

Motorhome

If you are traveling by self-contained motorhome, you will find your trip easy and enjoyable with your animal companions. A motorhome is indeed your "home away from home." All pets can fit into the lifestyle of traveling by motorhome. They quickly become adjusted to their mobile house and are less likely to become nervous or anxious. If you own your motorhome or can rent one a couple of days early, you can accustom your pet to the strange environment before you set out on vacation.

A motorhome is the transportation of choice for long-distance or lengthy travel. You should make reservations ahead of time at parks and campgrounds where you want to stay. Regulations and restrictions regarding pets may apply, so be sure to ask and get your reservations in writing. This again means good preparation and planning well in advance of your vacation.

STAYING AT MOTELS WITH YOUR PET

If you are staying at a motel, a few extra suggestions will make your trip more enjoyable. When you make reservations and again when you check in, question the manager about any recent chemical use. A freshly exterminated motel room can make your animal companion sick or could be fatal. Fresh paint, carpet, outdoor pesticides, and other chemicals should also be investigated.

Alone in the Room

Some motels have rules regarding leaving animals unattended in your room. You surely cannot blame them; many doors, carpets, and furniture have been ruined by nervous, stressed-out pets left in their motel room by their caretakers.

If you do leave your pet in the room, make sure that she is well secured in her crate or cage. Your animal should have plenty of toys to keep her occupied. Leave a litter box for your cat. Do not leave your pet alone for long periods. Return soon so she does not get nervous and start misbehaving. You also need to exercise her and reassure her that you are not abandoning her in this strange place.

It is a good idea while you are away to hang a "Do Not Disturb" sign on your door. This eliminates the possibility of the maid coming in when you are not there. You may also want to pick up your own linen at the front desk so that you will not have to worry about anyone disturbing your pet. Leave the television on to keep her company; it also makes the room seem as though it is occupied. There is also the risk that your pet could be stolen from the motel room.

Motel patrons and personnel may have had to deal with screaming, whining, or barking lonely animals that disturbed all the other guests. It only takes one bad experience for the motel to change its rules and make it more difficult for the more caring pet guardian. If the motel will not allow you to leave your pet unattended but you would like to do so for a short time, discuss the use of the crate with the manager. You may be able to get permission. If you do, make sure that all goes well. It will assist the next person who stays there with his or her pet.

Cleanliness

Keep your pet off of the furniture to limit the amount of hair left behind. If your companion is one who sleeps on your bed, bring your own blanket or bedding from home. If you do find hair in your room, clean it up. Bring your favorite hair collection tool.

Set a good example and help increase the acceptance of pets in the hospitality business by cleaning up your motel room and leaving no obvious signs that an animal has been there. Use a small broom and dust pan to sweep up any kitty litter or bird debris and get rid of most of the hair. Clean up after your pet while traveling and taking rest stops. Always clean up after she relieves herself.

USING A CRATE
TO KEEP YOUR ANIMAL SECURE

Your pet should have a crate if you plan to leave her unattended at the motel. Some motels that do not allow animals as a general rule may allow pets if they are assured they will be confined to a crate. You may have to be persuasive. Ask the desk staff when making reservations and get confirmation in writing.

When using the crate while traveling, it should not be placed on the floor because of the danger of carbon monoxide poisoning and fluctuations in

The author's rabbit Amelia travels safely in a crate secured with the seatbelt.

temperature. Place it out of direct sunlight, and shade it with a light-colored towel. The towel also helps calm excitable animals. Remove any swinging or hanging toys in crates or cages.

A water bowl is impractical because it spills and makes a mess all over the cage and animal. You can use a water bottle as long as the animal already knows how to use one or give your pet high-water-content snacks. Be sure to offer water at stops along the way.

A Calming Effect

A crate helps a nervous animal settle, and either a crate or small travel cage is an absolute necessity for rabbits or birds. If you are traveling with your pet bird, a bolt-on perch allows her some time outside of her cage or crate. A cat also benefits from a crate by staying more calm and feeling more secure.

Crates Increase Safety

A crate is a great safety device because it keeps your pet restrained and out of the driver's way in a car. If secured in the seat by a belt, a crate can help reduce injury in an automobile accident. In the event you are in an accident, your crated animal will not be running loose at the accident scene and will not get harmed. Some dogs guard their beloved caretaker, and emergency personnel sometimes must destroy the animal to help the person.

Safety Belts

If your dog or cat won't travel by crate, you can use one of the many belting devices specially designed for pet travel. You may also place your pet in a halter collar and leash and attach the leash to a belt. This is great for restraining but may not offer protection in an accident.

AIR TRAVEL

If you are traveling by plane or other public means, you will have to meet more requirements, and you must plan far in advance. You should find out all regulations and follow them to the letter. Get reservations to take your pet in writing. Get all information regarding requirements for health certifications and carrier specifications and meet them. You do not want to be turned away as you are getting on the plane to leave for your vacation because you have the wrong carrier or incomplete paperwork. Each state has differing rules on what is considered a "current" health certificate, so inquire about each state where you will be stopping.

Freight Compartment Versus Cabin

Most often when you fly, your friend will be traveling via the freight compartment. This is not the most desirable way for an animal to travel. Although airlines attest to their safety record and many pets do travel safely this way, it is risky and you must weigh the odds heavily. Make reservations well in advance and ask for a written confirmation assuring your animal a place in the cabin. Most airlines will allow a predetermined number of animals per flight in each cabin. She will have to be a small pet because she must fit in a carrier that can be placed under your seat. Call the individual airlines to get exact measurements.

If your pet is too large to fit under the cabin seat, she will have to fly air freight. Discuss with the airline that you are shipping a live animal and make sure that you fully understand all regulations and follow them accurately. To be certain that your animal is completely healthy, a visit to your veterinarian is in order. Your veterinarian can supply you with a record stating the good health of your pet.

If your animal is to fly in the freight compartment, it is absolutely mandatory to have a strong, well-built carrier. Each airline has its own requirements regarding the carrier design; so check with your airline before purchasing one. Your pet should be able to stand up, lie down, and turn around in her carrier. The bottom should be solid and furnished with a comfortable and absorbent lining. The carrier should also have good ventilation and cross ventilation. A strong, sturdy lock is also important.

The crate must be clearly labeled that it contains a live animal. Your pet must be identified, and care instructions should be easily located.

When to Travel

To make the flight easiest on your animal, choose to travel during slow or off-peak periods. Ask for a low-attended, uncrowded flight, which lowers the amount of luggage crowding your pet in the cargo hold and increases the likelihood of more personal attention. Ask how and where your animal will be taken off the plane, and arrange for your companion to be carried off. You do not want your animal to be released onto the luggage carousel. Do your best to reserve a nonstop flight. If you have no choice but to stop, find out if you have to change planes. This begins to get risky and difficult. At this point, you may change your mind and decide it isn't worth the risk.

If the weather is warm, schedule your flight for early morning or late evening when it is cooler.

Using Tranquilizers

Some animals are naturally high-strung and nervous. If your pet is one of these and you have no choice but to send the animal in air freight, then you may want to talk to your veterinarian regarding tranquilizers. Tranquilizers depress breathing and slow the animal's heart rate, so if your pet is old or sickly you may not be able to use them. The cargo area of an airplane may have little air circulation if its takeoff is delayed, which makes it more taxing on an already inhibited respiratory system. You want to see how the tranquilizer affects your animal companion before you take off, so try them a few weeks before your departure. Get to your veterinarian soon enough to discuss this concern, and give the drug a trial run.

TRAINS, BUSES, AND OCEAN LINERS

Trains and buses generally do not allow pets; most won't even transport them in the cargo area. The government does not allow animals to be carried in freight compartments that are not temperature controlled, and you wouldn't want your animals to be traveling there. These companies would have to spend billions of dollars to make their cargo areas temperature controlled — something that is not going to happen in the foreseeable future. In other countries, pets are welcome in the passenger areas of trains; if you are traveling abroad, check into this.

A few ocean cruise lines are friendly to pets. Some even have kennel areas on board. Ask your travel agent. Research requirements at every port you are scheduled to stop at, or you could get somewhere and be stuck for a thirty-day or longer quarantine.

QUARANTINES AND ATTITUDES

Some foreign countries have little or no restrictions for visiting pets, while others have a three- to six-month quarantine. Obviously this would be a massive disadvantage to traveling abroad with your animals. You may need to have an inspector check your pet's health and review your paperwork. Make sure you arrive at your destination when the inspector is on duty; otherwise, your companion may be held until the next shift.

You can even find punitive restrictions in the United States. Hawaii and Alaska have longer quarantine regulations than many foreign countries. Hawaii has a 120-day quarantine. Avoid a stopover in any of these restrictive states or countries.

Many foreign countries also have differing views on animal companions. Some are lenient and allow animals to be a part of all aspects of life; others take a dim cultural view of pets. Find out this kind of information before you make plans to travel with your animal. Contact the country's consulate in the United States to research this information.

HELPFUL TRAVELING HINTS

Some hints and suggestions make traveling with your animal companion more enjoyable. Remember, sometimes the little things can make a big difference.

As you garner more experience traveling with pets, you will find your own personal system and equipment that work best for you and your animal companions. The first trip with your pets may not run as smoothly as you had hoped. Don't give up. You will learn quite a bit the first time, and each time thereafter you will increase the ease of traveling. It is a rewarding experience, so give it a go!

Warm Weather Travel

Warm weather travel calls for extra precautions to keep your animals comfortable and safe. Never leave your animal companions in a car when temperatures

The author's Bouvier Retta is too large to fit in a crate in this car, so she is wearing a halter that is attached to the seatbelt with a short leash.

exceed 80 degrees, even for a couple of minutes. Even if you leave windows down, the risk is great. Cars and heat are a lethal combination.

If you don't want to invest in permanent window tinting (some of the new tints are subtle and yet keep intense sunrays from penetrating the windows), individual shades are available that attach to the window of your car. They are designed with the protection of children in mind, but they work for our precious animal passengers as well. You can pack a cooler with wet towels. When you stop for a rest, throw one on your pet to cool her down. The wet towels can also be draped over crates and travel cages to keep creatures cool. Bring a spray bottle full of water and when your pet seems to be getting overheated, you can gently spray her with the bottle and cool her down.

Grooming

You experience a more enthusiastic welcome in your travels if you start your vacation with a clean, well-groomed animal. Get your pet squeaky clean and sweet smelling, trim all nails, and trim your bird's wings.

Food and Water

Bring a supply of familiar food. If you use a brand that will be available during your travels, you can buy the bulk of it on your trip. The night before you depart on your trip, fill several jugs of water from your tap. Your pet's system may be upset by a sudden change in water, especially when she is already stressed from traveling (remember, even good stress is still stress).

Once you have reached your final destination, you can slowly help your pet adjust to the water by mixing half of the native water with half of the water that you brought from home. If you will be traveling for a long period, you can accustom your animals to a commercial bottled water and buy more as you need it along your trip.

Tools for Control

A mandatory piece of dog equipment is the ever important leash. Most cities have leash laws that you must adhere to, and you want even the best trained dog to be safely in your control in strange environments. A retractable leash is ideal for more vigorous exercise and exploration while retaining control of your canine. Your dog should understand "wait" so she doesn't just jump out of the door every time it is opened. Your cat and rabbit should be accustomed to a halter and leash to allow more freedom in exploring, and the retractable leash is also great for these pets. Keep a crated animal in her crate while driving and when stopped. Snap the leash on your pet before the car door is opened.

Phone Number Card

Before you leave home, prepare a three-by-five or larger card with a listing of important numbers. You need your veterinarian's phone number, the American Animal Hospital Association Veterinary Emergency Information number (800-252-2242), the Humane Society's Lost Pet Hotline number (900-535-1515), National Animal Poison Control Center phone number (see appendix), your emergency contact person's phone number, and any other important phone numbers or information. Have the card laminated, either by yourself or at a copy shop for a small fee. It is important to carry this card with you at all times; leave one in your glove compartment permanently.

Necessary Supplies

You also need dishes, toys, bedding, grooming equipment, and plenty of towels for accidents and messes. Toys should be of the silent variety so that you don't disturb any other guests at motels or your nerves in the car. See the suggested packing list below. Use it or create your own customized version and check the items off as you pack them. Then check them off again as you load everything in the vehicle. This double-checking helps assure you didn't forget anything.

PACKING LIST

- Pet first-aid kit
- Identification
- Health certificate
- Rabies certificate
- Food and water bowls
- Jugs of water
- Flashlight
- Grooming necessities
- Crate or travel cage
- Bedding
- Pre-moistened towelettes
- Necessary medications
- 3 x 5 phone number card
- Food for each day
- Extra leash
- Collar and leash for dogs
- Pooper scooper
- Scratching post
- Paper towels
- Treats
- Toys
- Written reservations
- Dish soap to clean bowls
- Photos for ID purposes
- Litter box and litter
- Towels
- Can opener
- Small broom and dust pan
- Halter and leash for cats and rabbits
- Retractable leash
- Spray bottle with water
  (for cooling hot animals)

WHAT TO DO IF YOUR PET IS LOST WHILE TRAVELING

If your pet becomes lost while on vacation, act quickly. Carefully survey the area you last saw your animal. Put into action the same searching strategy discussed later in this chapter. Call the police department (not the emergency number) and the local shelter, leaving the necessary information with them. If you haven't located your companion in a couple of hours, make your flyers and post them. Make sure you use the phone number of a friend, relative, or veterinarian that will be readily reachable. Call this appointed contact immediately so he or she will know your pet has been lost and will be prepared.

If you must get on your way but haven't located your animal, get the address and phone number of the local newspaper. You can subscribe to the paper for a month or so, scanning the lost and found section. You can also place an ad begging for the return of your pet. She may have lost her collar or tags along the way, so you want to put out the best effort you can.

Your animals should wear collars and securely attached identification tags at all times while traveling. A good recommendation is to have tags made before your trip that identifies a friend, relative, or veterinarian's phone number at home. If you have a cellular phone with you, include this number. You can check in with your appointed person to see if someone has called regarding your pet.

Bring the identification information from your observation/record book. In case your companion is lost, you can use this information and the recent photo attached to make flyers. Under such stressful conditions, you may forget any distinguishing marks or you may be so upset you can't even remember your pet's age.

Home alone during the day

When you are away for most of the day, you should take measures to keep your animals entertained. If you work full time, this is the reality of your lifestyle, and you need to make your pets feel as comfortable as possible. If you don't work outside of the home, there are times when activities dictate that your animals spend most of the day alone. In either situation, you'll need to be prepared and have a plan for your absence.

If you have only one pet or if you have more but they are not granted freedom to be together, your animal companions will probably be lonely when you are not home. Loneliness and boredom create behavioral problems. Your pets may become excessively noisy, destructive, or make frantic attempts to escape. You can help your animals deal with this loneliness and boredom by planning, training, and understanding the needs of your companions.

If you give your pet a balance of attention, play, training, and cuddling, your pet will be fine, even when you are away for most of the day. It is not impossible to work full time and have a multi-animal household; it will just take devotion and dedication from you.

BEFORE YOU LEAVE

Begin by giving your animals adequate attention when you are home. If you are working a full-time job and you have other responsibilities, you can suddenly find yourself overwhelmed, especially if you have haphazardly adopted too many animals.

Before you leave in the morning, each companion needs and deserves some time with you. Vigorous play expends excess energy and tires the animal. They can then spend most of the morning relaxing and resting. They benefit from your attention and game playing along with some cuddling.

Grooming is another activity that accomplishes a care objective and also has the benefit of "together" time. If you give your bird a shower before you leave, she spends hours preening and perfecting her feathers while you are gone. A secure relationship (that grooming helps develop) will go far to ease the mind of your animal friends.

ANIMAL-TO-ANIMAL RELATIONSHIPS

In a multi-animal household, pets have the company of other animals. This is a great way to combat loneliness, and if they have positive relationships, you will probably not have a problem with stressed-out pets. Two animals can possibly get into more trouble than one if they are so inclined. Evaluate the personality of your pets to see if they will be okay when you are not home and let experience be your guide. Two young animals of the same species are usually the spunkiest combination.

Can you assure the personal safety of each animal when you are not there? An underlying hostility could result in a fight or an attack, so introduce your animals carefully and slowly and be aware of the quality of their interactions.

Finding a friend for a lonely pet is not a good reason in itself to get another animal, though. If you are not ready to take on the added responsibility, then you should find other methods of keeping your companion entertained when you are away.

Some animals will not be able to socialize directly. As mentioned previously, birds find the antics of ground-dwelling animals quite entertaining and even instigate mischief at their expense. You do not have to have two dogs; your cat can be good company for your canine friend. Rabbits and cats are notorious friends. Read chapter 2 regarding introductions and use your intuition to make sure that your pets are enjoying the camaraderie.

SPECIFIC THINGS YOU CAN DO TO COMBAT LONELINESS

Your animals should have plenty of safe, fun, and interesting toys. Not supplying toys for your animals forces them to find some of their own. If you don't want your dog chewing up the couch cushions or your cats dragging houseplants all over the carpet, have toys available for them.

Bag of Toys

A small paper bag filled with toys and special treats can be given to your animal companions shortly before you leave in the morning. While the animals are busy digging in their "fun bag," they won't be as traumatized as you walk out the door.

Canine Playground

If you keep your dogs outside when you are away, you can add activity equipment to the yard. Tunnels, elevated walkways (not too high and not near a fence), hanging tires to beat around, and large indestructible balls encourage physical activity and keep canine minds occupied. Use caution if you decide to provide "playground" equipment for your dog. Offering equipment that is either beyond the physical capabilities of your canine or unsafe is dangerous.

Also, your dog should not be wearing her collar while alone; the risk of strangulation is great and this is especially true if she is playing on equipment in your yard.

Your Dog

If you will be away longer than four hours and there will be no one to let your dog out to relieve herself, you must leave her outside. Providing a doggy door may work if your cats or rabbits do not have access to it, or you can get a magnetic pet door. Although an expense at first, these doors are handy. They open only for the animal who is wearing the "key" or magnetic collar. Have a door leading into the garage or a back patio from the yard. This gives your companion an opportunity to find shelter from the weather.

If you keep your dog outside, she may become an escape artist due to boredom; there are so many interesting things going on outside of her boundaries. If your dog gets out or is destructive, you may have to build a kennel or dog run. This is for the protection of the dog, and most dogs like the feeling of security a run gives them. As long as your dog is with you most of the time when you are home, she will not suffer any emotional distress while in a kennel.

The run needs to be of adequate size. Your pet must have room to romp and play, a place to get out of the elements, fresh water, plenty of exercise, and toys for distraction. Confining your pet in this manner protects your yard and outdoor possessions, and this increases your appreciation of the animal. If not abused, this kind of confinement is healthy and beneficial.

Human Company during the Day

If you work full time, you may want to come home on your lunch hour to check on your animal family. You can use this time to let your dog out to relieve herself. If you need to rely on a crate for your dog, you must let her out once every three hours. Crates are great training tools and can be an invaluable aid if not overused or abused. A crate should be seen as a step in your dog's training. It protects your home and belongings when you're not there to supervise, but eventually your dog will learn the manners of the household and should behave herself

when alone in the house. With your guidance, she can graduate to more freedom. She will learn to cope with your absence without anxiety through repetition and experience.

If you work far from home or otherwise cannot make it home for lunch, consider hiring someone to check on your animals. Cats, rabbits, and some birds will be fine alone for eight hours, but for periods longer than this, you'll want them to have human companionship from someone they trust. Dogs and most birds find it more difficult to be alone this long. You know your pets and best understand their needs, so rely on your instincts.

Having a teenager or senior citizen visit your pets once during the day can make their day much more pleasant and not so lonely. Hire a responsible neighborhood kid to come over after school and feed the animals and play a bit. You may be able to find someone who loves animals, and friendships can blossom under these conditions.

Diversions for Birds

Birds are noisy and excitable in the evening, especially if you have been away all day. One way to lessen the impact of your return is to set the television or radio on a timer, having it turn on an hour or so before you come home. If you leave them on all day, your pet learns to tune them out and they have no impact. Many birds love to watch television, and this diversion helps them be more settled when you return home. Any animal benefits from this, especially pets who are alone with no other animal companion. Timers are inexpensive, easy to install, and easy to use.

Coming and Going

Most animals become very excited at your homecoming. This excitement can be overwhelming when you are tense from the day, still have evening meals to prepare, and haven't had time to unwind. Bad habits develop by coming home excited and lavishing emotional loving on the animals when you walk through the door. Make it as matter-of-fact as possible and keep your energy levels low. Dogs especially become quite nervous about your comings and goings if you make a big deal out of them. Telling your dog again and again "I'll be back. Don't worry. I'm so sorry, but I have to go. You be good, now. Don't chew up the recliner. Please, please, be a good girl!" will give her plenty of cause to worry. Greet each of your pets briefly when you arrive home. Wait until you have settled down before you dole out loads of attention.

Birds are especially sensitive to the departure and return of their family members. In the wild, members of the flock do not leave and return without making sure the other members are quite aware of the event. With birds, you should make sure to say hello when you arrive home and give them a minute of your time. It doesn't need to be emotional or dramatic — just an announcement and greeting.

Finding a lost pet

You have seen the flyers and posters hanging on streetlight poles and buildings pleading for a Good Samaritan to bring back a beloved pet. The thought of one of your animal companions being alone in the great big world is scary. It is truly a vision that sends quivers down the spine of the most stoic animal lovers.

In chapter 6 you will learn about what can happen to animals if allowed to have their freedom outside of your home and yard. The truths to the violent and uncaring society that pets suddenly find themselves in are quite horrible. These thoughts permeate the mind and hearts of caretakers when a pet is lost.

IDENTIFICATION

Investigate methods of identification and discuss them with your veterinarian. Some methods, such as tags, will lead the finder of your animal to you, and other methods, such as microchips, will help if there is a question about the animal's identity. This is especially true of animals that people consider difficult to distinguish from one another, such as birds.

One good way to identify your pet is to take close-up, clear pictures of any unusual markings or deformities. Place your driver's license in the picture so that it can be identified as yours and be used to gauge the relative size of the distinguishing marks. (See the information on creating a record book in chapter 3.)

Be careful. Keep your pets as safe as you can, but realize that uncontrollable situations may arise and your pet may become lost. Forget the guilt and find your pet as soon as possible. The following plan describes the best opportunity of locating your lost animal.

WHAT TO DO
Search

If your pet becomes lost, don't panic. This may sound difficult, but you will need to think clearly and act quickly. Stay calm and begin your search immediately.

Start by making a sweep of your entire house and yard. You may have accidentally locked your pet in a cupboard, closet, or appliance (such as a dryer). Listen carefully for any faint sound of your pet alerting you to her distress. Check closets, drawers, washing machines, dryers, and boxes — anything your pet could fit in and one size smaller. Animals, like children, have an amazing way of getting into trouble where you would never expect.

If your home search hasn't turned up your pet, enlist the help of as many people as possible and search the neighborhood. Knock on doors and ask the neighbors if they have seen your pet. Bring a picture to show them. Offer neighborhood kids a couple of dollars to help you look. Children are very active and will take a personal delight in searching for your pet.

Walk through your neighborhood and ask your neighbors and local business people if they have seen your pet. Many people see a loose animal and do nothing about it, but they can tell you when and where they last saw your pet and you can search there.

If it has been a couple of hours without a sign of your pet, you will have to extend your search. Call your local animal shelters and ask if any animals that match your pet's description have been received. On the first day you realize your pet is missing, visit the shelters in person. It will be easier for the busy people working there to attach a face to the situation, and

IDENTIFICATION METHODS

Even if you keep your cat indoors and are cautious about keeping your dog in your boundaries, escapes can happen. If your animal manages to wander off because of curiosity or a crisis (e.g., fire, storm damage, or earthquake), you can only safeguard her return by having up-to-date identification on her. Having a permanent means of identification assists in recovering your pet if she is stolen or you otherwise need to prove she is yours. Keep accurate records of your animal's physical identity along with recent photos in your record book, and look into the following methods of identifying your companion.

TAGS

Tags are the most obvious identification, and your pet should have a set to wear when you take her out and about. Collars can be dangerous if left on your pet when she is unsupervised. Tags make it easy for Good Samaritans to contact you.

Make sure the tag is current and has the animal's name and your phone number. Your dog should have her current rabies and license tags attached. If she bites someone, the victim can have the numbers researched and your dog's safety is better protected. To keep the tags from jingling, you can place back-to-back sticky wall mounts used for pictures between them or use double-stick tape.

The tags must be securely fastened to a well-fitted collar. The collar should be a buckle collar, not a training or choke collar. If you want to leave the collar on at all times, choose one that has an elastic or breakaway section. Cats must have a collar like this, allowing them to get away if they get stuck.

The problem with tags is that they can become separated from the animal. If this happens to your pet, a backup system of identification helps prove that the animal is yours. The following identification methods are supplemental to tags and should not be considered replacements.

TATTOOS

Most research facilities won't purchase animals with tattoos, so tattooing is a good deterrent to thieves. Talk to the veterinarian or technician who performs the tattooing about the best area on your animal's body to place it. If the tattoo is on an ear or even an appendage, determined thieves can amputate and rid the animal of the tattoo. Some shelters don't even check to see if an animal is tattooed due to ignorance and lack of time. This is one reason not to forgo using tags.

When choosing a registration number, don't use your phone number, address, or driver's license number. Use your social security number or other more stable identification number. The tattoo number will have to be registered, and you must pay for both the tattoo and its registration.

CONTINUED ON NEXT PAGE

IDENTIFICATION — CONTINUED

MICROCHIPS

The microchip, or radio frequency identification, is as small as a grain of rice. Your veterinarian implants it through a small incision directly under the skin of your companion. Each microchip is programmed with its own one-of-a-kind number that transmits a radio signal. The signal is read by a special scanner.

Herein lies the difficulty with microchips. In order to read the signal, a scanner is necessary. The three microchip manufacturers have three incompatible signals and scanners. Someone looking to identify your pet would first have to have a scanner (a yet uncommon piece of equipment in many shelters and animal facilities) and would then have to have your brand of scanner. This makes the venture a bit more risky. Pet guardians must also rely on the companies to stay in business.

Using microchips is definitely a good method of identification. If the companies can manufacture a compatible reading system and the scanners can become more widely available and cost efficient, then this method of identification could become the standard. In the meantime, you may want to use it as a backup method.

they will understand your genuine care. Bring a picture of your pet with you. Fill out a lost animal report and attach a photo.

Make sure you note any unique physical or personality characteristics that can help the staff identify your pet. Leave a phone number where they can either reach you personally or leave a message. Call every day for at least a week or two. Check with the shelters in person as often as possible. They are busy, and you don't want to risk your pet slipping through the cracks.

When to Call the Police

If you suspect your pet was stolen, contact the police department. Call dispatch; do not call 911 (if you have this in your area) unless the crime is currently taking place. Pets are stolen often right from your own yard. Parrots, especially the valuable ones, are often targets of break-ins and robberies. This is a good reason not to show off your prized parrot in a front window or take the cage outside in the front yard so that she can sun herself. Pets are stolen more than most guardians realize.

When you call the police, they will take a report, or if you live in a big city they will let you fill a report out yourself. Complete it thoroughly. Express to them how serious you take this situation and then keep in contact with them if you truly believe your pet was stolen. Stolen pets are difficult crimes to solve, so be patient and keep looking on your own.

Make Posters

Make your flyer easy to read from a distance by using large, clear letters. It should contain any information that helps the public know when and where your pet was lost and how they can identify the pet as yours. Include the date your pet was lost, the area last seen, what kind of pet, breed, color, sex, age, and any characteristics that make her unique. In large letters across the top of the flyer, write "LOST!" Don't forget your name, address, phone number, and a picture of your animal. Some people feel uncomfortable having their address on the flyer, and that's okay; just make sure that you give a phone number where you can be reached. You may also want to add a plea for the return of your beloved pet and mention a reward.

Another trick that some people use is to mention that the animal is mean or needs medication. The theory is that if you reduce the value of your pet, whoever has her will want to return her to you and collect the reward instead. This is especially true of purebred animals and birds. You do not want to give the impression that the pet is valuable and that the finders will be able to make money. You want them to return your pet as soon as possible.

Once you have made your flyer, make copies and hang them everywhere in the area where you lost your pet: on poles; in the notice area at supermarkets, feed stores, pet stores; and at veterinary offices. When you find your pet or after a couple weeks of looking, you will have to go back and take every flyer down. Put them up and be prepared to remove them.

Place an Ad

Place an ad in the lost and found section of your local newspaper. You may also want to place a second ad in the animal or pet section. The lost and found ad is usually free, but the one in the pet section will cost you. In your ad, give a general description of your pet (save the more complete descriptions to prove she's yours), mention the area that your pet was lost in and offer a reward. The reward is important because some people will not bother to return a lost pet if no reward is offered. If your pet is returned, you must pay this reward, so be prepared. Read both sections of the classifieds daily. Your pet may also be listed as found.

Home Again

Finding your lost pet may take weeks. Don't give up. You may get frustrated, but you must keep looking. When you do find your pet, take her to your veterinarian for an exam to check her health and be sure she didn't suffer great trauma. If your pet was missing for more than a day or two, you may need to give her special attention. She may be hungry or dehydrated. Of course, you won't mind giving her the extra attention because you have missed her terribly.

ESCAPED BIRDS

Clipping the wings of your bird helps keep her safe in your custody. It also prevents your bird from escaping through open doors or windows, and if she does escape, it may prevent her from gaining altitude. Checking the wings of your bird frequently is the best way to prevent her from flying from your life. Even if the wings are clipped, a well-balanced bird with just the right upwind can take flight to the tops of the highest tree and be unable to come down.

Walking around outside with an uncrated bird is an invitation for heartbreak. Secure your bird in a carrier when you are transporting her from one place to another. If you are outside with your parrot on your shoulder, a barking dog, a horn honking, or other loud, sudden noise can frighten your bird and even though she loves you more than anything in the world, her natural instinct will cause her to take flight. She may not know how to come back to you no matter how much she wants to. Facing this crisis is avoidable with the right precautionary care.

Enticing Your Bird Back to the Ground

Catching a bird that has taken flight is a difficult venture. Many pet birds are forever lost this way. Some birds have been recovered after they have swooped to freedom, and these successful recaptures provide valuable information.

First, you must stay calm. Your feathered friend may want to return to you, but a bird that escapes may not know how to safely fly lower. Inexperienced flyers are not comfortable flying downward, they get higher and higher as they fly from treetop to treetop. In order to regain custody, you need to do everything in your power to persuade your pet that it is better to risk coming down than to keep flying up.

Place a white sheet on an open area of the ground. Your pet's food and water dishes should be arranged on the sheet. This feeding station serves as an enticing beacon for your bird. If you and your family sit on the sheet and eat while making a big fuss about how great the food is, a well-bonded bird will hardly be able to stand missing out. If she is able, your pet will attempt to join you.

Recapturing Small Birds

If you are attempting to recapture a small bird, you can try the two-cage trick. If your pet has a buddy, you can use it as a lure. If your bird does not have a buddy, ask a friend if you can borrow his or her bird. Using a bird similar to your pet makes the attraction stronger. Place the enticement in a securely latched small cage, and then position this cage in a larger cage. Remove the door to the big cage to prevent it from accidentally closing before your bird is captured or while she is entering. The object of this exercise is to attract your pet using her desire to be with a companion. The encouragement may compel her to risk a flight down to the yard.

Recapturing Large Birds

If you are attempting to recapture a large bird, this cage-in-a-cage idea is impractical, but other approaches can be used.

Birds are most active at dawn and dusk, so these are the most opportune times to get a bird to fly down to your yard. You will be using a food enticement as well as a companion lure — you. Birds like the highest spot, so she will probably take refuge in the tallest tree. The safest avenue for your bird to return to you will be to climb down from the tree. Tempt your pet from the base of the tree and encourage her to climb toward you.

Have a towel ready to catch your bird. Use a neutral color towel and keep it discreet; don't wave it around and make a fuss. When your pet gets close enough, use a pocket full of her favorite food as bribery. It is frustrating to coax your pet very close to you only to have her take off again.

Catching Your Escaped Bird

If you want to climb the tree after your pet, you must be careful. Coming down is often the hard part, and if you catch your escapee, you will have your hands full. Have someone on the ground help you keep an eye on your bird and alert you to any movement she makes. Climb slowly and deliberately not only for your safety but also so you won't frighten your bird and cause her to take flight. Talk reassuringly to your pet; keep your thoughts positive and confident.

If you get close enough to catch her, do so as swiftly and as gracefully as possible. Grab her just tightly enough to hold her. Don't squeeze your bird's delicate chest, but don't let her slip away either. You may not get another chance at recapture. Do not let go, even if she bites, and bites hard. Quickly get your pet to safety. Clip her wings as soon as possible. Take her to your veterinarian for a full exam, even if she was free for only a short time. Be especially gentle and calm with her for a few days; she has had quite an experience and needs your reassurance that everything is okay now.

If it just isn't working

Occasionally even with the most thorough research, planning, and best effort, the relationships in a multi-animal household are difficult or impossible. What do you do in such situations? What do you do with the dog that will not quit chasing the cats? What about the two cats that violently fight whenever they are in the same room?

You have taken on a big responsibility, and you owe it to your animal companions to do everything possible to make your home a peaceful, safe haven in which to live. If you cannot remedy a negative relationship and if the risk of harm is present, then take steps to ensure the safety of your pets.

Be prepared for this reality before you bring a new animal into your household. Sometimes the companionships happen like magic — right from the first meeting. Sometimes the animals need a little more time to develop a comfortable level of interaction or tolerance. Other times they simply will not adjust to each other. If you introduce your pets according to their own personal tolerance level, you will increase the likelihood of harmony in your home. If you are patient and have trained them well, you will find that most trouble spots can be corrected before they get out of control.

If you have done everything you can, tried every avenue open to you, given your pets adequate time to adjust and learn their manners, and yet there is one making life hard on everyone, then you may have to consider finding the animal a new home.

Take into consideration how much disruption your lifestyle can tolerate. Some people are able to make extreme sacrifices and take great measures to keep their animal family intact, but some lifestyles permit little flexibility. You and your human family must agree on every aspect of any adaptations necessary to keep your pet. Like any decision, you must use your present life situation and current knowledge to make the best choice for you and your animal. After you make a decision, let go of guilt or apprehension and take action. This is a difficult and heavy-hearted decision and should not be done quickly or taken lightly.

WHY?

First analyze why your pet did not work in your household if the reason is not obvious. Find a home for her that does not contain any of the elements that made your life difficult. For instance, if your dog will not stop chasing cats even with your best training efforts, then you know you will have to find a new home that is not inhabited by cats.

The reason may not be so obvious, and you may have to reflect on what gets your pet upset and causes the misbehavior or difficulty. Is it the noise level? The energy level? Does she need a home where she gets more exercise? Does she need to be with others of her own species or separated from others of her own species?

Take these reasons and develop a vision of what her new home should be. Write this information down so that you have it for reference when interviewing prospective families. Later, as the search goes on, you may out of desperation decide these things are not as important. The rule of thumb is to stay loyal to your first standards. Obviously, that is the kind of home your pet needs. If she is not going to be better off in another home, then it is your responsibility to make it work in yours.

STARTING YOUR SEARCH

Once you have decided what kind of home you want to find, start your search by getting the word out. Notify the breeder if you purchased her from one. A responsible breeder will either accept the pet back (usually at a monetary loss to you) or, more likely, help you search for a solution. Tell your friends and family. Call your local humane shelter and ask them for names and phone numbers of organizations that find homes for pets. If you own a purebred animal, call your breed club and ask for the number of the rescue group for your breed.

Run an ad in the newspaper if you want, although you may want to limit your advertisements to a more select group of people. You can do this by advertising at your veterinary hospital. Hang flyers at grocery stores in the area of town near you or in an area you think your pet would do well in, such as the country or in a neighborhood with older residents and fewer children. You may also want to put flyers at feed stores or pet shops. Distribute flyers to places where you feel responsible people may see them, such as the library, health food stores, churches or synagogues, and employee lunch rooms.

Never advertise your pet as "free." Always ask a purchase price. This limits impulsive adoptions and puts a damper on the revenue opportunities for people looking to resell the animal or use it for training purposes and lab research.

BEWARE!

Many uncaring, devious people are out there, so beware when you are looking for a new home for your animal companion. Many people adopt a pet without considering what is necessary to make the animal's life a good one. They have little regard for the pet's well-being and will not take time or extra measures to ensure a good relationship. These people then sell the animal or take her to the shelter. This poor pet gets shifted from one home to another, making any negative characteristics of her personality worse or creating new undesirable traits.

Even if you tell the prospective caretakers everything about your pet, this terrible cycle may continue. If at that moment a barking dog doesn't seem like trouble to them, one night with constant noise may find your pet in the shelter. Also, don't assume that if you ask them to return the animal to you if it doesn't work that they will call you. Many times they are too embarrassed, don't want to bother, or think they can make some money if they get rid of the animal some other way. You would be heartbroken to find out that your former companion stayed only a couple of weeks or days with the family you thought would love her, only to be passed on to another unknowledgeable person and you have lost all control over the situation.

Choosing the family or person your pet is going to live with is difficult. You must talk to them extensively and get a feeling for their level of commitment. Understanding their intentions thoroughly aids you in finding a secure home. Some people buy animals and then sell them to labs for research. People who want to train their dog for fighting, who don't know what they are doing, buy pets (either dogs or cats) and use them to train their fighting dogs to kill. Smaller animals, such as rabbits, may be bought to feed snakes. Unscrupulous criminals even come to your home with children in tow to camouflage their intentions. Your pet may become the victim of neglect and mistreatment.

INVESTIGATING PROSPECTIVE HOMES

Investigate any families you are considering by asking for references and follow through by checking them out.

You need to ask pressing, almost intrusive questions, to find out the most applicable information. You took responsibility for your companion's life when you adopted her and just because it is not working in your home, you cannot simply abandon your obligation. You need to find the right home for your animal this time, so be picky and stringent in your search.

Questions to Ask

Ask about their home and if it would adequately house your pet. A large parrot will need plenty of room for a huge cage and play stand. Your dog may require a large, secure yard or must be provided with increased opportunities for exercise. Where do they plan on keeping the creature? Will they let her sleep indoors? Do they have room for adequate freedom and exercise? Do they rent? Are they allowed to keep pets? Ask to see their rental agreement that states this

or contact the owner or manager.

You may want to know the schedule of the people in the family. Will your pet be left home alone for long periods of time? Do they foresee any changes in their schedule? Have they moved many times, or do they plan on moving?

If they have had any pets in the past, where are they now? You should get a good idea of their commitment to their animal companions. Do they presently have pets? Do they have too many animals? They may be animal "collectors" and not give enough quality attention to each individual.

Is there anyone in the family who opposes the adoption? If there is one person who is opposed, it can make the whole process a failure. What about children? See how the children interact with your animal.

Pet Care Philosophy

Make sure that they understand basic pet care. You will also want to question them on their personal theories of animal behavior or psychology. If they regard parrots as interesting animals to watch and to add to the decor of the home but do not understand the unique requirements of interactions and personal attention, then they are not the right people. They may have plans to immediately declaw or debark your animal — what are your feelings on these elective surgeries?

If your pet is not spayed or neutered, do so before the animal goes to her new home.

Your Last Opportunity to Scrutinize

Set up a plan for the return of the animal if it doesn't work. If they have difficulty with the animal, you do not want them to take her to the shelter or drop her off on her own. Put in writing that you are to be notified if there are problems. If you are supportive and friendly while discussing your pet and the adoption, the new family will be much more likely to look to you for guidance if they have any questions or problems. Demonstrate how much you care, and they will be less hesitant to contact you. Never belittle the new family when communicating with them. If they feel inferior or self-conscious, they may be too embarrassed to ask you for advice or assistance.

When you think that you have found a new home for your pet, take the animal to the house yourself. Have them pay you when you take the animal to their home and only after being sure you are totally comfortable. If you deliver the pet to their doorstep and don't approve of what you see, you can still back out.

Insist that they have the animal checked by a veterinarian in a twenty-four- or thirty-six-hour period; put this in your bill of sale. Work out an agreement so you can visit once or twice to check on the animal. Some people may feel threatened by this, but try to have it stated in the bill of sale.

No matter what, call in a couple of weeks to see how things are going. If there is any hesitation or problem, offer to come pick up the pet and return any money.

Your animal companion's physical and emotional well-being is your most important consideration. This difficult decision can be successful if you are cautious and loyal to your commitment.

Protecting your pets when you're not there

What will happen to your pets if you are incapacitated or die, leaving behind your animal household? Without prior preparation, you have no control over what happens to them because you will not be there to voice your desires. Before any situation occurs requiring displacement of your pets, have a plan ready.

Your animals will be confused at your absence. They have to deal with the stress of not having you there to care for them and adapt to someone else. The disruption in their routine can be unsettling and painful. If you have kept them on a rigid schedule, they will be less likely to adapt smoothly. Although having a general routine comforts and gives your pets security, being slightly flexible teaches them to accept change more readily. Maybe you always groom your pets at night before bedtime, but sometimes you do a quick brush with more play, sometimes a thorough combing, and sometimes you skip it altogether. This kind of flexibility within a schedule makes handling small changes in routine easier. If you leave

complete instructions describing the care of your creatures, then the caretaker will be able to maintain a semblance of the same schedule, lessening your pets' discomfort.

If you are caring for an animal that has lost her caretaker, you must treat her like you would want your animals treated. Be patient, sympathetic, and loving. Remember that the animal has just lost the most important person in her life. Let the behavior of the pet guide your treatment. Increasing your interaction helps the creature feel more secure. Quietly talking to and petting the pet help her relax. Grooming her, eating and sleeping with her, and taking her places outside of the house help the sad pet bond with you. Suggestions for building relationships with your animals are mentioned throughout this book. Apply some of the techniques, but remember to take it slow and gentle.

SHORT-TERM CARE

Although you would rather not think about it, there is always the possibility that you may be the victim of an accident, become ill, need an operation, or become incapacitated. Prepare a plan for your animals in advance.

Some caretakers are fortunate to have family members willingly take care of their pets until they are back on their feet again. They don't have to worry and know their pets are getting the best of care while they are unable to provide for them.

Selecting someone who will be guardian of the animals and providing monetary support are two of the most important considerations in your plan. Providing a schedule for the caretaker to follow also helps greatly.

WHO WILL TAKE CARE OF THE ANIMALS?

When choosing someone to be caretaker of your pets, be picky. This person will be responsible for the physical and emotional health of your beloved animals.

Choosing a Caretaker

The person who will take care of your pets should understand their emotional sensitivity and be gentle and sympathetic. A kind, caring person helps ease their pain. If you can recruit someone who already knows your animals, it will greatly smooth the transition. If you have a good friend or family member who frequently visits your home and interacts with your pets, they will more readily accept this person as their guardian.

Because of your inability to care for your pets, the person you choose to take over will be fully responsible. Find someone who understands the complexity and enormity of this responsibility and who shares the same outlook on animal life that you have.

The Difficulty of Multiple Animals

In a multi-animal household, there are special considerations. You may never find someone willing to take on the awesome responsibility of a number of animals. Appointing several different people to accept a portion of your peaceable kingdom may be the only solution. Some animals may be very good friends and would suffer if separated, so arrange for them to stay together. Make sure you discuss which pets you are considering when you discuss the plan with your caretaker of choice. Your sister, who may love your dogs and be more than willing to take responsibility for them, may be terrified of your cockatoo. If this is the case, find a great home for your bird elsewhere. Don't push your pets on someone. For the situation to be successful, it must be as stress-free as possible.

Executors

If you are looking for a short-term solution, find help from a combination of different family members and friends. When considering what to do with your pets in a permanent situation, you must find dedicated caretakers. If you are unable to find someone willing to take complete responsibility, you must make other arrangements.

In this situation, appoint someone as executor of your animal household. It must be someone you completely trust. Upon your permanent incapacitation or death, this executor can be in charge of finding good homes for your animal companions. Make provisions in your plan for special circumstances such as the two cats that cannot be separated. Provide the executor with several names of people to contact to

help find homes for your pets. In addition, clubs, breeders, organizations, and friends may be able to help.

Making It Official

Once you have discovered the perfect person to care for your pets, fully discuss the matter with him or her. The person you choose as caretaker must readily accept the responsibility and be fully capable to take on the obligation of pet guardian for your pets.

Appoint an alternate caretaker. If something happens in the life of your first choice, such as a move or a change in living arrangements, you will be assured that there is someone to pick up and help out. Discuss your plans and get acceptance from your second caretaker.

Once you have made an agreement with the people who will care for your pets, you must get it in writing. Getting the help of a lawyer is highly recommended. You will feel more comfortable knowing things are legally recorded. This protects your pets and your caretakers and assures you that a stranger or someone you don't trust won't be able to step in and ignore your desires. The agreement is proof of your wishes and a guideline for action to benefit your animals.

Making the Information Accessible

Keep a copy of this agreement along with your plan of care in a number of key locations. The glove compartment of your car is one place. Of course, a copy of this information should be stored in your home. Place a notice by the doors of your house stating where the information can be found. Give your appointed caretaker a copy, and your lawyer will also have one. A trusted neighbor or landlord needs to have a copy so he or she knows who will be taking care of your pets in your absence. This person may also have a house key to gain access to your home if necessary. If you rent your home, give your caretaker a key and written permission to enter your home. A copy of this permission should also be left with your landlord.

In case you are in an accident, you want your caretaker to be notified that the care of your animals needs to be addressed. Next to your identification, keep a small, preferably laminated, card handy that states (1) you have pets who need immediate care, (2) who should be notified for their care, and (3) where further information is located. Leave the name and number of an alternative person in case the first person cannot be reached.

INFORMATION PACKAGE

The first step in assuring that your pets are taken care of when you are not available is to prepare an information package that includes everything that the caretaker needs to know to properly care for your pets. It should also include a copy of your care agreement. This package should accompany you when you travel to be sure that your pets are cared for in case of an accident.

When creating a detailed plan of care, your record book will be of great benefit. Copy much of the data from the records directly to your care plan. Mention the location of the record book because your pet guardian may be able to use this information.

Identifying Your Pet

Prepare a complete description of each creature, including species, breed, color, sex, date of birth, and identification numbers. Also include at least one color photo with the animal's name on the back of the photo. This identification will aid in locating each pet if the person assigned to their care is not immediately available.

Care Routine

Include in the information package your care routine (your plan of action from chapter 3 will be useful). Your caretaker will then know the animals' schedule. He or she will not be able to duplicate this schedule exactly but can use the schedule as a beginning point. It will also help the caretaker understand any difficulties in adjustment.

To help ease the transition even more, include care tips for the different animals. If your dog must play fetch for ten minutes a day or else she becomes a psychological mess, then you will want to mention this point. If your cat will only eat chicken-based food, include this in your care tips. How do your pets like to play? How much exercise do they regularly get?

What are some of their personality traits? What are some of the animals' likes and dislikes? What kind of relationships do the different animals have? What are any special needs of your pets? What is your grooming routine?

List the type of food and amount for each animal and include a suggested place to purchase the food and supplies. Mention the amount of water your pets drink.

Make a note of where you store all of the animal-related equipment. Locations of leashes, bowls, extra food, toys, grooming supplies, carriers, books on animal care, and record book should be listed.

Supplying General Information

Including training tips and disciplinary techniques will be a great help if your caretaker does not know how you prefer your pets to be treated. Leave the title of a book that you use and trust. Leave the name and phone number of a trainer or behaviorist. If your pet has a difficult time adjusting to the transition, your caretaker can then seek the advice of this person and you will feel better knowing your pet is in the best hands. When your caretaker understands your philosophy on animal discipline, then you know that your pets will benefit from the continuation of their routine. Discuss these philosophies with your caretaker when you are getting permission to make the person your pets' guardian.

Other information that can aid your caretaker includes articles and information on poisonous plants, first aid, safety precautions, and general care of animals; you may suggest a book that covers this information. However, suggesting too many books, especially to a nonreader, can be overwhelming. Mention basic care guides for the initial care of your pets. Offer the books that you own, possibly mentioning the most beneficial sections of the books.

Useful Names and Phone Numbers

It is important to include your veterinarian's name, address, and phone number. Having your animals see the same veterinarian will aid in the care of your pets. Your veterinarian will know them, their medical history, and their personality and will be able to help the caretaker understand and care for the animals. Make sure you discuss ahead of time with your veterinarian that you have assigned a caretaker for emergencies and give your veterinarian the name of that person.

Your information package should contain the names of people who have watched your pets for you during vacation. If you regularly have a pet sitter, then you will feel better knowing that if your assigned caretaker went away for awhile, your pets would have a familiar and trusted sitter to care for them. If you have a helpful friend or relative, mention these people, including their names and phone numbers.

Emergency Cash

One of the most helpful things you can do for your caretaker is to include emergency cash with the package to purchase food, litter, medicine, or other incidentals that may be needed. Include enough cash for two weeks worth of supplies for your pets. Even if they receive monetary support later, the cash will assist them in the interim.

Recording the Information

If you are dreading the idea of recording all of this information in writing, you can record it on an audio cassette. It may be easier for you to just chat away in the microphone. Include backup information in writing. A simple care plan can be recorded on video. You can demonstrate the way your pets like to be cuddled and played with, your daily regimen on care, your grooming methods, and other activities that translate well to video.

If your animals will be separated (often the case in multi-animal households), you need to make a package for each home. Put all the information in a large envelope with the name of the designated caretaker on the front. Mark the envelope "Animal Care Information." Make sure to include emergency cash in each envelope. You need at least four copies of each package. Give one to the designated caretaker and one to the executor of your will, put one copy with the will, and keep one in your home. Place a note by the doors of your house stating where the information package can be found.

Update the Information

You must update your plan regularly. Situations change, your designated caretaker may move, you may have changed vets, or you may have adopted another pet. It would be wise to read, listen to, or review your plan once a year. Amend the plan with new information as needed, keeping it as current as possible.

IN THE EVENT OF YOUR DEATH

If you live alone or have no immediate family members who will care for your pets, your death may result in a terrible end to your animals. They may be sacrificed to a shelter and euthanized when adoption by a new family does not occur. Your creatures will be frightened, stressed, and traumatized by their predicament, and all because you failed to plan ahead. Make the effort to ensure your companions are treated with dignity in the event of your death.

Your animals deserve the continuing good care you have committed yourself to offering. The previous section regarding choosing your guardian should be referred to when assigning a caretaker. Design your care plan as previously described.

You Need a Lawyer

In order to assure a legally binding arrangement, you must see a lawyer. In the event of your death, only a lawyer will be able to prepare the necessary paperwork that makes the transition an easy one. You never know if someone will challenge your previously detailed plan, but if you have a lawyer provide the correct paperwork, you will not have to worry about the care of your pets.

It is important that you get a lawyer's assistance when creating a means to financially support your pets; otherwise, your animals will be the ones who lose. Caring for your pets can become quite expensive. You do not want your animals to become a monetary hardship to your caretaker, so find a way to financially support them.

Your lawyer will probably suggest a living trust. A living trust makes the transition of your pets to your designated caretaker inexpensive and allows your pets to immediately become a part of their new family. Other arrangements would require a probate process. This would delay your animals' getting the care that they deserve and would make a lengthy transition period. Discuss with your lawyer the differences between possible arrangements.

Most states do not allow you to leave property of any sort to your animal friends. You can leave your assets or a portion of them with a designated person, either your caretaker or another person, stipulating a percentage that goes toward the care of your pets. The balance of this amount would then be passed on to the caretaker in the event of your animal's death.

The worst-case scenario: Your designated caretaker becomes selfish and uses little of the money provided during the pet's life and then allows the pet to die prematurely. Sound awful? Even with careful choosing, you never know what could happen. If you leave money directly to the caretaker and request that the money be used only on your pets, you have no guarantee this will happen. Also, in a situation like this, your relatives may challenge the arrangement and attempt to collect the cash for themselves. You may tempt wrongdoing by leaving cash without a backup system.

Implementing an honorary trust may be the best solution. This requires assigning a trustee who gives the money to the caretaker as needed for the care of your creatures. The trustee and caretaker can be one in the same, but you may have the same problems as mentioned above. If you choose two separate people, you eliminate selfishness. Your trustee must understand the cost of caring for animals and be sensitive to the needs of the caretaker. Conditional bequests are another choice. An executor distributes the money as needed to care for your pets.

Taking out a life insurance policy on yourself, payable to your caretaker in the event of your death, is another solution. Request that the caretaker use the money to care for your animals. Of course, you are losing some of the assurance that the money will be used in their best interest. But there is really no way to guarantee that your caretaker will remain faithful to your wishes. You must choose carefully and be comforted by the fact that you have considered the care of your pets in advance.

Alternatives to a Caretaker

If you are unable to find a caretaker willing to assume the obligation of your pets, you still have a few alternatives to consider.

If you have parrots, this is an even more difficult situation. The large birds will probably outlive you. After your death, they may still have many years ahead of them. Prepare carefully because the responsibility of care may extend for thirty or more years. This is a big commitment for someone to undertake.

• **Sanctuaries** — Look into a sanctuary. Ask your veterinarian or members of a club for references. Sanctuaries will match pets in need of a home to people in need of a pet. Most sanctuaries are dedicated to the well-being of your pet and check on her to make sure all is working out. If an animal is adopted by a disabled or elderly person, sanctuaries often offer transportation and care when needed. Investigate the benefits that the sanctuary offers. Check references carefully.

• **Zoos** — Often people who care for parrots think that they can donate their pet to a zoo. Zoos are risky because they usually have plenty of animals, especially birds, and do not need to add another to their population. If they do not need your bird, you have no control over where she may end up. They may reject your pet and sell your feathered friend. Even if they did keep the parrot, the bird often suffers from depression at the major change in her life. A parrot at the zoo will receive no one-on-one attention; zoo birds are not pets and are not treated as such. You would be better off finding a caretaker, checking into a sanctuary, or talking to bird people in your area to see if there is a placement organization that finds wonderful homes for birds in need.

• **Executor** — You can assign a trusted person to find homes for your pets when you are gone, as previously mentioned. This person could follow a prepared outline for choosing a new home for your animals. Of course, you supply this person with money to care for your pets while they find them a family.

• **Shelters** — You may also leave your pets to a shelter or adoption organization. Leaving money for these organizations for the care of your pets is usually necessary. Request that the group find a good home or that they keep the animal indefinitely. Some people ask that if a good home is not found in a number of months, the animal be euthanized. This should be a last resort; every effort should be made to locate an organization that can provide care for the lifetime of the animal. Make sure you contact the organizations in advance. You will be required to make plans with them before you declare them in your will. Contact your local shelter first and then proceed to other groups. Ask your veterinarian for suggestions.

• **Euthanization** — Some people request that their pets be euthanized upon their death. These people may fear that their animals will only suffer when they are gone. This is unnecessary; your pets should be offered the opportunity to find a new home if you can no longer provide for them. Don't give up too soon and resort to this. Also realize your pet's adjustment to being without you may be long and difficult, but it is not impossible. Give your devoted animal companion an opportunity to go on with life.

Passages

• • • • • • • •

Your animal companions are such an integral part of your consciousness that it is often hard to accept the changes that occur with the passage of time. To those who share their lives with pets, this is probably the most difficult subject to discuss.

Your animals become an essential component in the functioning of your being. It is accepted without thought that your dog will greet you enthusiastically after you have been gone, your cat will rub against your legs when it is time for dinner, your bird will yell out "hello" every time the phone rings, and your bunny will perform an acrobatic dance for your entertainment upon being let out of her cage in the morning.

The fulfillment that pets offer is often taken for granted, not in a manner of nonappreciation but of the total acceptance that it will continue until time itself is over. You are comforted by their effect on your life without always being aware of it, and changes to this existence are not a part of your vision. Adjusting your vision and expectations as animal friends change with the ebb of life is the same truth you must confront in any relationship.

When your pet dies, the grief is immense. You suffer the loss of a friend like no other: one who accepted you for all your faults and failures, and one who showered you with unconditional love and acceptance. Often you must face the sense of guilt that accompanies the death because of your belief in mastery over the natural world. You must go through this grieving; it is a large loss. You must also help the others in your life, both human and animal, grieve and carry on.

COPING WITH DEATH

When a pet dies, you suffer the same loss as if a friend or relative has died. The same emotions are felt: sadness, anger, depression, fear, and guilt are all feelings that accompany the death of a pet. Each is felt to some degree or another. Most people work through their grief and come to a place of resolution. You won't be "over it"; you will always miss your dear friend.

But you can come to a place where reminiscing about the pleasures your pet brought to your life won't bring you pain. You can recall events and smile with the joy you experienced because of the spirit of the creature.

This is where you will be — later. But first you must grieve. When a pet dies, let yourself feel the hurt and work through the grief.

Human Relations

Although the sadness felt at the death of your animal companion is very real, it isn't always accepted in society. Employers often don't understand the turmoil you are feeling and are unwilling to give you time off from work. Uncaring people will make comments on how silly you are; others may criticize you in a hostile way.

The people who belittle your grief simply do not understand. They are confused by your intense pain and don't know how to help you. They may avoid the whole affair, being careful not to discuss your experience, or avoid you completely. Some people who don't have pets or have different relationships with their pets may think your grief is unnecessary and invalid.

Do your best in this sad period of life to surround yourself with caring people — people who understand that what you feel is not only real and intense but unavoidable. Find someone you can confide in — a sympathetic listener. Find someone who can appreciate the value of your animal companion in your life, maybe someone else who is a caring pet caretaker.

Support groups are sprouting up all over the country, and if you have one near you, you may find much help in attending.

Magnifying Your Responsibility

You are responsible for the pets in your care, but there comes a point where no matter how responsible you are, you cannot control everything that happens to them. It is difficult to handle the death of your animal companion when you know your obligation was to keep her alive and healthy.

What if you did have something to do with the demise of your pet? What if you made a mistake? Didn't take her to the veterinarian as soon as you should have, missed the warning signs of trouble or decided against a form of treatment? What if? Maybe you could have.

These thoughts can haunt you forever, but you must learn to let them go. They are a part of your past, your history. Learn from mistakes and carry on. The difficult thing to remember is that you are only human; you can only do so much. You make decisions using your best judgment at that moment, in that situation, and you act on that knowledge.

Sometimes it is right and everything goes well; sometimes the end result would have been better if you would have done something else. But you can't make decisions in retrospect, you can only act on your feelings at that moment. Accept this and know that your pet would never hold it against you.

Stages of Grief

There is no right way to work through grief — you have no wrong feelings; you feel what you feel.

Grief is a natural reaction to an intensely sad experience, and mourning becomes a problem only when a person is unable to feel the emotions and cope with them. Prolonged grieving or being stuck in a stage of mourning may indicate a problem. Also, in order to fully reconcile the death of your animal friend, you must complete the grieving process. You must deal with your feelings in order to find resolution. If you don't and you only suppress them, then they haunt you in many ways. Often you will not even recognize the pain you feel months or years later.

Although the resolution of grief is not a predictable process, grief counselors recognize five stages of grief: shock, denial, anger and blame, depression, and resolution. These stages may overlap, and they may not necessarily be experienced in this order. People also feel the emotions with differing intensities and duration. Many become stuck in one or more mourning stages and don't even know it because they have learned to live with the sadness. This pain may carry on for years.

Although the pain is intense, you will come to a place of resolution if you confront your emotions and deal with them. Experience them and then let them go. It is not a betrayal of your loved one. It is in her honor that your heart is filled with good, happy memories. Smiling when you think of your friend is the greatest compliment you can give her life.

• Your Personal Coping Abilities — How you deal with the death of your pet depends on your relationship with the animal, your emotions about death itself, the level of stress in your life at the time, and the emotional support you receive from your family and friends.

You may want to see a counselor or talk to a grief counselor to help you work through these feelings. It is common to need help in dealing with this kind of a loss. The emotions are very intense, and the experience is a difficult one. Don't be afraid to talk to someone who can help you through this. Give yourself time and permission to grieve.

• **Shock** — Shock is often the first stage in the grieving process. Shock is a stage of disbelief. You may be numb, and the reality of the death may be beyond your ability to comprehend. Shock is a defense strategy; you are protected from feeling the intense pain of your pet's death.

• **Denial** — Denial is the stage of mourning where time doesn't seem to be affecting you. Nothing outside of your pain exists. This stage may be very short-lived or extend for long periods. You may fantasize that the death of your pet has not really occurred. The entire situation doesn't feel like reality.

• **Anger and Blame** — When your pet dies, you feel victimized and frustrated at your inability to maintain control over the situation. This creates anger, which leads to blame. You blame yourself and other people. You may even blame your pet. "She knew better than to run into the road!"

Watch for your anger exhibiting itself at the expense of other people. Recognize it and control it. If you are having difficulty with your anger, see a counselor who can help you with strategies for coping.

• **Depression** — Depression is felt by most people to some degree or another and is usually overwhelming. The intense sadness a depressed person feels is draining, emotionally and physically. There is no desire to participate in life, no desire to do anything. The depressed person is extremely fatigued, and his or her sleeping patterns are altered. The depressed person may also have a loss of appetite.

Depression is so controlling and unbearable that it may be accompanied by thoughts of suicide. If your depression is this controlling, seek help right away.

CHILDREN

For children, death is confusing. In order for children to cope and resolve the death of their dear animal friend, you must help them. Children learn most from following examples of the people they look up to, so learning to cope with death yourself is helpful. As you handle the death, so will your children. If you let yourself feel your emotions, deal with them, and then resolve them, your children will learn by observing your experience and do the same.

Hiding Feelings

You cannot hide your feelings from your children. They know even if they aren't aware that they know. If you attempt to shelter them from the pain, it creates great emotional turmoil. Often by attempting to ease their troubles, people overprotect their children. In reality this overprotection can have devastating effects.

Let them know the way they feel is valid. They need to grieve in their way just as you need to grieve in yours. You cannot take away their sadness by denying its existence. You cannot shield your child from hurt by denying them the truth of the death of your pet.

Your child or children may feel embarrassed for having the feelings they do. They may think what they feel is wrong. If you are not truthful with your children, they know there is more to the situation that you are not acknowledging and it confuses them. It lessens their importance in your life and the life of the animal if they are left out of the grieving. By denying them a place in the sorrow, you deny them a place in the happiness. This in turn makes them feel shameful that they are not "good" enough to be trusted.

Helping Children Overcome Grief

If you are unable to deal with your own grief, can you successfully help your children deal with theirs? Absolutely. Being honest is the first step. If you are confused, tell them so. Explain to them how you feel. Sharing your feelings honestly and openly helps your children discover and relate to their own emotions.

• **Death as Punishment** — Your children may think their pet was taken from them because they did something "bad" — they misbehaved and their pet died, or they thought bad thoughts and their pet was taken from them. They may have yelled at the animal the week before and now feel responsible.

If your children feel like they are responsible, they need your reassurance. Make a point to tell them they did not say, do, or think anything to cause the death of the animal. They may not be able to articulate their feelings or may be afraid to share them, so reassure them that they had nothing to do with the loss, even if they don't express these feelings to you. Feelings of guilt are very strong and have much control. If guilt is not dealt with, it can have lasting complications throughout the life of your child.

• **The Child's View — You Fill in the Blanks**
Ask your children to explain what they think death is and what the death of their pet means. This will give you an indication of their level of understanding. Death is such a complex subject for adults that we are often surprised by the matter-of-fact attitude children have about death.

After experiencing the death of one of our rabbit friends, Lucky, my youngest daughter, three at the time, was most concerned about where and what Lucky would eat and if she would get enough food. Once I explained that when you die you don't have

The death of an animal is often the first encounter children have with this emotional experience, and a compassionate adult can make the difference in a child's understanding.

to eat anymore, my daughter was at ease. Let your children tell you what they understand about the death of their pet; you can fill in the blanks and answer any questions they may have.

• **Explaining Death to Children** — Adults have a tendency to oversimplify their explanations to children, using euphemisms. Children are often hungry for more information than the simple one-sentence answer provides. Oversimplifying the event will trivialize it, which makes the child's sadness seem out of sync with reality and creates confusion. Treat your children as intelligent, sensitive human beings and adjust answers according to their emotional development.

It may be helpful to read a good book about explaining death to children before you are confronted with the tragedy. You will have the knowledge to help your child through this difficult time if you are prepared. Let your child know you are available for discussing the issue at anytime. Be there for security, reassurance, sympathy, or just a shoulder to cry on.

• **Being There for Them** — Be aware that your child may not come to you and say, "I really need to talk about this." He or she may exhibit signs that alert you to the need to bring the subject up. They may act out, become grouchy or withdrawn, or cry. These are the times to ask if they need to talk.

Children, like adults, deal with death in a very individual manner. And like adults, they go through the same stages of mourning. The expression of their grief may take different outlets, so being sensitive and understanding during this period is paramount.

It is helpful to reminisce about your pet. Let your children tell funny or loving stories about the much-loved animal. Take out pictures and talk about your memories — memories keep the spirit of your pet alive and are healthy for emotional happiness.

Ritual

It can be helpful to provide a ritual of some kind signifying the closing of your animal companion's life. The ritual provides a format for your child, and for yourself, to say good-bye to your pet.

If your city allows burials on personal property, you may want to have a burial service in your own yard. If you cannot bury your pet in your yard, you can have a memorial service dedicating a monument or symbol to your pet. A plant, tree, bird bath, fountain, or statue can be added to the landscape as a dedication. By giving everyone a chance to say good-bye and making the death a reality instead of something completely nontangible, rituals provide a helpful initiator in the healing process.

OTHER PETS' GRIEF

Don't forget the feelings of your surviving animal companions. Your animals, like children, may exhibit misbehavior in order to unburden their stress. In a multi-animal household, the dynamics of the interrelationships need rearranging. This may result in a few tiny squabbles or out-and-out wars. Watch for this behavior; let them work it out on their own as much as possible (while ensuring the safety of all involved); and most importantly give them time.

Do Animals Grieve?

Scientists would like to believe that animals do not, but by experiencing the reactions of animals, it is obvious that some do mourn the loss of other pets.

Animals understand things have changed, and companion animals do miss other pets. Some demonstrate obvious distress at the loss, which can cause problems for them and their caretakers.

A definite connection exists between the strength of the friendship among the animals and how great of a loss they experience. If they were very close and spent a great deal of time together, a greater difficulty in accepting the loss is felt.

The ability to deal with the loss of a playmate is also determined by the individual temperament of the animal. If the animal is sensitive, she will feel the absence of her friend more profoundly. If she is social and strongly attached to the pet, she will be more likely to react to the departure with increased anxiety. If she is independent, with little involvement in the social structure of the household, she may likely exhibit no reactions to the death.

Even animals that didn't interact with the pet may miss her after she has died. Dogs may miss the rabbit; birds may miss the cat. Some animals may have a difficult time accepting this absence. Dogs may whine while standing at the empty cage, and birds may repeatedly call out the cat's name. Helping animals deal with the loss by comforting and consoling is necessary.

Parrots

Parrots are highly intelligent and sensitive animals. They may experience grief (symptoms such as depression, lack of appetite, lethargy, and withdrawal from activity) for many years after the death of a significant partner in life, whether human or bird. They eventually adapt, but it takes time. Occasionally this grief is never healed and the parrot spends the rest of her life in a pitiful existence. Because there have been many documented cases of this sense of loss, we can assume this is an example of birds' ability to feel great pain and grief. Some may doubt that any animal can feel this level of mourning; however, those who have known parrots understand this to be the reality.

Veterinary Check

One of the first things to do if your pet is exhibiting changes in her routine, appetite, or activity is take her to your veterinarian. Stress creates a state of lowered immunity to illness and disease. If your pet is compromised physically, it will be more difficult for you to help her emotionally. For both these reasons, be certain your pet is physically healthy. Additionally, eliminate the possibility that she is suffering from the same illness that caused the death of your animal companion. If they are the same species, have the surviving animals examined by your veterinarian as a precaution.

Keeping a Routine

Keeping the life of your household as routine as possible goes a great distance in helping the other animals and people cope with the loss. Changes are stressful, and some stress is inevitable.

Your pet may not want to eat without her buddy to keep her company. Changing the time of feeding or type of food causes more stress, so continue as normally as possible. Eventually she'll return to eating. Your bird may stop all vocalization without her "talking" friend around, but she will begin again. Make sure that you have cleared her health with your vet, and if changes such as these continue for prolonged periods, contact your veterinarian and discuss them. Keep things as normal as possible, and soon everyone will get back to being as normal as possible.

Consoling Grieving Animals

If you reinforce any of your distressed pet's grieving behaviors by overindulging her with attention, you inadvertently encourage her to continue these behaviors. Well after the loss of the pet is felt, your animal may still be displaying the symptoms as an attention-getting device. This can cause many problems in the future.

Don't scold or punish your surviving pet. This does nothing to alleviate her stress and only confuses her and makes it worse. A balance must be accomplished because your animal friends do need increased support and consoling. Engage them in distracting activities to keep them busy and assure them with

your continued affection. Although you may be emotionally drained, the people and animals who share your life will benefit, and ultimately you will also, from your continued interaction and comfort.

GETTING A NEW PET

Each animal is an individual, a unique personality all her own. Even though this realization has been expressed again and again throughout this book, its relevance becomes even more significant in the context of the death of a pet.

Often after a pet dies, people will rush out and immediately buy another pet. They may adopt an animal similar to the one they lost — the same species, breed, color, or even from the same parents. You cannot replace your pet; there will never be another like her. No matter how close in appearance your new pet is to the first, they will never be like each other. You will experience great disappointment if you attempt to replace your animal companion.

When?

When should you get another pet, if ever? Everyone deals with this question differently. It depends on your feelings about death, how you have dealt with the death of your pet, how the others in your household have dealt with it, what your expectations are, what the situations in your life are presenting you at this moment, and if you feel like you can fully accept a new pet.

The decision of adding a new pet is very complicated, but there are some things that can help you decide. If you want another pet immediately to fill the void left behind but are willing to acknowledge the unique personality of the new pet, then by all means go ahead.

If you have children, you may want to wait a little longer before adopting another pet. Children may not have fully resolved their loss, and replacing the pet too soon may teach your children that life is expendable. Life should be treated as sacred and each individual as valuable. They may also feel that you are telling them to stop grieving before they have resolved their emotions, which could cause them to feel pressured to suppress and ignore them. Give your children time to complete their mourning process before adding another pet.

If you are considering adding another pet to the household, take the surviving animals' feelings into consideration. Are they ready for another pet to become a member of their family? Would it be too difficult on them at this time? Don't assume you can replace the deceased pet for either yourself or your other animals. It is not a guarantee that your animals will accept a new pet and feel the same for her as they did for the other.

If your pet died of a contagious disease, discuss adopting another pet with your veterinarian. You may need to follow a waiting period before bringing another animal into your home.

Emotional Considerations

If you are not fully ready for another animal, you may start feeling resentful toward that animal. If someone tries to replace your pet to make you feel better, they are doing you and the animal a great disservice. You may feel as though you are being disloyal to your first pet if you love your new one too much. This may make you push her away and never form a strong bond with her. She will feel it, and you could create many difficult behavioral problems. Of course, you wouldn't do this intentionally.

Resolve your emotions about your first pet. Your grief must be reconciled, and you must be completely ready before adopting another animal. If you live in a family with other people, every person must be ready. If you are at all indecisive, then wait until you know in your heart of hearts that you are truly ready. Some people may take only weeks; others may take years. You will know.

When you do adopt another companion, it is most important that you give your new pet an opportunity to express her own individual personality. Give her the freedom to blossom as her own unique creature. Appreciate her for who she is, and resist the temptation to compare her to your other pet.

It is your responsibility as a partici-pant in the community to take the comfort of your neighbors into consideration.

Responsibility to your neighbors and reducing overpopulation

So far you have learned how having multiple pets can influence and shape your life; now you are going to look at the bigger picture. How does having a house full of animals affect your responsibility to your neighbors?

As an animal lover, you already appreciate the benefits and delight that you experience with those in your animal kingdom. Unfortunately, your friends, family, and neighbors may not understand the joy you find in surrounding yourself with the furry and/or feathery faces of your animal friends. You are a spokesperson for the benefits of animal friendship. If you allow only negative experiences to be observed by the yet-to-be-converted animal appreciators, you will further alienate these people, rather than convince them of the rewards of living with pets.

It is your responsibility as a participant in the community to take the comfort of your neighbors into consideration. It is your duty, and should be your pleasure, to show naysayers that sharing your home with animals does not automatically mean it will be filled with odors, messes, and dangers.

Negative encounters won't help convert nonanimal lovers into pet enthusiasts. As a responsible animal caretaker, try to eliminate any negative associations with your pets that can damage the reputation of not only the animals but also the people who care for them. By doing this, you will find that the people in your life are happier, your homes are cleaner, and your animals are healthier and safer.

The high cost of freedom

Dogs and cats have been allowed to run free through the streets for so long that most people don't even recognize this freedom as a problem. Loose animals are threats to themselves as well as to other animals and people. The risks related to roaming were not as serious as recently as a few years ago, but times have changed. Towns and cities are much more crowded, with more homes, people, and cars. The attitudes and behaviors of the citizens have changed, and your pets are not safe when exposed to strangers.

I have come across pet care books written in the 1970s recommending that your dog run free if you lived in the suburbs. And until recently, most people believed that cats had to roam the "wild" frontier of neighborhoods to be psychologically healthy. These myths cannot prevail today without causing risk to animal lives or violating restraints of complex animal control laws. With so many dangers and risks, freedom like the kind given to your pets "when you were a child" is simply unacceptable.

THE TERRITORIAL INSTINCT OF YOUR ANIMAL FRIENDS

Wild animals may naturally roam their territory, but your pets are domesticated, not wild. Preventing them from roaming is not denying any of their natural instincts. Your ancestors brought these animals into their homes and made them a part of the human world. They developed, through breeding, a creature that is dependent on people, and it is the responsibility of pet caretakers to assure them safe living conditions. Roaming is not safe.

Cats

Cats do need their own territory, but their territory does not have to be the equivalent of a cougar's in the wild. Domestic cats only require a specific place to call their own and it does not have to be large. As long as you have not overcrowded your living area, your cats can find their own territory. They may share or overlap territory, but they know which is theirs. A cat may decide his territory is just a corner of the living room or everything down the hall in the back of the house. The cats in your home will work it out. If there is enough room and you offer whatever is needed in the way of beds, scratching posts, litter boxes, and food and water, the cats will develop a comfortable territorial arrangement.

To offer cats new sensory stimulation, you can walk them on a leash attached to a halter. You can also construct safe enclosures in your yard for your cats to play outdoors. Cats can have a full and good quality life without being exposed to the dangers of roaming.

Dogs

Dogs have a desire to explore and experience new sights, smells, and sounds. Walking your dog on a leash, allowing him to smell and explore as you progress, is a good way for him to get out and about. Taking your dog on short fun trips is also good for both of you. Get outdoors and take your beloved canine swimming in a creek. Take obedience classes so your pet can meet others of his kind. Go visit a dog-owning friend's home, and while the people visit, the dogs can romp. In some communities dog parks have been established and these fenced areas are great for dog play and exploring. These are all safe ways to allow your dog to stretch his natural curiosity muscles without being in danger.

LOOSE DOGS CAUSE MANY PROBLEMS

Loose dogs are a particular menace to people who are responsibly walking their dogs on a leash. People who are following the law and being good neighbors will have no way of protecting themselves and their companion from a loose and determined dog. A leashed dog that is attacked by a free-roaming dog may be permanently damaged by fear.

Walkers, cyclists, skaters, and runners are all at the mercy of roaming dogs. The excitement of the chase is often too much for a free dog to resist. Many children and adults have been terribly frightened by a loose dog chasing them; some have been injured or attacked.

Recently, while jogging, a friend of mine was bit on the behind by a loose dog. The path he was jogging is well traveled by cyclists, walkers, and runners. It was a surprise attack, and it worries me for other people. I've seen the dog several times, and Retta (my dog) thinks it is her personal duty to keep him away from us. As long as the dog does not decide to attack Retta, we'll be okay, but what about children on bikes? A number of older citizens, some recovering from illness, frequently walk this path. Are they going to be safe? The bite was a quick snip this time, but will the dog become more territorial and tenacious? To make it worse, the owners of the home have a fenced yard. Why can't they put their dog there?

WHO IS THIS DOG?

When roaming, dogs often take on completely different personalities. They may be fearful, dominant, or aggressive — you have no way of knowing. Your sweet, loving pet may become a fierce member of a hunting pack, which is not uncommon. While allowed their freedom, many dogs form a pack and injure and kill livestock, wildlife, and smaller dogs and cats. Your loose dog may be on the receiving end of the pack and be killed or injured while roaming the neighborhood.

Your dog's personality will probably be different on the streets, even without the benefit of pack affiliation. If your pet wouldn't hurt a fly while at home, while loose he may be aggressive. He may bite children who try to play with him, adults who try to get him to leave their yard, or anybody minding his or her own business that he sees as a threat. Do not think that your dog is too kind to bite.

We once had two loose dogs stay at our house for a couple of hours; they would not leave our front yard. They were friendly and I could pet them and talk to them, but they had no tags so I could not get in touch with their caretakers. They seemed to be well behaved — until my daughter's school bus came to the house. One of the dogs jumped on the bus, and any attempts to remove him were answered with growls and bites. The bus driver and I began to worry because children were on the bus. Finally, I lured him out with food, but it took ten minutes, and we were not sure what was going to happen. My point is that this dog was probably someone's beloved pet that had never done anything threatening. I'm sure his caretaker would have been surprised by his actions.

DANGER ON WHEELS

More than a million cats and dogs are killed by cars each year. The roads are so crowded that they have become very dangerous places for everyone, especially a free-roaming pet. Most of these deaths are accidents, but the harsh reality is that many are deliberate. Cats are especially vulnerable to this kind of ignorance and violence. Too many people will go out of their way to run over a cat.

I learned this reality firsthand many years ago while riding in a truck with an acquaintance who swerved in an attempt to hit a cat. Obviously, I immediately began chewing off a good piece of his tail end only to learn this was a habit of his and his buddies. I am no longer an acquaintance of this fool, but it made me realize that even perfectly normal-appearing people may have a violent, uncaring side to their personality. I will not allow my pets to be victimized by these crazy people. Do you want your beloved feline to die at the hands of such an individual?

Thankfully, most people are not like this and attempt to swerve around an animal that wanders into the road. Unfortunately, it puts everyone in danger. Drivers slamming on their brakes or swerving quickly to get around the animal causes accidents that injure themselves, their passengers, or others on the road. Would you want to live with this guilt? Anytime injury or damage is caused by loose pets, the caretakers of those animals can be held criminally and financially responsible. So think about the consequences before you allow your pet to roam.

Cats can run loose in the neighborhood, using flowerbeds as litter boxes and clean cars as feet warmers, creating tense relations between neighbors.

HEALTH HAZARDS

Your animals could also contribute to the spread of disease, fleas, and ticks by eliminating their waste in your neighbors' lawns. They may pick up these troubles from other nearby animals. Also, children who play in sandboxes are at risk of disease spread by cats and so are people who enjoy gardening.

Getting into chemicals or pest controls is another common problem. Dogs and cats find it difficult to resist automobile antifreeze, and letting your pet roam free negates your efforts to keep these kinds of poisons from him. Your free-roaming pet is more likely to get poisoned or contract an illness, and all of your precautions to keep your home clean and healthy will be wasted energy.

Your dog or cat could also get rabies from wild animals. Even if you are not in a rural area, raccoons and other animals may be infested with rabies or other deadly diseases. Your pets may also get injured during fights for mates. Whether or not they are spayed or neutered, they are not totally safe from overzealous lovers. Fights for mates are violent and can be fatal.

THE WRATH OF AN ANGRY NEIGHBOR
Cats

Even though cats running free are common fixtures in neighborhoods, they offer a unique perspective into the relationship of animals and neighbors. Just the simple action of a cat walking across the hood of a freshly waxed car with dirty paws is enough to sever all friendships between neighbors. The resentment of people who live next to a cat household is fueled when they cannot leave the windows down on the car because a cat may jump in and urinate on the seats. Constantly having to deal with the waste of your animals when they want to enjoy their own yard makes your neighbors despise your pets and become increasingly hostile toward you. Neighbors who were once good friends can become bitter enemies over loose animals.

What about the neighbor who has gone to great lengths to attract birds to a feeder and bath? Cats hunting birds is a problem few people are aware of. More and more people live in bird territory as our city boundaries extend into formerly wild areas, and these people are beginning to own more cats than in the past. As a result, entire populations of birds are in danger. Many areas in the country exist where native species have almost become extinct because of the high population of cats. This is another good reason cats should be kept indoors.

We have so many loose cats in our neighborhood that you cannot park your car outside with windows down without being welcomed by the pungent odor of urine. No vehicle is free of paw prints for longer than a couple of hours. Several people I know have given up gardening because they can't work in the yard without dealing with handfuls of feces and the odor of urine. People must pick up cat feces before mowing their lawns.

One neighbor was told by a cat-owning family that this is just the way cats are and that it wasn't just his yard the cats used. But this particular neighbor has to sleep with the smell of cat waste because they use the garden area under his window for a litter box. And he should just accept this? Wonderful, caring people release their anger by wishing all sorts of terrible ends to the feline population.

What about the neighbors who do not have such high moral and ethical boundaries? Do you think some of these "solutions" have been acted on? Definitely. It is a problem in some areas. Your pet is not immune just because you love him so much.

Dogs

Dog feces is a particularly frustrating problem. I'm amazed at how many people still do not pick up after their dogs while they are out and about. This is the very reason that many parks are now off limits to dogs, and some cities have even had to ban dogs on the streets. It is not hard to pick up after your dog. It may be unpleasant, but considering the consequences of stricter regulations, it is definitely worth it. Always take your scooper bag when you leave the house. Of course if you are not with your dog, you will not know, so keep him with you.

Dog feces on the street, in the park, or in someone's yard is disgusting. Even if you are a "dog" person, you will not take too kindly to stepping in something mushy in the grass or on the sidewalk. Even

though I always carry a bag and pick up if my dog goes in the street, I've still been reprimanded for dog messes. I guess the idea is that if you cannot catch the actual criminal, get anyone with a dog. If a stranger walking down the street goes out of her way to stop me as I'm jogging along and lecture me on picking up after my pet, I realize the situation is becoming intolerable to many. The reality that my dog and I may one day have to pay the price for irresponsible dog walkers is maddening. Pick up after your dog!

Farmers and ranchers may shoot your dog while protecting their livestock, and your cat could be shot if chasing chickens or other fowl. Your pet could also be poisoned, either intentionally or accidentally. He could be the victim of a trap set to catch other varmints. If you live close to the country, your pet could be accidentally killed by hunters. Cases of this type of misidentification are common.

IF SOMEONE CAPTURES YOUR PET

Research labs are always purchasing dogs and cats, and there are people ready to supply the demand — sometimes with your precious pets. Each year, 500,000 dogs and 200,000 cats are used in research labs. Most of these animals are supplied by pounds and thieves. This is a terrible fate to imagine for your animal companions.

Dogs and cats may also be stolen for pets. Loose animals may be lured or captured and kept by their finders who think they are unwanted. Other pets are caught and used by violent humans as a misguided means to train dogs for fighting. These pets are torn to pieces by dogs that are being taught to kill. This may sound harsh or too awful to be true, but it is a sad fact of life, and you should protect your pets from this torture.

Roaming dogs and cats are picked up by animal control. Depending on the laws in your area, you may be cited and have to pay a fine to get your pet back. Your pet could also be a victim of mistaken identity and kept at the shelter if it is suspected that he has bitten or harmed someone. There have been cases where an innocent pet was put to sleep because it was believed that he had caused great harm to someone. The worst part is he may have done it and you would not even know.

YOUR PET'S ACTIONS ARE YOUR RESPONSIBILITY

Whatever damage your pet causes while he is roaming is your responsibility, and you will be held liable. If your dog causes an automobile accident, you can be sued for damages. In the present litigious environment, this is a very real threat.

Loose animals cost taxpayers $500 million a year. With more and more people living with more and more animals, the tolerance for roaming pets is declining. Laws are becoming more restrictive, and sometimes the conscientious pet owners are the ones who suffer. There are towns where it is against the law to have a dog outside of your backyard within city limits — they can't be in the car, on a leash for a walk, or anywhere outside of your yard. These stringent laws have been caused by the uncaring, unknowing owners who allow their pets to run free and wreak havoc in the streets and your neighborhood.

Don't think that your pet hasn't caused any of these problems. He may have and you are not aware of it. Even if you have been lucky and have not experienced misfortune by letting your pet run free, don't be comforted by thinking if it hasn't happened, it won't. It only takes one bad experience to ruin it for your pet, yourself, and someone else. Do the responsible thing and keep your pet confined.

HOW TO BRING AN OUTSIDE CAT IN

Indoor cats live longer than outdoor cats. The poor feline souls who are restricted to the great outdoors live an average of one or two years. If your cat is allowed indoors as well as outdoors, he may live five years longer than his outdoor counterpart. The lucky, soft-pawed cat that is limited to staying indoors averages a fifteen- to eighteen-year life span. This illustrates how dangerous life in the big, open world is for your feline friends.

If you have decided that it is best for your normally outdoor cat to be inside for his protection and the comfort of your neighbors, you will have to teach him the manners of being an indoor resident.

THE ADAPTATION PROCESS

You can take a cautious and slow approach by keeping your cat inside your house for longer periods at a time. By increasing the length of stay indoors, you are gradually accustoming your cat to life inside. Many people feel that this is the best way to bring an adult cat indoors, but your cat can also adjust spontaneously.

Cats may be slow to adapt to change, but they will adapt. As long as you meet all their needs, they will become accustomed to this change in lifestyle.

PROVIDING THE NECESSITIES

In order to make the adjustment from a wandering cat to a safe indoor cat, make sure you are offering him all that he needs. Providing him with adequate substitutions makes his newfound perspective on the world happy and healthy.

CONTINUED ON NEXT PAGE

HOW TO BRING AN OUTSIDE CAT IN — CONTINUED

Your cat needs a good litter box. Show your cat the litter box, and he will probably begin using it without persuasion. Also provide a sturdy, functional scratching post.

Your furry feline also needs a comfortable place to soak in the sunshine. There should be an accessible sunny window, with room for each cat. You can provide a bed that hooks onto the window frame or you can purchase a cat tree and place it in front of the window to make it comfy.

Although your cat will greatly appreciate the warming from the window, an indoor cat loses a portion of the health benefits of full-spectrum light. Sunshine is important for your animal friends as well as yourself. The window glass blocks out beneficial sunrays and therefore you need to provide your pets with alternatives. You can provide full-spectrum lighting by purchasing special light bulbs found at pet shops that provide equipment for exotic pets. These lights may not provide the health benefits of full natural sunlight; there is no conclusive evidence to suggest they are a complete replacement for the sun. Providing natural sunlight is most beneficial.

You can let your inside cats experience the great outdoors and receive the benefits of full sunshine by providing them with a safe place to play outside, such as a secure porch area. Some caring owners have even created fully enclosed runs. These runs can be as simple as a cage attached to a window so the cats can step outside whenever they feel the urge or as elaborate as a fully furnished run with plants, grass, trees, and other fun climbing adventures. You can let your cats bask in the sunshine while secure in a special cat cage, a wire crate, or a commercially manufactured enclosure. Make sure the cats can get out of the heat to cool off if they get too warm.

VARIATIONS IN ACCEPTANCE

Bringing an outdoor cat permanently indoors can be difficult at first. Some animals will not even bat a whisker and enjoy staying inside, but other cats may whine and cry nonstop for days or weeks. If you see your cat heading for the door, intercept him and offer him a treat, game, or affection as a distraction. The secret is to never, never let your cat out while he is crying, even if you are using the gradual approach. This only aggravates and increases the whining. Ignore him no matter how hard and do not weaken your resolve. Remind yourself that it is best to bring your cat indoors, and don't let the opinions of well-meaning friends sway you. If after a month he is still crying at the door, you can resort to the use of a spray bottle or squirt gun. As soon as he leaves the door, reward and/or praise him. Whether a simple or a difficult experience, bringing your cat indoors will be well worth the effort in the end.

Noise

• • • •

Noise can be a problem for you and your neighbors. Multiple notoriously noisy animals only make the problem larger and more difficult, but not impossible, to manage. You want to begin with sufficient forethought and planning and use good management skills to control as much of the noise as possible.

If you live close to your neighbors, and especially if you live in an apartment, carefully consider the noise that your pets generate. Keep noise level in mind when doing your research about what breed or species to adopt. Some ideas to control noise are suggested in the following sections.

If you live in a rowdy neighborhood with children playing and other animals making noise, your concern is different. Will all this ruckus cause a normally quiet creature to turn vocal? Possibly. Will your nerves be pushed to the limit if you add yet another voice to this chorus of disturbance? Maybe. Will your pet simply blend in without disturbing anyone further? Hopefully.

If you live where your neighbors are not affected by the noise level from animals in your household, you only have to consider your own tolerance levels.

DOGS

Some breeds of dogs tend to bark more than others, and some breeds are known to be more discriminate in their vocalizations. If you have multiple dogs and one dog begins barking, it usually gets the others barking. If you have two quiet dogs, adding another that barks may get them all sounding off, probably not the other way around. Barking is just too contagious, too habitual, and too much fun.

It is difficult to offer guidelines regarding how much noise is acceptable. The amount of barking tolerated by your neighbors depends on them. Most people are aggravated by excessive barking, and some people may make a formal complaint if your canine friend barks once at a cat on the fence. Laws differ in each city, but if someone repeatedly complains to the animal control office that your dog is a noise nuisance, he may cause you some legal problems as well.

Why is Your Dog Barking?

When designing the solution to cure a problem barker, you must identify the underlying problem. Pay close attention to when your dog is making the most noise. For example, does he bark at every child who walks by the fence? Then keeping him indoors when the school children are walking to and from school alleviates this disturbance. Eliminating as much provocation as possible helps the problem diminish naturally.

• **The Nervous Dog** — Other dogs, usually the high-strung variety, bark out of nervousness. They may be bored, lonely, or scared because you are gone, and these dogs also resort to chewing, digging, and self-mutilation. Without properly dealing with the root of the problem, curing the barking alone only stimulates other bad habits to form. If you have a healthy relationship with your dog companion and he has a sound mind, you will probably not have this problem. Try the suggestions mentioned in this chapter, and if you are unsuccessful find a good trainer or behaviorist.

• **The Spoiled Dog** — Dogs that are spoiled and babied will be emotional messes when you are not home to pamper them. There is a balance between giving your pet enough attention and giving him too much attention. An overindulged dog will whine, howl, and bark in your absence from shear lack of knowledge about what to do with himself without you. He will bark from stress at his perceived abandonment.

If a dog has been exposed to different stimuli throughout his life, he will more likely take the activities that occur during his day in stride rather than react anxiously. This experience makes him feel secure, and he will not feel the need to sound the alarm at any new sound, sight, or smell. A well-socialized, intelligent canine accepts the world with enthusiasm and calm curiosity.

Making a big production out of leaving escalates the fear in these dogs. Your dog may become anxious if you make a big fuss out of coming and going, turning him into a stress barker. Your departing and returning should be treated as matter-of-fact events. Your dog will follow your example and remain calm.

• The Bored Dog — Is your dog barking from boredom? Spend more time with your pet. Exercise works wonders for burning excess physical energy. Training, and whether it's the basic obedience commands or more advanced specialty training, burns excess mental energy as well as gives your dog some important lessons in self-control. Also provide your dog with something interesting to play with while you are away.

• The Value of Barking — You must get your dog's barking under control as much as possible, although you will not be able to eliminate it completely. It is beneficial for your dog to alert you to the presence of strangers on your property, and you want your dog to warn potential troublemakers that they should go elsewhere lest they face the wrath of an angry canine. Protection is valuable in even the most prestigious neighborhoods. It's not necessary your dog be attack-trained for you to feel more secure and safe; having a well-trained dog that can bark on command is a valuable tool for self-protection. If you use a drastic measure, such as surgery to cure a barking problem, you eliminate this asset.

The author's dog Retta has been trained to cease barking and sit while a visitor is greeted at the door. There is no reason visitors should have to deal with unruly, uncontrolled dogs.

"De-barking"

De-barking surgery is controversial and should be your last resort. It is a procedure that deserves much thought, so discuss this option thoroughly with your veterinarian.

Two types of de-barking surgery can be considered. The most commonly performed practice is one where the dog's voice is made quieter. His bark may become high pitched or hoarse. This method is temporary, lasting from a few months to a few years. The veterinarian anesthetizes the dog's mouth and removes a portion of the folds of the vocal cords. The other course of action for permanent bark inhibition is to remove all of the vocal cords. This surgery is more painful and requires an incision through the dog's throat.

The advocates of de-barking say that they do not notice any psychological or emotional difficulties in the dogs after the surgery has been completed. The dog that has been de-barked will still "whisper" his bark as if he doesn't even realize his voice has changed. Other dog experts report depression and trauma following the procedure. Many veterinarians see this as a cruel and unnecessary operation and refuse to perform it on any dog.

It is a tough decision. If your dog got you into trouble with his barking and you have done all you can or are willing to do, you may be considering this radical solution. If it means choosing between sacrificing your pet to the shelter for almost probable euthanasia or de-barking, the choice gets burdensome. There are so many other solutions to cure a barking dog that such a resolution appears to be extreme. Try other ways of curbing the barking first.

Shock Collar

An electronic shock collar is an unnecessary and aggressive training aid used as a shortcut by those who do not want to put effort into training their dogs. The shock a dog receives when he barks can cause him to become fearful, and you could create a fear-biting problem. Your dog may also become aggressive from constantly being "attacked." A barking problem is easier to deal with than an aggression problem. A shock collar is not a training tool that builds mutual respect or creates the desired behavior through willingness to please. The use of a shock collar to train dogs has left a legacy of pitiful animals that are more like robots than emotional creatures. Avoid the shock collar and make a bit of effort instead.

Bringing Your Dog Inside

If your dog only barks when he is left alone outside, you can keep him in. If you are going to be away from home for four hours or less and your dog is an adult, you can keep him confined to a crate indoors if he isn't yet trained to behave in the home. A young puppy won't be able to wait longer than three hours, and you should have someone let him out or confine him to a safe room where he can relieve himself if necessary. Crate training is an advantage with most dogs. Your dog feels safe and happy in his "den" if introduced to it compassionately.

If you do keep your dog inside, either in a crate or loose in the house, he may still bark — possibly for the same reasons that he barked when outside. With less stimulus, your pet may not have as many excuses to voice his emotions, but the reasons will not disappear completely. The main advantage to keeping him inside is that you have more control over how much noise is exposed to your neighbors.

Turning on a stereo or television conceals some of the noise. Because the stereo or television camouflages the outdoor stimulus, your pet has less reason to be alarmed and may naturally become quiet. Make sure you shut the windows. If you shut the curtains also, your dog will be less exposed to visual activity outside and may be able to stay more calm and relaxed.

Make sure you provide a confined dog with plenty of activity to keep him busy. Boredom is trouble. Exercise your dog before putting him in his crate. He can rest and relax with more ease after he has exercised his body and his mind and has expended some of his energy.

Barking on Command

Although this book is not intended to be a book on training, one simple training technique can make a difference in the quality of life with a barking dog.

The idea is to teach him to bark on command. If you can train your dog to bark on command and then be quiet when told to do so, you will have better control over the situation.

If your dog begins barking at someone or something, give him the command that you have decided upon, such as making a hissing sound or a quiet, whispery "Watch 'em." This is a useful tool to demonstrate to strangers that your dog is protecting you. You will have control over when you want your dog to exhibit this protection.

You then want your dog to be quiet on demand. Very gently wrap your hands around your dog's muzzle, holding it closed while you command "quiet." It is important that you be gentle and nonaggressive when using this technique — your dog should not feel this is in any way disciplinary. Holding the muzzle is only a way for you to demonstrate to your pet what the word "quiet" represents, and it is a gentle teaching tool if used correctly. Holding his muzzle roughly nullifies the lesson. You want your dog to listen to your commands with respect and do so willingly; aggression on your part only creates resentment.

Never forget to praise your dog when he stops barking. For the initial training, give him a food treat when he ceases barking. This helps the lesson stay with your pet. He can't bark while chewing, and food has a way of cementing knowledge in the canine brain.

If Your Neighbors Complain

Before they tell you, ask the people who live near you if they hear your dog barking, howling, or whining while you are away. If your neighbors come to you and complain about your noisy dog, you've got to act quickly. People must get quite irritated before they actually complain, and if they are complaining to you, then your dog has pushed their tolerance.

Some people do not appreciate the furry friendship of a dog. It is sad but true. In any event, these people are the ones who find fault in the canine existence where there is none. They may complain that your dog is barking when perhaps he is not.

One way to check on the activity of your pet while you are away and check the level of noise your dog is creating is to simply leave a tape recorder on

DOG BITES

YOUR DOG

If your dog bites someone, you are responsible according to the law. Dog bites must be reported to the local health department, and you will be required to show proof of your dog's current vaccinations. You may have to confine your pet for observation. If your pet is a wolf or wolf hybrid, he may be "sacrificed" and put to sleep for investigative surgery.

How do you know if your dog has the potential to bite someone? Sometimes you have no warning, but sometimes your dog is provoked and bites in defense. Usually owners of biting dogs can tell you the signs they failed to recognize and take seriously until it was too late.

If your dog growls, snaps, or snarls, he is expressing his desire to control the interaction. Whether instigated by pushiness or fear, this could be a precursor to further action. If he lays his teeth on someone, you must immediately deal with the problem. Warnings leading to a biting dog usually start small and escalate. If your dog growls at someone, take it as a sign to get help. If you feel frightened of your dog at anytime, even for a fleeting moment, get help. It is beyond the scope of this book to help you with a potential aggression or biting problem. Read chapter 3 to get assistance in finding a competent professional. Never assume it will go away or that your dog will never bite anyone. Read the signs, and trust your gut feeling. You know your dog better than anyone.

By exposing your dog to many different people and situations while he is young (socialization), he will be more accepting of strangers. He will still be a good watch dog, and instincts will dictate his protective nature, but he should accept people if you want him to. Explain to someone who approaches you and wants to pet your dog that they should not be boisterous or rough. You can even help them find your dog's favorite petting spot.

OTHER DOGS

Never assume that every dog you meet will immediately be your friend. Not all dogs are friendly. Sometimes because dog lovers enjoy their dogs so much, they want to get to know every dog that they come in contact with. You can avoid bites from other dogs by using common sense and exercising caution. Instruct your children on how to handle strange dogs.

If a dog is wandering by himself, it is best to leave him alone. As mentioned earlier in this chapter, roaming dogs have unpredictable personalities. Don't chase the dog or try to catch him. Some dogs are very friendly and love to make friends as they roam about the neighborhood; others are fearful and will bite with no provocation.

DOG BITES — CONTINUED

If you are out and about and a strange dog comes at you, don't run. Running stimulates him to chase you. This is difficult if you are riding a bike or performing another fast activity. Slow down. If the dog seems aggressive, do not turn your back to him. Never stare into the eyes of a dog; focus on the space between his ears. Staring is a threat, and you may get bit. If you are attacked by a dog, don't try to run away. Cover your face, squat to the ground, and be still.

Of course, you know better than to reach into a car or over a fence to pet a dog. And leave a chained dog alone. The smaller the area to defend, the more furiously a dog defends it.

If you get bit, remember every possible detail about the dog's description and the situation. Write it down at the next available moment so that you don't forget. It is important that the health department get as many accurate details as possible, and report this information immediately. Clean the wound well and call your doctor.

while you are gone. If you find that your dog is indeed well behaved, you will have to enlist the help of dog-friendly neighbors for support.

If you introduce your neighbors to your dog as soon as you get him and show the people who live next to you that your pet is a nice, well-behaved canine, then you may eliminate some of the complaining. How can someone who knows your dog is nice possibly mind an occasional ruckus? On the other hand, introducing your pet to a person who finds no joy in animals will do neither of you any good. If you know that the people living next to you dislike animals or dogs greatly, keep your pets away from them.

Communication is the key to good neighborly relations. If you know your neighbor works the night shift and must sleep during the afternoon, you can keep your dog indoors or quiet during this time. A new baby next door? Is your neighbor recovering from surgery or illness? You will only know to take extra measures if you and your neighbor have open lines of communication.

Respect the feelings of your "nondoggie" neighbors. You may find discrimination against your multi-animal household from people who do not understand animal companionship. Respect their views and do everything you can to show them your level of responsibility and peacekeeping.

CATS

Cats can be noisy and disruptive. An unneutered male or female can be an incredible nuisance, and the howling may be unbearable to your neighbors. Some cats will come to the windows of each house yowling at the cats indoors, which is both irritating and frustrating.

Your cat may meow sweetly to people who are outside. You may find this endearing, but there are people out there who do not. Keep your cat out of their auditory range, especially at night.

If you have a problem with your cat disturbing your neighbors, the first step is to get him or her neutered or spayed. You can keep him inside your home if he is making noise that is unrelated to sexual needs. The comfort of your neighbors is worth bringing your cat indoors. If your neighbors complain to you about your feline, trouble could be right around the corner. In order to complain, nerves have to be pushed to the extreme. Casually ask your neighbors if your cats are too noisy before they confront you. You'll have a better chance at soothing relationships if you catch a noise problem before it gets too irritating.

BIRDS

If you have birds that scream with delight, impatience, joy, or all the other wonderful bird emotions, the decibel level may offend your neighbors.

Behavioral Advice

The first step you should take is to determine why your feathered friend is screaming. It may be that he is simply expressing his joy at being alive like any healthy bird would. This kind of vocalization should be expected and tolerated if you are going to live with parrots. If the screaming is consistent and continuous, lasting for a large portion of the day, you should find a solution to the problem. Getting advice from a bird behavioral specialist is wise. Turn to the breeder that you purchased the bird from to get information, and read magazines and books. (Very few books help a bird lover understand the behavior of their pet or offer sound, nonaggressive solutions to correcting undesirable behavior. It is hoped that in the near future, more knowledgeable, sensitive people working with birds will be putting their ideas onto paper.)

How Loud Is Loud?

If you are looking for a bird to adopt, remember that some species tend to be less noisy or less likely to use their voice than others. Even a normally quiet cockatoo can upset very close or noise-sensitive neighbors if he lets out his joy cry even once a week.

If you haven't been around birds, especially big parrots, you may wonder if this is a concern since the bird will be inside the house. However, once you have heard one of these parrots let out his unrestrained voice, you will believe. My neighbor behind me, separated by two backyards, teases me about my macaw. Even with all the windows closed in both houses, he can still hear Salsa calling out for me in

the afternoons to be let out. He doesn't mind, and because it is a distance, the sound is muffled by the time he hears it. If he were closer and noise sensitive, this could be a problem.

Things You Can Do

No matter why your bird is screaming, take measures to keep this from disturbing your neighbors. Acoustic board or foam can be applied to the walls surrounding the bird area. This helps cut down on the noise reaching the outside world by absorbing a good portion of it. Even nailing a carpet remnant on the wall blocks the noise a bit. Keeping your noisy bird in the area farthest from the closest neighbor also helps. None of these ideas will totally eliminate your neighbors' share of the ruckus, but they will soften the audible blow and improve neighborly camaraderie.

Responsible breeding and compassionate neutering

You have probably been exposed to a vast amount of material regarding the overpopulation of companion animals, yet even with this information many people are unable to comprehend the enormity of the problem. Most are unaware of the role they play in the perpetuation of this horrendous mess. It is your responsibility as an animal lover to understand the problem and educate other people who may lack the information necessary to make a difference.

The issue is controversial, with persuasive arguments from all sides. The only right solution is to learn as much as you can and be open to the positions of all involved. Remember, there is no single right answer. Your personal situation and the conditions of the area where you live are the deciding factors for your feelings on the overpopulation issue.

THE STATISTICS ARE STAGGERING

Although varying figures exist on the number of animals euthanized yearly in animal shelters, the average number of dogs and cats that meet their end in a shelter is between seven and thirteen million. In a litter of five kittens, four of those five will be euthanized in a shelter. There are currently estimated to be about seventeen million animals in shelters throughout this country waiting for families to adopt them. Each of these animals is an individual, each is a live animal capable of love and devotion. Only one in six will find a home.

As described below, the problem becomes more difficult as you begin to look closely at the statistics. Currently, people are devising methods to better research this problem so that more efficient solutions can be found. For the time being, some facts make the problem difficult to remedy.

Most puppies and kittens brought into shelters are adopted, and some areas have waiting lists for them. Also, most puppies and kittens bred by backyard breeders are adopted into new homes.

LACK OF COMMITMENT

The main problem does not seem to be that people don't want a pet; they just don't want a pet after it begins to grow up. Most dogs, cats, and rabbits that are surrendered to shelters are adolescents and adults. The majority of birds looking for new homes are adolescents. These misunderstood creatures have outgrown their cuteness and are beginning to challenge their owners with their verge-of-adulthood quest for independence and dominance.

The largest obstacle then is to get people who adopt pets to keep them. Why do people give up on their animals? The answers are yet to be fully understood. Maybe it is another manifestation of a throwaway society. Maybe the aggressive training methods that have become popular in the last twenty years are backfiring and producing uncontrollable pets. Maybe mass production breeding has consistently provided animals that do not instinctually know how to live in the world of humans, and people don't know how to teach them. Maybe it is conflicting messages or inexcusable advice offered by some professionals. It may be the inability of people to acknowledge their responsibility. But more often than not, it is probably a simple lack of understanding.

RESPONSIBLE BREEDING

If the overpopulation problem is so great, is there room for breeding more animals? Yes and no. Animals should only be bred to better the gene pool. You may think your animal companion is the best pet in the world and breeding him would allow you to have more of the same, but this never works.

Evaluate your reasons for wanting to bring more animals into the world, even though you have no guarantee they will find a home, by asking a series of questions like those that follow. Being honest and caring when considering such a complicated puzzle is paramount.

Questions to Ask Yourself

Do you have the necessary knowledge of genetics? Genetics is an extremely complicated subject. Years of research and a great deal of education are prerequisites for understanding the genetics of a species. A person must specialize in his or her particular breed for years to fully understand the complexity of this science.

Are you active in programs or organizations that promote the benefits of your breed? If you are interested in dogs, do you participate in sport or obedience as well as showing? You must strive to better the working intelligence of your breed as well as the physical qualities.

Does the individual you intend to breed have a stable and desirable temperament? Although not all behavioral qualities are inherited, you should strive to breed only the animals with characteristics that you would want passed from generation to generation.

Is your pet in good health? Is your animal genetically sound? Good health is important when having to endure the rigors of reproduction as well as for ensuring the health of future generations.

Is the pet you would like to breed one that you adopted from a reputable, responsible breeder? Do you have a three- to five-generation pedigree? Is your animal's family physically and psychologically sound? Are there members of your animal's family that have titles or hold special honors given by organizations striving to better the quality of your breed?

Further Analysis

If you were able to answer yes to all of these questions, you may indeed have a pet that would be considered breeding quality. Does this mean you should breed your beloved? Think very carefully about this choice — it entails much work and dedication. You are responsible for every baby, and you play a part in the responsibility of every offspring for generations. Do you want such a burden?

If you cannot answer yes to each of these questions, have your pet neutered. There is no sense in breeding your pet and adding to the explosive population of unwanted animals.

These questions do not apply to pet birds. Breeding parrots is an entirely different situation. Many of the bird species kept as pets are endangered, and captive breeding programs may be the only means of keeping many of these species in existence. Does this mean you need to sacrifice your pet to a breeder or that you have to get your pet a mate? No, and please read the special section on this subject to better understand the issue.

If you have decided to breed your pet, continue on in your search for knowledge and read the following myths regarding breeding.

Myth #1

The biggest myth of all is that you can make money at breeding animals.

People who breed animals are doing so generally at a cost to themselves. If the breeder is caring and conscientious, then there is rarely profit or only a surviving level of it. Breeding animals is expensive.

Veterinary expenses for prenatal care, assistance that may be required during a difficult birth, supplemental feedings of the babies if needed, and inoculations are quite substantial. You also need to support your animal family with equipment, housing, food, and then you will have the expense of finding the babies new homes.

Responsible breeders will keep any babies that are unable to find good homes. This is another expense and obligation.

If you think that having a male alleviates any of these hardships and he can make you some cash, think

again. Breeders will not want to breed their female and pay a fee for just any male. You will have to prove that your stud is special. You will have to pay more for a higher quality pet to begin with and then put money into proving he is worthy of a fee by working for applicable titles.

So did you make back the money you invested? Doubtful. If you include the price of the parent animal and any stud fees, you have probably spent more than your return. You cannot view breeding animals as an income source — it is more accurately viewed as a hobby expense. It should be something that you do for the love of the creature. You will be lucky, like all breeders of animals, if you break even.

Myth #2

Some people want to breed their pets as a way of sharing the miracle of birth with their children. There is no way to guarantee that their experience will be one of happy rejoicing.

If you are fortunate enough to be there with your children when your pet does give birth, what may happen during this incredible event may not be a good experience for you or the kids. Complications may arise, and your children can find their beloved pet being rushed to the veterinarian in panic. The babies may be born dead or deformed. There is blood, pain, and noise — and your pet could conceivably die. Would you want your children to experience this trauma?

Teach your children true responsibility by having your pet spayed or neutered. Responsibility to the general community should make more of an impression than the sacrifice of lives. If you feel it is important for your children to see the miracle of birth, you can rent or buy video tapes that allow your children to witness the birth of animals.

Myth #3

Another common myth is that in order for an animal to be "whole," it must experience reproduction.

To say that an animal needs to reproduce to be emotionally well adjusted or physically healthy is absurd. Animals live only in the here and now; they do not linger in the past nor do they wish they had been able to produce offspring. They also do not wish that they had their sexual organs. You are not depriving your pet of "love." Your creatures look to you to fulfill their social needs, and they will not miss love affairs never experienced.

The Health Factor

Physically, neutering your pet is in his or her best interest. The risk of many hormone-induced conditions is either partially or completely reduced when your pet is neutered. Testicular cancer, prostate disease, breast cancer, ovarian and uterine tumors, infections of the testicles, venereal tumors, and chronic endometritis are just a few.

Unspayed female cats have a seven times greater risk of developing mammary cancer. A cat's eggs are not passed through her body like in humans. She stores them until she is mated. A couple of heats can make these eggs cystic. The more heat cycles a female experiences, the greater her risk of developing mammary tumors.

Spayed and neutered animals are less stressed since they do not have the worries about or the desire to mate. They also do not have to go through the physical challenge of reproduction. Spayed and neutered animals do not gain weight. Only inactivity and too much food make your pet gain weight.

All in all, neutered pets are healthy animals that live longer, calmer lives.

THE CONSEQUENCES OF AN UNNEUTERED PET

If you are the owner of an unneutered pet, you face increased responsibility. The comfort levels of your animal, your home, and your neighbors are all affected by the pet that sees his or her purpose in the world as reproducing.

Female Cats

Unspayed female cats call incessantly when in heat; the call is bone chilling. They yowl, howl, and sound as if they are in pain, and nothing you can do will stop the noise. You cannot train or threaten her to be more quiet. The sound even travels through the walls of your home. Your nerves, as well as those who live nearby, are on edge.

A female cat also solicits an invitation to mate when you pet her by raising her rear and hooking her tail to the side. Going through heat after heat is difficult on a female cat. It can be very tiring, and she may become thin and nervous.

Female Dogs

The female dog must be securely confined because male dogs will come for miles and do just about anything to get to your "lover girl." Even if you are constantly supervising, a male dog may aggressively mate with your female, and you may not be able to do anything about it.

Your companion becomes a messy problem and must live in confinement, unable to freely roam the house due to her bloody discharge. She is also not allowed to venture outside freely. Again, this can cause nervousness and a high level of anxiety for your pet.

Male Cats

Unneutered male cats are notorious for spraying everything with urine to mark their territory. You cannot train an intact male cat to cease spraying. To make matters worse, their urine has a strong odor. No one can mistake the home that contains an intact male cat; the smell is a dead giveaway. Even breeders who have stud cats do not let them roam in the house. The stud cats are usually in a separate area from the living area and are kept in runs or kennels.

Male cats are messy in their litter box, and no matter how often you clean the box it will smell — strongly. If a male cat is neutered, his urine will not be as pungent. He will probably stop, or decrease, spraying. Cats that have learned the habit or those that possess strong territorial urges may still occasionally spray. All cats, male and female, may spray if they feel threatened, a new member is added to the house and they feel the need to demonstrate their dominance, or they are anxious, upset, or ill.

An unneutered male cat can become tense and nervous if he cannot service enough females. He can become uncomfortable, aggressive, and intolerant of your handling.

Unneutered male dogs will break out of your yard if they decide to find the female they smell is in heat. Once out, they can get into all sorts of trouble.

Male Dogs

Both male dogs and cats who are unneutered have a strong desire to wander. They will roam looking for available females. Many get into fights, and some of these fights can be harmful or even fatal. They may also become noisy when they smell a female in heat and can disturb you and the people around you.

Male dogs may become overly territorial and protect their home with a vengeance. This level of protection can bring you many problems, including disturbing the peace, biting, attacking people and other animals, and creating fear in people who come near your home. Intact male dogs are also aggressive with other male dogs and may not listen to the commands of their caretakers in the heat of an encounter. This loss of control can have devastating effects. The dogs can be injured, and you could be facing litigation if the other dog has extensive veterinary bills or is killed.

The unneutered male dog will also be inclined to demonstrate his dominance. The struggle for dominance can lead to trouble. Most dog bites are from unneutered male dogs between two and three years old. When a dog reaches his sexual peak, he does not want to listen to you, comply with your demands, or tolerate what he considers irritation, even from children. He has more important things on his mind — he is concerned about proliferating his genes.

An intact male dog is a sexual being and as such he will mount, ride, sniff, and lick both inanimate and living objects. This is embarrassing for you and the recipient of such lusty demonstrations. Behavior such as this can be dominance motivated, and you won't be spared even if your female dog is bossy and strong-willed. Most embarrassing to the average caretaker is the blatant arousal often demonstrated by a male dog that he usually reserves for the presence of children ("Mommy, what's that?").

THE NEXT GENERATION, AND THE NEXT, AND THE NEXT

You are accountable for all baby animals born to your pet. This means the ones that you plan, the ones that happen by accident, and even the ones that you may not know that your male animal contributed to. These animals are your responsibility for the rest of their lives. You are also responsible for the offspring of the offspring. Generations of animals will have you to thank for their existence. In a perfect world where every living creature is valued and cherished, this would be fine. In our world, it is a heavy obligation.

Will you be able to find all of the babies new homes — homes where they will be cared for, have good veterinary care, get good food, be protected from dangers, and loved forever? Your friends who say that they absolutely admire your pet and would adopt one of their babies may not be there when the babies are available. They usually back out on you because their lifestyles change, or they may have been offering you a compliment with no intention of taking one of the babies.

As you search for people who believe a lifetime of care is their duty to their pets, you will encounter a shortage of conscientious homes. Offering your home as a refuge for the offspring of your animals once they are unwanted by their new families will be a heartbreaking responsibility.

GETTING YOUR PET SPAYED OR NEUTERED

The best time to get your pet spayed or neutered is before she or he actually hits puberty and all the undesirable hormone-induced behaviors become habits. Your companion's risk of disease is dramatically lowered the earlier he or she is neutered or spayed.

Different species and breeds mature at different rates, and each animal is an individual so the age your pet explodes into puberty is difficult to pinpoint. An increasingly younger age is being recommended, with some veterinarians advocating neutering and spaying while the animal is only two or three months old. Ask your veterinarian when you should have your pet spayed or neutered.

When you bring your pet home, let him or her sleep off the anesthetic. Give your pet comfort, attention, warmth, and security after surgery. Do not allow the other animals or family members to disturb your furry friend. Keep the noise level low and the comfort flowing.

Spaying and Neutering Your Rabbit

Although it has not been the focal point of much media attention, overpopulation of rabbits is a large problem. The same sad facts are true of abandoned pet rabbits and their fate in animal shelters. Rabbits are especially vulnerable because they are viewed as less emotional and psychologically developed, which is far from the truth. They are considered low maintenance, which is also not true, and the "no hassle" pet becomes burdensome. Their biggest fault is they are so adorable they are hard to resist adopting in the first place.

If you have an unspayed female and an unneutered male rabbit, you will have baby rabbits. You may not have to worry about rabbits wandering in search of reproduction opportunities, but you do have all of the other problems that are associated with unneutered dogs and cats.

There are numerous benefits to having your pet rabbit neutered or spayed, such as

- Unspayed female rabbits have a strong urge to burrow. This means torn carpets and shredded furniture.

- Much destructive chewing may be caused by rabbits with increased hormone levels, which spaying and neutering lessens.

- Spaying and neutering reduces or eliminates spraying in both females and males. It also helps your rabbit become a more talented litter box user.

- Four out of five unspayed five-year-old rabbits develop uterine cancer. You never have to worry that your spayed female will develop uterine cancer.

- The chance of your rabbit developing urinary infections is reduced.

- Spaying and neutering lessens territorial aggression. If you have more than one rabbit, this helps promote harmony among them.

- Spaying your female rabbit eliminates the possibility of her developing ovarian or mammary tumors.

If you are not taking your rabbit to a veterinarian who specializes in exotic pets and has a good knowledge of companion rabbits, you may get conflicting advice. A livestock or small animal veterinarian may advise you to forgo having your pet rabbit spayed or neutered. The belief that rabbits only live for about five years and therefore do not warrant risky surgery is an outdated one. Rabbits that are protected from common cancers, receive care from educated owners, and benefit from the increase in veterinary education are living longer and longer lives. By giving affection, security, and good health, you may be surprised at how long your rabbit friends will be with you.

Males can be neutered sometime after they are three to four months old or after their testicles have descended. Females should be between six and eight months old. Your rabbit can have the surgery at any age, and you will be helping to keep your rabbit healthy. If your pet is over one year old, your veterinarian will advise you to have a pre-operative blood panel. He or she will be looking for anemia, kidney function, and elevated liver enzymes.

Because rabbits are sensitive creatures and anesthesia is more risky, surgery is a bigger challenge for them than it is for dogs or cats. Taking your rabbit to a veterinarian who has extensive experience performing surgery on rabbits is critical.

Rabbits do not vomit, so you will not need to deprive them of food before surgery. Keep them full and healthy. Give your rabbit time to recover and offer lots of love, warmth, and security. Strictly follow your veterinarian's advice, and contact your veterinarian if any complications arise. Be aware that neutered pairs of rabbits may still engage in the sexual act — they're just that way.

Should You Breed Your Parrot?

The fact that the wild population of parrots is so jeopardized creates a quandary for caring bird guardians. You may be swamped with advice from well-meaning, but not completely informed, people telling you it is your responsibility to place your bird in a breeding situation. The truth is that unless you are the caretaker of a rare species and your pet is needed to increase the gene pool, there are enough birds in breeding situations. It is not your obligation to part with your beloved friend. Your parrot can be your lifelong companion, and you should feel no guilt.

• **Sexual Maturity** — When parrot guardians are confronted with a particularly difficult behavioral problem, they are often advised that they have a sexually mature bird on their hands and it would be better to give the bird a mate or put him in a breeding program. This is nonsense. This advice is given even to caretakers who have birds that are six months old. A parrot may be three to five years old before sexually mature, although he may play mating games when younger. Misbehavior is too often wrongly blamed on sexual frustration. Knowledge of parrot behavior and sound behavioral modification is usually the best cure for misconduct.

• **Why Are They Suggesting This?** — If you are offered this advice, evaluate it for any secret motive

the person may have. If a pet store gives you this advice, are they interested in selling you another bird? Is a breeder offering you this advice so that you will take another baby and trade a part of the purchase price for your bird? Is your veterinarian who offers you this advice one who specializes in avian medicine? If not, you may be getting incorrect information.

If you are having behavior problems with your bird, seek the help of a parrot behaviorist and read information in books and magazines (suggestions are listed in the bibliography) about behavior modification and parrot personalities.

• **Using Understanding** — If your parrot is sexually mature and exhibits sexual behavior, you are still not obliged to relinquish your friend to a breeding program. You can learn how to handle the fluctuation of behavior. Understand the life cycle of your pet, and adapt your handling to create the most serene environment.

• **Part-Time Breeding?** — Birds cannot be part-time breeders. They cannot be bred during breeding season and then separated and kept as pets. Parrots bond for life and become emotionally attached to their mate. Once a parrot has a mate, neither of the two birds will be very interested in you. If you are having difficulty with one bird, your difficulty will only be increased if you put two birds together. You will have a very hard time keeping them bonded to you because they will be more interested in their own species. It has been done, but it takes time, patience, dedication, and birds that are very bonded to their owner.

• **Myth of the "Perfect" Life** — Many people think their birds would be much happier in a breeding situation. They imagine the easy life of a large, well-accessorized flight area, a loving mate, good food, conscientious care, and a touch of the wild life that they have been unable to experience. This may be far from reality.

Breeder birds do not always live the ideal life. Birds that have been raised in a home environment may find it difficult to adapt to a breeding situation. Often they are thrown together with a mate they find incompatible and possibly even violent. This is, of course, if they don't spend the next couple of years in a cage in a back room waiting for the right bird of the opposite sex to be found.

Irresponsible breeders treat breeder birds like egg factories, taking the eggs as soon as they are laid and pressuring the birds to produce more.

• **Choosing a Breeding Situation** — If you do have a rare species, a wild-caught bird that has not adapted well to captivity, or have otherwise found that it is necessary to place your pet in a breeding situation, find the best possible breeder. You want a responsible, reputable breeder who cares deeply for the emotional needs as well as the physical care of the birds. Many breeders who fit this description have closed aviaries and will not accept new birds, so your search may be a long one.

Ask your avian veterinarian for recommendations. Once you have some names and telephone numbers, you can begin interviews. Ask many detailed questions and try to get a feel for the emotions behind the answers. Are they sincere? Honest? Do the answers feel contrived? This is an important decision — don't take it lightly or make a quick choice.

Here are some questions you may want to ask:

• Do the breeders share their home with permanent pet birds? Many loving and affectionate breeders have pets that they care deeply about.

• What do their birds eat? Only seed? Pellets? You want your pet to get lots of healthy vegetables and fruits and an array of other good stuff to eat.

• Are the birds offered toys? Branches? Chunks of wood? Even breeder birds need stimulation, and they like to play and exercise their beaks.

• How are the birds introduced? The birds should not be thrown together. They should be introduced gradually and with sensitivity.

• How are their aviaries maintained? Are there people coming and going at all times, disturbing the birds? Do they have a high quality of hygiene?

• How many babies do they raise a year? Experience is good, but if they are a baby factory then they do not give their birds the attention that they deserve. Birdie mills are no better than puppy mills.

If you decide to breed your parrot yourself, you are in for an involved experience. Breeding birds is extremely time-consuming, all encompassing, and emotionally taxing. You need to get educated, so talk to other breeders who will take you under their wing (so to speak). Read everything you can get your hands on. And good luck!

7

Your pets depend on you to help protect them from danger and to act quickly in any dangerous situation that may arise.

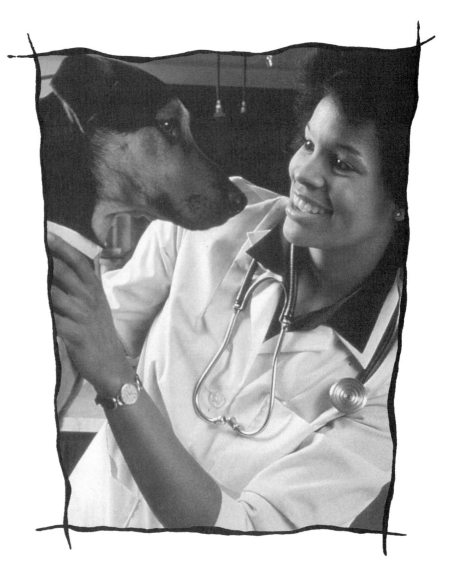

Keeping your animals healthy

Ensuring the health and safety of the animals in your care is a constant, crucial responsibility. Ironically, it is often the area that caretakers neglect. The thought of your animal friends becoming sick or injured is often too difficult to accept.

Because your pets rely on you to fulfill their needs, you want to control everything connected to their existence. However, the truth is you cannot control everything that happens to your animal companions. You care for them and protect them, but sometimes they succumb to harm in spite of your efforts. When they do, you may feel you missed some sign of illness or overlooked a possible source of accident, and you may feel ashamed and guilty or be in a state of denial.

Many veterinarians have witnessed defensive clients exonerating themselves of guilt over their pet's predicament. Have you ever felt like you needed to "explain" to your veterinarian that you did everything right and you don't know why "it" happened to your pet? You must do the best you can and release yourself from guilt. People make mistakes. You may wish you would have acted differently, but you are only human.

Being immobilized to take action is the biggest mistake. Continually evaluating the safety of your home and following through with needed changes

THE STRENGTH OF YOUR ANIMAL COMPANION'S IMMUNE SYSTEM

The strength of an animal's immune system is vital to her health and longevity. Many factors determining the effectiveness of the immune system can be manipulated to benefit the animal.

Malnutrition is a major cause of weakened ability to fight off harmful microorganisms. Offer your animal companion a well-researched, nutritionally abundant diet. A reluctant eater can be persuaded to adopt a nourishing fare with patience and perseverance.

Oversupplementing your pet's diet (hyper-supplementation) also plays a role in making your companion more susceptible to the damage of pathogens. Before supplementing her diet, talk to your veterinarian and breeder. Even exceeding the nutritional requirement of some vitamins and minerals by a small amount can weaken the immune system. An overworked body must rely on smaller resources of energy when fighting for good health.

Stress is one of the most detrimental conditions to an immune system. There is always a level of stress in life, but stress is not entirely bad. You need stress for motivation, and a life devoid of stress is no more functional than one with excessive anxiety. However, a limit exists as to how much stress each individual can handle and stay healthy. Your responsibility as guardian is to know each animal well enough to understand the level of tolerance and to keep the anxiety the pet experiences to an acceptable limit.

Your animal companion has also inherited a genetic pre-disposition to immunity strength. If you are looking for an animal, information on the parents may give you insights into the offspring's health.

Remember, an animal with a strong immune system may withstand an environment that is laden with germs and still retain her health. An animal with a weakened immune system may succumb to minute amounts of germs in the cleanest of environments.

help lessen the possibility of accidents. Giving your animal companions the best veterinary care, both needed and preventative maintenance, increases your pet's chance for a healthy life.

Some people don't worry about safety because they have never had to. They are the lucky ones. They may have spent a lifetime with animals and never had an accident or an emergency. These are the rare folks who are pushing fate. The natural order of life says to be ever alert.

Some live with animals that never seem to get into anything or into any trouble. These people fall into the trap of comfort; it takes only once. Even though they may recognize a potential problem, they do not feel the need to act on it because their pet is so well behaved. Later they may be burdened with guilt by their lack of preventative action.

These caretakers may need some encouragement to make their homes safe. Set aside a weekend day for establishing a hazard-free home. Do it before it's too late and you learn firsthand how fragile safety is.

Some animals are always into something, and the guardians of these pets know safety and prevention are critical. People whose animal companions have had an accident have discovered the significance of safety the hard way, but they are also the most likely to keep their homes hazard proof.

Your pets depend on you to help protect them from danger and to act quickly in any dangerous situation that may arise.

Your partner — your veterinarian

Your veterinarian is your ally in the perpetual obligation to your animal companions' health. Consequently, having a good relationship with your veterinarian is the most significant alliance you develop with an animal professional. A veterinarian you can trust and feel comfortable with is a crucial part of your life and the life of your animals.

HOW TO CHOOSE A VET

Choosing a veterinarian should be done before you bring your animal companion home. Most veterinarians specialize in certain species or types of pets. Many are knowledgeable about dog and cat health, and some even devote themselves entirely to one or the other. If you are looking for a veterinarian who concentrates predominantly in exotic animal medicine, your choices will be more limited, and you may have to travel a distance to see one.

Begin your search by asking other animal people for a recommendation. Word of mouth is the best way to get a few names to begin your quest. Ask the breeder you adopted your pet from, your friend who has a wonderful veterinarian he always brags about, the local pet store if it is a good one, and members of clubs and organizations. The worst way to get a veterinarian is to go to the nearest one. You are fortunate if the best veterinarian for you is also the closest, but this is not the only issue you should base your decision on.

Specialty Vets

Veterinarians who do not routinely see birds or rabbits will not be as enlightened with up-to-date information as exotic pet vets. They may not attend conferences that educate on the rapidly advancing research and findings. To get the best care for your exotic friends, find a veterinarian who specializes in your species.

You can also ask a trusted veterinarian who doesn't routinely treat exotics for a recommendation. If you can find an avian veterinarian who is board certified in avian practice, you are very lucky. Only a few veterinarians have earned this honor of expertise. Look for one who is at least a member of the Association of Avian Veterinarians.

Avian medicine is constantly improving due to continual research and discoveries. Ask if the veterinarian attends continuing education courses in avian medicine. Avian and exotic devotees must expend much energy keeping their knowledge current, and their efforts benefit your pet.

Rabbits are considered exotic animals in the veterinary field. Search out an exotic veterinarian who specializes in rabbits as pets. Often the same veterinarian who treats birds will treat your rabbit.

I live in a relatively rural area, so the vets are

familiar with rabbits only as meat and fur animals. The methods used to treat rabbits kept as pets have a different emphasis. Farm rabbits grow quickly and do not live long. The lack of emotional attachment means that fewer measures will be taken to keep the animal healthy. These vets still care, but their education and knowledge just have a different emphasis. You may have to travel to find a veterinarian educated in the newest advances who will deal with your rabbit as a beloved pet.

Learning about the Vet

Once you have a few names, call and set up an interview. Some of the questions can be asked of the staff at the front desk but reserve other questions for the veterinarian. Because a vet is so busy, have him or her call you when it's convenient if you want to talk first on the phone. Ask one to two key questions that give you the best indication of the practice.

A basic question to ask is the hours of the clinic. Also, how will your animal be treated for after-hour emergencies? Will your veterinarian be on call? Will another vet from the same office alternate being on call, or will you have to go to a different hospital? Does the veterinarian routinely attend continuing education conferences and lectures? Is he or she familiar with your species or breed?

You may be interested in grooming and boarding facilities offered by the veterinarian and, if so, inquire about these. You may need to consider the cost of the services and compare those with others. If you are going to do a price comparison, ask for the cost of several procedures because one procedure may not give you a clear picture. Remember, cost isn't everything — you want the best, most pleasant veterinary care for your creatures.

If your research is positive, you hear many good things about the veterinarian from other people, and you like the front desk staff, set an appointment and see the facilities in person with or without a phone interview. Take your pet in for routine care such as a nail trim. If you would like a tour of the facilities, be sure to tell the front desk staff so they can arrange enough time. Taking your pet in with you for this meeting is useful because you can see how the veterinarian and the pet interact.

Possible Problems with Clinic Staff

Even if you think that your veterinarian is the best one to care for your animals, there may be times when you have difficulty with the business side of the relationship. If you find that the front desk staff is inconsiderate or ineffective, inform the vet. You can explain that you appreciate the wonderful care your animal receives, but it is difficult to get through on the phone, that the front desk staff seem uncaring, or whatever your complaint may be. If you are honest and kind, your veterinarian should not be offended and should appreciate your input.

COMMUNICATING WITH YOUR VETERINARIAN

Communication is the cornerstone of a good relationship, and this is especially true when the health of the animal you care for is at stake. Your veterinarian should listen to your questions and answer them fully in language you understand. Your job is to listen carefully so you can accurately perform any procedures you are asked to do at home. A good habit is to write down the instructions as the veterinarian gives them to you.

A veterinarian should be able to kindly and gently share with you things you are doing that may not be in the best interest of your pet. Keep an open mind and listen to these suggestions. You can learn much from an intelligent, educated vet.

If you feel that the veterinarian is always putting you down and you disagree on most issues, then you may be more comfortable elsewhere. No matter how much education a veterinarian has, it is never justifiable for him or her to belittle people or make them feel incompetent and unintelligent.

A good veterinarian considers all aspects of animal care and discusses vaccinations and preventative medicine with the caretaker. These are vital to the health of your companion, so listen intently and follow the advice.

Finally, be wary of the veterinarian who does not seem to care for your species or breed of pet. They are human and come to their practice with preconceived perceptions regarding different kinds of animals. Most good veterinarians can overcome this prejudice and be quite capable with individual animals. Some cannot. If yours seems to dislike your pet because of her species or breed and it influences the relationship, find another veterinarian.

Your veterinarian will share more information regarding your pet's health concerns when he or she discovers your intense concern with the well-being of your animal companion. This gives you more knowledge for care, treatment, and future problems. Don't be afraid to ask questions and launch a lifetime of learning.

THE RELATIONSHIP BETWEEN YOUR VETERINARIAN AND PET

You found the veterinary clinic you like best, you like the facilities, you like the staff, and you like the doctor. Now you must see how your veterinarian and pet relate to one another.

Most creatures are nervous and a bit uptight when they go to the clinic. There are many strange smells, sights, sounds, and possibly bad associations. Even in this uneasy setting, your pet and your veterinarian should get along. Some may hit it off immediately.

The veterinarian should talk gently and soothingly to your animal — not that there has to be cooing or gooing — there should be friendly tones and gentle but firm handling. If your animal doesn't react positively, you still may not need to worry; the tenseness of the situation may be causing it. If your pet is usually a kind and friendly animal and she is being obstinate with this doctor, there may be a personality conflict.

Even if you can find no reason for your pet to dislike your veterinarian of choice, she may. If everything else about the clinic is satisfactory and you feel like the doctor is doing everything possible to build a good relationship, then continue. Even difficult relationships may blossom with the efforts of a caring veterinarian.

All in all, you should feel comfortable with your veterinarian. You should be able to communicate easily and develop a trusting relationship.

A VISIT TO THE VETERINARIAN

A visit to the veterinarian can be a stressful time for you as well as your pet, even if the appointment is for routine care. The animals are usually tense, and you are usually anxious.

What if my dog jumps on someone? Will they think I can't control her? I didn't comb my cat in the last couple of days and she has a couple of knots on her belly; will they think I don't care? I need to trim my bird's nails and didn't have time; will they think I can't take care of my own pet? Even during low-key, run-of-the-mill appointments, these fears can make you anxious. When you are anxious, it only makes your animals more tense, so be prepared and be organized.

If you have a multi-animal household, you may be tempted to take several animals to the clinic at once. Ask if this will save you time or money. I prefer taking one animal at a time. It is less chaotic, and my veterinarian and I can concentrate fully on the health of my companion. Bringing in multiple animals makes it more difficult to concentrate and the appointment more hurried.

It is your responsibility to get in contact with your vet's office as soon as you sense your pet is ill. Waiting to call and then realizing during the middle of the night or on the weekend that you are dealing with a major emergency is unfair.

Treating your pet yourself for long periods without consulting your veterinarian is extremely careless. When you can do no more and you fear your pet may die, you call for help, expecting your veterinarian to bring a pet back from the edge of death, which is irresponsible and unfair. It is vital to contact the veterinarian as soon as you suspect that something is out of the ordinary with your beloved animal companion.

The Appointment

When you call the office, give the front desk staff information regarding the behavior and physical condition of your pet. When they ask you questions, be prepared to answer as accurately as possible. This shouldn't be difficult if you are observant and have been taking notes. The staff will then make an

WHEN TO CALL THE VET

Knowing when to call your veterinarian can make all the difference in the outcome of an illness or injury. Acting quickly if you suspect an emergency situation decides the life or death of your pet. It is better to err on the side of caution if you are deciding on whether to call or not. Here are some tips:

- As soon as you suspect a problem, begin acute observation and take notes in your record book.
- If you can, see the same veterinarian each time. This gives the doctor a chance to get to know your animal.
- Know the signs of illness in advance. Purchase a good health guide on each species that uses language you can understand. Find a book that is well designed so that you can find the information you need quickly and easily. Read it and know the symptoms that may be present in your pet.
- Remember that you know your animal companion best and if things just "don't seem right," make an appointment with your veterinarian for a checkup. You may have sensed something that didn't have exact physical manifestations or you may have missed the symptoms.

CALL YOUR VETERINARIAN IF YOU NOTICE THESE SIGNS:

coughing
runny nose
runny eyes
fever
change in appetite
lethargy
diarrhea
bloody stool or urine
bloody vomit
vomiting
enlarged joints
head shaking
walking in circles
staggering
convulsions
jerking motions
shortness of breath
unusual posture
confusion
rapid and weak pulse
straining to urinate
swelling of eyes
excessively bloodshot eyes
pale or bleeding gums

sneezing
any swelling, lumps, or bumps on body
fur loss
parasite infestation
weight loss or gain
accidents (repeated mistakes in the house)
foul odor from nose, mouth, or ears
bleeding from anywhere on the body
change in urine (odor, frequency, color, amount)
sudden change in water intake
unexplained change in behavior or physical appearance

Special Considerations for Birds
Be aware of any symptoms mentioned above, as well as the following:

change in droppings
feathers that are not replaced by new growth
new feathers that look unusual
consistently ruffled feathers
falling off perch more than once
tail bobbing
droopy wings
not talking or vocalizing
soiled vent

appointment and inform you on how to proceed. If they ask you to bring samples into the office, completely understand their directions and follow the procedures exactly, writing everything down. Plan enough time to arrive at your appointment promptly.

A carrier is the best way to travel, and it keeps your pet safe while in the waiting room of the clinic. If your dog is too large to travel in a carrier, bring her to the office on a leash. When traveling in a vehicle to the veterinarian, use the same cautionary advice offered in chapter 5 regarding travel with your pet.

Talk soothingly to your animal, reassuring her during your trip. Keep the music low and relaxing. Make the ride as comfortable as possible, especially if she is ill or injured. Your emotions are reflected in your pet's attitude, so stay calm and loving.

When you are at the clinic and waiting for your appointment, keep your pet confined in the security of the carrier. Even if she is usually relaxed, she may become nervous or excitable at the clinic. Another animal could be brought in who may not be so friendly or may be sick. It is safest for everyone, but especially your pet, if you keep her confined.

Bring with you any requested samples. Also bring in your record book and any other notes or questions regarding your concerns and observations. Do not assume you will remember these things once you get to the clinic. The anxiety of the appointment can make even the most gifted memory have lapses.

The Exam

During the examination, you will be asked questions regarding your animal friend. Answer each question honestly and thoroughly. If you think of a question, you may want to jot it down to ask at the end of the examination; refrain from asking at this point. If your visit is an emergency, this is even more significant. The doctor needs to concentrate on diagnosing your companion's health and condition and will fully explain the results of the examination when finished. You will be offered an opportunity to ask questions afterward.

Your veterinarian will outline a course of action or make suggestions regarding treatment or preventative care procedures. Each of your questions should

have been answered clearly. It is extremely valuable to write down the information as it is discussed with you. If there is something you don't understand, don't be too embarrassed to ask for an explanation. Your animal's health is on the line; no question is silly. The only silly question is the one not asked.

You may need to make follow-up calls if you have an important question regarding the initial treatment procedures or if you feel that there is a matter of concern regarding the outcome of the treatment. Remember, your veterinarian is a caring but very busy individual, and time is valuable. If you have a question that you forgot to ask but it is only a matter of curiosity, then keep the question in your record book for your next appointment. If you have many animals sharing your home, you will find yourself at the clinic soon enough.

Getting a Second Opinion

If you feel that you would like a second opinion on the recommended treatment or course of action, say so. Sneaking around behind your veterinarian's back will get you nowhere. The second veterinarian you consult will have the benefit of access to your pet's records if you are open and honest with everyone. Diagnostic tests and reports performed by the first veterinarian will be available, and you will not need to have these procedures repeated, costing you time, hassle, money, and possibly the health of your animal.

PET HEALTH INSURANCE

Veterinary science has made incredible advances. Using many of the technologies developed for use on humans, veterinarians can now diagnose and treat more conditions in your beloved pets. Organ transplants, CAT scans, open-heart surgery, and a number of cancer therapies are not limited to humans, and your animal friends can enjoy the benefits of such technologies. Currently, much research involving genetics, pharmaceutical treatments, and other areas specializing in animals are being perfected.

With this advance in veterinary science comes a price — a high price in many situations. Animal lovers are willing to spend what it takes to keep their pets healthy. However, this is getting more difficult.

Enter the insurance industry. Insurance companies are now offering animal caretakers the opportunity to buy health policies for their animals. This gives people the option of getting treatment for their pets when they may not otherwise be able to afford it. Some treatments can run into the thousands of dollars. Would it be wise to get an insurance policy on your animal family members? Maybe, but you have to do your homework.

Ask your veterinarian for information. You can discuss what insurance companies have been used by his or her clients and how beneficial those companies were to the families involved.

Stability

Insurance companies that sell health insurance policies to pet guardians are a business. Like any business, there is risk. While working out the system of this new kind of insurance, many companies have disappeared; find a company that has stability. The company you choose should have been in the industry for a number of years. Find a company with good backing that can weather the financial highs and lows.

The insurance industry is regulated by each state through the state's Department of Insurance. Check with this government department regarding the insurance company you are considering. Also check with the Better Business Bureau for any complaints against the company.

Policies

Carefully examine the policy you are being offered to be sure it matches your needs. Most policies have many exclusions. Most genetic defects, such as hip dysplasia, are excluded, as is routine preventative care, such as vaccinations, spaying, and neutering. Check each company; you may be able to find one that covers all the conditions that you would like covered. As in choosing health insurance for your human family, weigh the pros and cons of each one to find the one best suited to your needs.

Some insurance companies offer a money-back trial period, which may work for you if you are uncertain about the benefits of insurance in general or the company in particular.

Cost

The price of these insurance policies is generally very reasonable. Most have yearly premiums, and some of the HMO-style companies offer prepaid options. Many offer multiple animal discounts. Some allow you to claim all your insured pets for one deductible, but you may still have to pay a premium on each pet. You should be able to find a policy that fits your budget.

Summary

Is pet health insurance the way to go? Maybe, maybe not. In other countries, it is a stable, profitable business offering peace of mind to many animal caretakers. The overseas policies generally cover more and are more reliable. Companies in the United States have some catching up to do. Some are no more than a ripoff; others can offer trustworthy assistance in trying times. Do your research and be cautious because you may find that pet health insurance is right for your animal kingdom.

There is a strong possibility that your pet will eventually suffer a serious illness or become injured. The comfort of knowing that the size of your bank balance will not determine the course of action you take is invaluable. A sizable savings account or insurance policy will lift this heavy burden, and you and your veterinarian will be able to concentrate on getting your pet healthy and back home where she belongs.

Common household dangers

Your home is your sanctuary. You feel safe and secure and enjoy a level of comfort you receive nowhere else. Conversely, it is also one of the most dangerous places for you and your animal companions. Household accidents are prevalent, and poisonous chemicals fill your home.

It doesn't have to be this way. With a careful inspection of your surroundings, you can take measures to prevent accidents. With a change of habits and new, safer ways of cleaning and controlling pests, you can make your home safer.

Your animals have smaller respiratory systems than you do, and they are more susceptible to many of the dangers in your home. They are closer to the ground and they also sleep on carpets that have been collecting pollutants that you bring in on your feet from outdoors and those from inside that settle to the carpet fibers.

Even though you are affected by pollutants and environmental hazards, you don't feel the effects as they are happening, so often they are ignored. However, these same pollutants and hazards affect your pets in more quick and obvious ways. Your creatures absorb poisons via the yard or floors and through their skin. They also lick the residue of environmental pollution as they groom themselves.

You can help protect your animals from these hazards by choosing less dangerous products at every opportunity and thoroughly cleaning up any chemical spills. Good grooming habits also help keep residue off of your animal's fur and skin.

Is your water safe to drink? Although this cat is just enjoying a cool resting place, you wouldn't want her to drink water that has the potential to make her sick.

On very smoggy days, keep your pets indoors. When building kennels or arranging dog houses, avoid placing them near the road or driveway. When you take your dog outside for exercise, choose a lesser traveled road with the least amount of traffic possible. Don't let your dog ride in the back of a pickup truck where the exhaust is very thick.

If you rent or lease, arrange with the manager ahead of time and have it in writing that you are to be notified in advance if they will be painting, spraying the grounds, or using any chemicals. Alert a new manager to your arrangement; don't rely on the new manager to read each rental agreement.

IS YOUR WATER SAFE TO DRINK?

How do you know if your water is safe to drink? Every water supply has a collection of the pesticides, chemicals, waste, and pollutants that are dumped into the earth. It is also the warehouse for many of nature's products. No water is absolutely "pure"; what you hope for is water that is the least dangerous to you and your pets.

WHAT'S IN YOUR WATER?

Getting your water tested is the first step in finding out if it is safe. If your water supply comes from a private well, this may be more difficult because many water testing companies will not test water on a single sample. Call your local city water district and ask them to recommend a testing facility in your area. If you are on a municipal water source, you can get the annual quality report from your local city hall. If they do not have an annual quality report, ask for their most recent test.

Once you get the report, you will know how safe your water is to drink. All water has microorganisms, minerals, gases, and dust particles. You just need to know if your water falls into the safety guidelines for health.

Some harmful microorganisms, such as giardia, can be found in munincipal water sources. You may find toxic minerals and gases in your water, such as arsenic, asbestos, copper, mercury, lead, chlorine, and fluoride. Some municipal supplies add chlorine to kill bacteria and fluoride for children's teeth. Both of these may be added in excess, and excesses are dangerous. If you have hard water, sodium chloride (salt) may be added to soften the water, but high levels of sodium chloride are also dangerous.

Remember, the damage to your pets is higher because of their more compact body systems. But don't panic when you get your water test results. Every water source in the world contains traces of all the above-mentioned pollutants. Just be concerned with high levels, which is where the danger lies.

Now What?

So you have water that is dangerous or at least not as safe as you would like it to be. Now what can you do? A number of solutions are open to you. The route you take depends on your individual situation, what dangers are present in your water, how much work you want to put into it, and how much money you are willing to spend.

• **Water Purification Systems** — If you are going to be living in your present home for at least a couple more years, you may want to invest in a water purification system. This solution is a larger investment initially, but over a period of time will cost less than bottled water. You won't have to lug bottles home, but you will have to perform some routine maintenance.

If your main concern is microorganisms or minerals, you can use a filtering system, which is quick. The sediments from organisms and minerals are trapped in a carbon filter. Follow the guidelines exactly, and change the filter when required. If you are lax in your upkeep, your water will soon be no better than it was before you began using the filter. Some filters can even add more pollution to your water; for example, carbon filters have been blamed for adding carbon to the water.

Ask around and find out if anyone else you know is using this kind of system, and then do your own checking. Carefully read the literature on the system you are considering. Ask for a trial period to be sure you are happy with the results.

If metals such as lead are your main difficulty,

then a filtering system will not work. The best solution may be investing in a reverse osmosis system, which is complicated and may need to be installed by a professional. It is slow and wastes quite a bit of water. A reverse osmosis system will not eliminate radon or chlorine.

The safest supply of water is distilled. This is a very slow and expensive process; it takes five to six hours to get one gallon of water. The advantage is that it gets most of the toxins out of the water. See the manufacturer's information to be certain that the system removes the pollutant that you are concerned about.

The latest purification system uses ultraviolet light to kill microorganisms and bacteria.

When all else fails, boil the water before using it. Boiling only removes microorganisms, not metals. Do not use aluminum pans to boil the water; choose stainless steel, ceramic, or glass. Only boil what you will use in a short period.

• **Bottled Water** — If you don't want to add a water purification system or if your water crisis is a temporary one, then you may consider bottled water. Few laws govern bottled waters and some are no better or worse than your water supply. Bottled water also contributes to more garbage in landfills.

Water marked "drinking" is the best source. If you are unable to find drinking water, look for "distilled" or "purified." Avoid any water that claims to be from a natural source. This source may have water that is more polluted than yours.

Also beware of the sodium content. Check the label and make sure that the water you are looking at contains 140 milligrams or less per eight-ounce serving. Buy your bottled water from a popular source so that the water hasn't been sitting on the shelf too long and is as fresh as possible.

Purchasing water from water vending machines is also a solution. The machines use municipal water, so check the safety of this water first. The vending machine should have a certification on it from the local health board.

Water specialty stores and delivery services also offer water for home use. Ask questions regarding the safety of this water. It depends on the source, and you want to know what is in the water. Remember, you are looking for a high-quality water supply that is safer than your tap water.

• **Making the Change** — Some animals are very picky about their water. You may have to transition your animals by using a half-and-half mix and then increase the percentage a bit at a time. Some animals do not like the dull taste of purified water. Experiment with different bottled waters to find one that they like.

COMMON HAZARDS

Common household hazards and dangers are described below. Read the sections and mark off each item after you have physically checked each hazard in your home. Routinely, perhaps once a month, make a survey of the house to ensure that nothing has become a danger. If there is a precaution you tend to forget, such as checking the dryer before closing it, hanging a reminder note helps it becomes habit.

Be watchful and cautious and be aware of your surroundings. Catch any trouble as it develops, and repair anything that needs to be repaired. Watch your pets as if they were small children.

EVERY HOUSEHOLD WITH A PET SHOULD HAVE THESE ITEMS
• Fire alarm
• Fire extinguisher
• First-aid book for each species
• First-aid kit
• Styptic powder
• Record book

Carbon Monoxide

This gas is especially dangerous in the winter months when your house is closed up and there is less ventilation. Carbon monoxide poisoning can cause convulsions in pets and humans. Leaks come from the heating system, pilot lights, paint fumes,

formaldehyde, insulation, and gas leaks. If your garage is attached to your home, you should back out before warming up your engine. Even if the door to your home is closed, the fumes can slip through and poison the inside air.

Although it may be a cold day, it is beneficial to open the window slightly, even for a couple of hours, to let fresh air pass through your house. If you have a gas stovetop, you should turn on the cooking fan and open a window in the kitchen while cooking. Make sure all vents to chimneys, dryer, or stovetops work efficiently.

These precautions are extremely important in a new home. Carbon monoxide detectors are inexpensive and available at hardware, discount, and some department stores.

Carpet

Commonly referred to as new-carpet syndrome, this series of troubles can occur even with older carpet. Symptoms include headaches, sinus problems, eye irritation, difficult breathing, fatigue, convulsions, memory loss, sporadic muscle pain, tremors, respiratory system failure, lymph node enlargement, and skin rashes. These symptoms may be experienced by both humans and pets. Your smaller animal friends are at the most danger, and fatalities are not uncommon.

The problem seems to stem from the carpet backing, not the carpet itself. If you have new carpet installed, you should air your home thoroughly for two weeks before you or any animals reside there. Sometimes this is not enough and over the years, carpet may present problems. At this time research has not been able to shed much light on which fumes cause damage and how they do it. There is much controversy surrounding this issue.

Do you really want to add carpet? Even if the carpet you choose emits no harmful fumes, you should consider the other problems with carpet.

Carpet is the most fertile breeding ground for fleas. It is like a sponge, soaking in and retaining all of the chemicals, dirt, pesticides, and everything else you step in outside and anything you use inside. It is almost impossible to keep carpet clean. Most environmentally concerned organizations suggest eliminating carpet from homes.

Ceiling Fans

Ceiling fans can be a hazard for birds who are allowed to fly throughout the house. Even if you keep your bird's wings clipped, they may grow back before you know it. Keep ceiling fans off when your bird is out of her cage.

Chemicals

This section covers many different types of chemicals. Some of them you may not have even thought of as dangerous, while others are more obvious. A partial list of some of the poisons you should keep from your pets is presented here.

As a general rule, all chemicals should be stored in an area that is inaccessible to your pets. Keep these toxins locked in cabinets or stored in high cabinets or containers with secure-fitting lids.

Remember, your pet does not always have to ingest these chemicals to be poisoned by them. Some of the chemicals expel fumes that can be harmful, and some are absorbed through the skin or in a residue that is cleaned off by the mouth of your animals. Even cleaners you use on the floor can eventually affect the health of your pets.

If you suspect your pet has been poisoned, you can contact the National Animal Poison Control Center (NAPCC), which has been in existence since 1978. The NAPCC is operated by the University of Illinois at Urbana–Champaign College of Veterinary Medicine. It is answered by veterinarians and board-certified veterinary toxicologists. You have two options of paying for this service. You can dial their 900 number; you will be charged $20.00 for the first five minutes and $2.95 every minute thereafter. Or you can dial their 800 number and charge a $30.00 fee to your Visa, MasterCard, Discover, or American Express card. If you call the 800 number, you will get free follow-up service. Place these phone numbers in your record book for easy access.

NAPCC
1-900-680-0000
1-800-548-2423

DANGEROUS CHEMICALS

Acetaminophen *(such as Tylenol)*
Aerosols (use pump sprays)
Antifreeze
Art and photo supplies
Auto products *(carburetor cleaner, brake fluid, gasoline, oil)*
Bleach
Bug spray
Chlorine
Cleaners
Cosmetics
Deodorizers
Detergents
Disinfectants
Drain cleaner
Dye
Fertilizers
Flea bombs
Flea collars
Fungicides
Glue
Hair spray
Kerosene
Laxatives
Mothballs
Oven cleaner
Paint
Perfume
Permanent wave solution
Pesticides
Rodent Poison
Rubbing Alcohol
Self-cleaning oven products
Shoe polish
Snail bait
Solvents
Suntan lotion
Toilet cleaning products *(continuous cleaners)*
Toiletries

**Anything that says
"Keep Out of Reach of Children"**
(This is not a complete list. Be cautious of any source of fumes.)

Chocolate

You may have a love affair with chocolate, but chocolate is toxic to your animal friends. Chocolate contains theobromine, which is poisonous to animals. Dogs, cats, birds, and rabbits can all get very sick from eating chocolate, even small amounts.

Don't leave food containing chocolate or chocolate candies out on a table or counter. Resist the temptation to share your special treat with your furry or feathered friend. Enjoy the whole thing yourself.

Cigarettes

You've already heard the concern over secondhand smoke. If it is that dangerous to people, imagine the poor respiratory systems of your smaller and more sensitive animals.

Also be cautious of lit cigarettes and matches. The matches can be toxic if ingested, and burning cigarettes can cause burns or fall to the ground or onto furniture and cause a fire. An animal can get nicotine poisoning from licking or playing with cigarettes.

Stop smoking. If you can't or don't want to stop, don't smoke in the house. It's that simple.

Coins

Your pets are in danger of any small items that can be swallowed and cause a blockage or problem in the digestive track. Coins are a high risk because they are often left within reach of animals. Pennies are zinc with copper overlay and will poison your pets if swallowed.

Cooking

With the irresistible smells of a cook in action, your animals may lose their self-control. The burners on the stovetop can burn animal feet. Licking utensils to get the savory juices of your food can cut mouths if they are knives, peelers, or blades to food processors. Food cooking in open pots can cause burns on curious animals, and birds who fly into cooking food will lose their lives. Tripping over an animal while carrying hot food is a common danger, so keep your pets out of the kitchen while you are cooking.

Doors

It is important to be in the habit of closing doors behind you. Your pets could get into trouble fairly quickly if you don't know that they escaped to the outdoors. Birds have been known to fly out open doors.

If you have children who aren't reliable door closers or you yourself have a habit of leaving them open, attach springs that close the door automatically as a safety measure.

Doors to cabinets, closets, and drawers could accidentally be closed after a curious pet has ventured in. Depending on where the entrapment occurs, this could be a serious problem.

All those who live with an animal must learn to look before they close any door. Doors that could cause serious trouble are on refrigerators, ovens, washing machines, dryers, dishwashers, microwave ovens, and other appliances. File cabinets with drawers left open can seem inviting, but the weight of a heavy animal can send the whole thing crashing to the floor.

Check first, then close.

Electrical Outlets

Curious pets can sustain electrical shocks through outlets. Another danger is an outlet close to a bird or rabbit cage. Either spilled water or rabbit urine can cause electrical arcs and may start a fire. Cover the outlets with plastic covers.

Electrical Wires

Electrical wires are often chewed by pets. All the pets mentioned in this book have the potential to be wire chewers. Electrical shocks can be fatal.

You can use plastic tubing on wires to keep them from your pets. Buy some clear plastic tubing at hardware or aquarium shops, slice it lengthwise, and then tuck the wires into the plastic. You can also purchase pre-slit black plastic tubing. If you want to invest more time and money and make your job more permanent, you can encase the wires in decorative wood grained or gold wire concealers. You can also hide the wires under carpet or behind furniture, although very curious and determined animals can find them there.

Electromagnetic Fields

Another environmentally controversial subject but one you may want to look into for your own comfort is electromagnetic field (EMF) danger. Everything that is powered by electricity has EMFs to some degree. The ones that have a high output of EMFs are being blamed as the culprits of a series of symptoms.

You can use caution by not placing cages or pet beds within a three-foot radius of high EMF output appliances, such as microwave ovens, radios, electrical clocks, or televisions. Try not to use a blowdryer on your pet too often because it has a high EMF output. Encourage your pet to keep away from the objects by giving your pet a better place to be.

Research this subject to get a clearer picture for yourself. If you want to find out the level of EMFs in your home, you can easily have them tested.

Fireplaces

The comforting picture of a dog sleeping by the fireplace can warm an animal lover's heart. Some may add feline, long-eared, and feathery friends.

The warmth and glow of a fireplace are like magnets on cold, blustery days and nights, so make sure that it is safe for your pets and yourself. Before each winter, have your flue checked and cleaned if necessary. To keep heat-seeking or curious pets out and hot coals in, make sure that you have a tight-fitting, secure screen. Keep any tools in a solid stand, and don't store wood indoors that could be poisonous to your pets. Never leave a fire unattended with pets in the house.

Garbage

The garbage can is like a candy store to your pets. Unfortunately, there are too many things that they could find in it that can be harmful.

You certainly don't want an overweight pet or one that is on a restricted diet to get into all the food goodies in the garbage. You also don't want your pets getting sick eating spoiled food. Many things that your animals may find in the garbage can be harmful, such as chocolate, potato eyes, onions, and chicken, pork, or fish bones.

Nonfood items can also be very dangerous: broken glass, jagged metal, and any of the other items mentioned in this section on hazards.

Keep your garbage in a strong, heavy trash can with a lid that can be locked down or difficult for your pet to get into. Store your trash under the sink or in a pantry where you can keep the door closed.

Holiday Dangers

The biggest danger to your pets during the holiday season is that in the hubbub of activity you forget to reassure them and give them the same quality care and attention that they are accustomed to.

Pay attention to the added hazards of decorations. If you have a Christmas tree and you have pets, take extra precautions. Keep your tree standing by securing it to the wall or ceiling with fishing line and eye hooks. Many a tree has fallen on rough-housing animals.

Be wary of glass ornaments that can break and ceramic ornaments that may contain lead. Sprayed "snow" is dangerous if ingested. The water keeping the tree green and any needles that fall to the ground can be toxic, so keep the water covered and vacuum frequently.

The extra electrical cords should be covered so that they won't be chewed through. Wire hooks used to hang the ornaments can also be a hazard. They could get stuck in paws or mouths. You can use ribbon to hang ornaments, which also looks beautiful. Watch for string, yarn, tinsel, garlands, and popcorn strands, which pets may eat.

Keep all candles out of reach.

Lead Poisoning

Lead poisoning is a problem that does not seem to be disappearing fast enough. Symptoms include convulsions, hyperactivity, chronic fatigue, colic, anemia, psychosis, high blood pressure, and mental retardation.

Some potential sources of lead are common in your household: auto exhaust, batteries, curtain weights, fishing weights, and lead-based paint. The bells and weights inside pet toys frequently contain lead. Many homes have lead water pipes, which poisons the water with lead. It is difficult and expensive to filter lead out of your water source. Leave the water running thirty to sixty seconds; use this water to wash dishes; then fill water bowls.

Cans also contain lead. Never leave an opened can of cat or dog food sitting with leftover food in it. Empty the food you don't use into another container to store it. If you can find lead-free cans, use that brand. One six-ounce can of cat food can contain 1.19 milligrams of lead. When you consider that 0.3 milligrams is considered toxic to small children, you can understand the concern.

Medicine

Prescription and nonprescription drugs should be kept away from your pets. Even seemingly innocent drugs, such as vitamins and fluoride tablets, can be fatal to animals. All these drugs should be kept in a secure area. After taking medication, be sure that you securely replace the lid and put the bottle back in a safe spot.

Do not give any medication to your pet without consulting your veterinarian. Many harmless human medications, such as aspirin, can be harmful or fatal to animals.

Nonstick Cookware

The answer to many a dieter's dreams is also the cause of much grief to bird owners. When nonstick cookware is heated to high temperatures, it releases polytetrafluoroethylene gas that can be instantly fatal to even large parrots. Remember the canary in the coal mine?

It used to be believed that the temperature had to be very high (530 degrees or higher), but more cases are being documented where the temperature of the cookware was considered well within the safety limit.

Nonstick surfaces can be found on pots and pans, stovetop burner rings, waffle irons, and clothes irons — and now it can even be found on the clothes themselves. Although there are no warning labels yet, many distressed bird owners are working to get the warning out to the public.

If it can be instantly fatal to your birds to use nonstick cookware, it must surely be detrimental to your other pets and to you. If you must, use the cookware with great care, making sure to use vent fans and open windows. I believe there will be more information on this as the public becomes more aware.

Plastic Bags

Just like children, animals find the sound and fun value of plastic bags intriguing. And just like children, animals can suffocate. If the bags are the kind with the handle holes, the animal may even choke herself.

Poisonous Plants

Plants are a wonderful way to clean the air in your environment; they act like a sponge, soaking up many toxins in your home and outside. The trade-off is that your pets may chew or eat the plants that you have in your home and yard. This is a natural activity for your animals, and there is no way to guarantee that you can keep them from ingesting a plant that could be harmful.

You can spray your plants with products that make the plants taste bad, but this does not always work, and you must keep up on the task. The best way to protect your animals is to keep only plants that are not harmful or keep the ones that are poisonous out of reach.

The following is a list of some plants that can be harmful. It is not a complete list, and some are more dangerous than others. This list should be constantly updated to include new plants (or their toxic component) or delete ones that have been proven to cause no harm. If you have any questions regarding the safety of a plant, you can call your veterinarian or contact the NAPCC or the American Humane Association.

Alocasia
 (elephant ear)
Amaryllis
Avocado
Azalea
Bird-of-paradise
Black locust
Boxwood
Buttercup
Caladium
Calla lily
Castor oil
 (castor bean)
Cherry tree
Daffodil
Daphne
Delphinium
Dieffenbachia
Eggplant
 (not the fruit)
English ivy
Elderberry
Foxglove
Goldenchain tree
Hemlock
Holly (berry)
Horse Chestnut
Hyacinth
Hydrangea
Indian turnip
Iris
Jasmine
Jerusalem cherry
Juniper
Lantana
Larkspur
Laurel
Lily of the valley

Lobelia
Marijuana
Mistletoe
Mock orange
Monkshood
Morning glory
Mushrooms (wild)
Narcissus
Nightshade
Oleander
Peach (pit)
Philodendron
Pickerelweed
Poinsettia
Poison ivy
Poison oak
Privet
Rhododendron
Rhubarb
Snow-on-the-
 mountain
Star-of-Bethlehem
Sweet pea
Toadstool
Tobacco
Tulip
Virginia creeper
Wisteria
Yew

Pools and Spas

If you have taken the proper precautions to keep children and uninvited guests from falling victim to your pool or spa, then you have probably protected your pets as well.

The more barriers and levels of protection you use, the less likely an accident will occur. You can include fences, covers, surveillance equipment, and alarms. Teach your animals how to escape from the pool if they should fall in. Keep fresh water available at all times so that your animal companions don't rely on pool water for drinking. Remember to store the chemicals in a safe, restricted area in the manner suggested by the manufacturer.

Radon

Radon is a colorless, odorless gas that naturally results when uranium breaks down. The gas can seep through the earth below your home and fill your house or it can invade your water supply.

Radon is a dangerous gas, and excessive amounts are blamed for nearly 20,000 cases of cancer a year. Your pets with their smaller bodies are at risk. For your safety and the safety of your animals, have your home checked for radon.

Some areas have a larger concentration of radon. The only way for you to find out if your home is a potentially dangerous source for your human and animal family is to use a radon detector. There are two types of detectors. The charcoal canister detector takes two to seven days to get an accurate reading. The alpha track detector takes one month.

Once you have a reading, refer to the U.S. Environmental Protection Agency standards to determine which course of action to take. If you have an elevated reading, you need to take action immediately. Remove your pets from the home until you can take measures to lessen the radon. Seal cracks and holes in your basement and crawl space. You may need to have a qualified contractor implement a radon control plan.

If the level is not in the dangerous zone, then you can simply make it a practice to frequently open the windows and air out your home. Don't use ceiling fans; they can actually draw the gases into a home.

Sharp Objects

Sharp objects can get stuck in the feet of your pets if they are left on the floor. Small objects and broken glass can get stuck in paws and fester, and cause cutting, slicing, and poking. They can also get stuck on the lips and mouths of curious pets. Beware of needles, safety pins, fish hooks, screws, nails, thumbtacks, staples, and broken glass.

Staircases

Obviously, falls are a concern, but banisters also pose a threat. Pets can get their heads stuck between the banisters. This is especially common with puppies. If you are having this problem or if you are worried about other smaller animals falling through the banisters and off of the side of the stairs, you can connect a mesh net or fabric along the inside of the banister.

Strings and Yarn

Anything that is long and thin can be a danger. Once cats and rabbits start swallowing a long piece of string or yarn they will be unable to stop. This can cause digestive problems, and surgery may be required to remove the item. These items may also tangle in the intestines, which is very serious.

If your pet does swallow something like this, don't attempt to pull it out. Call your veterinarian immediately. Animals can also get tangled in these objects, cut off circulation in appendages, and even suffocate themselves if they get them wrapped around their throat. Check toys for any long pieces attached.

Watch for string, yarn, thread, ribbon, garland, pantyhose, balloons, and rubber bands. Also watch for miniblind cords. The loop of these cords should be cut so that there is not one continuous loop. These can be very dangerous.

Use your imagination when checking your house for these long, thin dangers. Think like a curious, playful animal. Does it look fun? Can it be a danger?

Sun

Animals with light pigmented skin can get sunburned. If your pet is outside enjoying the sun, you can apply a children's SPF 15 (sun protection factor) or higher sunscreen on her sensitive areas, such as her nose.

The same application requirements for humans should be followed for your pet. Rub in a generous amount of sunscreen thirty minutes before going into the sun. Reapply every two hours or if your pet goes for a swim.

Spray sunscreen is now available for pets. It is convenient for large body areas but should not be sprayed on your animal's face. You are also going to pay more for special sunscreen.

Tablecloths and Appliances with Cords

Appliance cords are especially pleasing to cats and rabbits as play items and to birds as something to chew. Dogs can get tangled up in the cord or the end of a tablecloth and pull everything down to the floor and on themselves.

While laying on my feet, my dog woke up from her nap, panicked, got tangled in the sewing machine cord, pulled the entire thing to the floor, and dragged it a couple of feet. Thankfully, she was okay. She could have easily been injured by the cord or machine, and I could have been hurt. Unfortunately, the machine took a beating and had to be replaced. It proved to me that even if I was right there, not even inches away, I could not prevent such an accident. Keep the cords out of the way of your pets.

Your pet could be injured or burned by falling appliances and could even become tangled in the cord itself and suffocate or cut off her circulation.

Toilets

Many pets have the habit of drinking water out of toilets. Supply your pet with plenty of fresh water in well-rinsed bowls and keep the toilet lid down. You may have to hang a sign for guests that visit your home if you find that it becomes a problem. Animals can easily fall into toilets and drown. Flying birds are at particular risk of this danger. In addition, continuous toilet cleaning products are poisonous if your animals drink the water in the toilet.

Toys

Although many toys are manufactured with the safety of your pets in mind, many others on the market can be very dangerous for the animals they were meant to entertain.

Small plastic toys can be broken into pieces by even the most seemingly gentle pet. These pieces can then be swallowed and cause choking and digestion problems. Especially check toys that you offer to birds because they are very destructive and strong. Also check toys for cats and rabbits because they are often not made with the strength or curiosity of these animals in mind. Small eyes and decorative objects can easily fall off during play and be consumed.

Look for strong, well-made toys that are designed for the animal for which it is intended. The problem in a multi-animal household, like that in a household with children of different ages, is that a toy intended for one pet may be played with by another. The small rubber ball that is perfect for your cat may become lodged in the throat of your dog. These are precautions that you will have to keep in mind when toy shopping.

You can buy toys for one animal in particular and then let the pet enjoy them during your playtime together. This way you can supervise the action and put the toy away after playtime is over.

If you give your pet toys that are edible or retain bacteria, such as fabric and wood toys, check the toys' condition regularly and dispose of them after they have been played with for awhile.

Windows

Open windows or ones with loose screens are very dangerous, especially to cats that enjoy viewing the world from a warm, sunlit window. If your window is on the second floor, a fall could kill your pet. You may think that this couldn't happen, but one small urge to bat at a passing butterfly and your pet could easily fall out. Screens may not be safe enough if they are not strong and secure. Pets may escape and become injured.

Having your dog around to keep you company while you work on the car may be good for you but could be disastrous for your pet. Just a few licks of antifreeze could make this dog very sick.

SENSORY INPUT

Your Pets and Their Sensory Input

Remember that your pets are more reactive to sensory input than you are. They have keener eyesight, smell, hearing, and touch.

Be kind by not wearing too much perfume or perfumed products, which will irritate sensitive noses.

You don't need to yell every command at your dogs; they have four to five times better hearing than humans do. If your dogs can hear a marshmallow drop on the carpet (my dog, Retta, comes running from anywhere in the house when she hears people eating in the living room, no matter how sneaky we try to be), then they don't need you to yell "sit" when you are only two feet away.

Keep this sensitivity in mind when you are interacting with your animals.

Flea control

If you have a dog or cat, sooner or later you will have fleas. Fleas are a problem especially in homes with many pets; their numbers multiply and the work becomes more time-consuming. Very few areas are not affected by this hardy pest. Once a flea population has been established, you will have quite a battle to gain control once again.

THE PROBLEM WITH FLEAS

Fleas are nasty little troublemakers; they feed on any warm-blooded creature. Most animals and people have an allergic reaction to some degree. If an animal is especially allergic, the scratching, chewing, and constant irritation produces a raw spot that often leads to a secondary infection. If your animal swallows a flea or its waste products while grooming, she can get worms. If you have a flea problem, you also need to take preventative measures against worms.

Fleas depress the immune system, thereby making your pets susceptible to other illnesses. Some heavily infested animals, especially young or physically compromised, have even died from fleas and secondary problems caused by an infestation.

NO MATTER WHAT YOU DO

Even if you are determined and diligent about your flea control plan of attack, you will find an occasional flea or the evidence of one particularly during the heavy infestation periods of the year.

The fact is that even if you are thorough and dedicated, your neighbors may be less so. No matter how clean your home and yard, no matter how healthy and well cared for your animals, some areas of the country are so heavily flea infested that it is a constant war. This is why it is so important to keep up with a flea abatement program.

SEE YOUR VETERINARIAN

If your pet shows signs of skin irritation or a skin condition of any kind and you suspect pests are to blame, see your veterinarian. You can be sure about what pest you are dealing with and have the input and suggestions from your veterinarian regarding a treatment program. If your animals are heavily infested with pests, they may be at risk of developing secondary problems due to a drain on the immune system. Your veterinarian will be sure your pets are in fighting condition.

PLAN OF ATTACK

The secret to the war on fleas is to act before the battle is too large and never let your guard down by waging attacks at regular intervals. Set up a program and stick to it. An effective flea-control plan includes the treatment of your pets themselves, the furnishings and carpeting inside your home, and your yards. If you fail to include one of these three areas, your efforts will be wasted.

Treat each of these areas simultaneously and then repeat the whole thing again in a few weeks. This is your initial attack on a flea infestation.

Once you have this treatment under control, repeat the whole process a couple of times a year, especially in early spring, before you notice any fleas. This may prove difficult because often fleas don't seem like a problem until they are a big problem. Once fleas are noticeable on your pet, then you have an infestation. Implementing this series of flea-control methods in the early spring enables you to control the flea population in your environment.

This is an extremely frustrating process. You can never let your guard down; you must be diligent about repeating the process in a couple of weeks and then again throughout the year. Why is repeating the program so important? The reproductive life of the flea is very fruitful. To better understand the reasoning behind the suggestions, it is important to understand the life cycle of the flea.

THE LIFE CYCLE OF THE FLEA

You find fleas on your pets or yourself because fleas need blood before they can lay their eggs. Fleas lay their eggs on the animal host, and the eggs then fall off into the environment. One female flea can lay two thousand eggs. Eggs survive in shaded areas such as carpet or under debris in your yard.

The eggs hatch in one to five days and become larvae, which feed on flea dirt. The larvae also feed on dust, dandruff, mold, and hair as well as flea "dirt" (those little brown specks that accompany fleas and are actually flea droppings). This flea dirt is recognizable when water hits it and it becomes a speck of blood. This flea dirt also falls off of the animal.

This is why it is so important to treat the area where your pet spends a great deal of her time. For example, if your cat sleeps on the window sill, it is essential to thoroughly treat the area where she jumps down; the shock of the landing jolts the eggs and flea dirt to the floor.

In ten to two hundred days the larvae spin a cocoon. This cocoon is often spun right into the fibers of your carpet. That is why vacuuming everyday is an effective flea control task on its own. These pupae bury themselves deep into the carpet and even into the backing and pad.

The pupae then hatch in another ten to two hundred days, depending on the environmental conditions and they become adult fleas. These adults find a host, your pet, and then begin the life cycle all over again.

The belief has been that only 5 to 10 percent of the flea population lives on your pet. The remainder of the population is in the egg, larvae, or pupae stage. Some researchers dispute this, saying a larger percentage of the flea population lives on your pet. Regardless, each stage of development needs to be controlled. This is why just one method of flea control will not work and treating once does little good. Getting rid of as many fleas as possible in their different life stages is optimum for gaining control.

Though there are methods of killing adult fleas, eggs, and larvae, there is not a way to kill the pupae, so it is necessary to repeat the process again in a few weeks after the initial treatment to get to these pupae that have emerged as adults. A double-whammy with a three-pronged attack (treating your pet, your home, and your yard) is the best way to stop an infestation.

FLEAS ON YOUR PET

The most common method of treating a flea problem is to treat the pet. This reaches the adult fleas, but remember that it is only a small percentage of the population.

A Strong Resistance

If your pet is healthy, she is less likely to get a heavy flea infestation and more likely to remain healthy while you treat an infestation. Keep your pet in good health by feeding her a high-quality diet (adequate protein has been credited with resistance to fleas) and receiving good veterinary care.

Grooming your pet can also help. A pet that has a squeaky-clean coat is less likely to be a "good" host. Remember, the flea also eats dust, dandruff, and hair and prefers dark, shady areas. If your pet has dirty, matted hair and unhealthy skin, she will be a flea's ideal home and restaurant. Keeping your pet well groomed helps make her less desirable.

Flea Combs

Grooming can also help by stirring up the fleas on your pet and then knocking them off. If you use a flea comb, you can also deliberately get some of the pests. When using a flea comb, dunk the comb in a bowl of hot water with a little detergent to drown the fleas.

Flea combs work easily on small or shorthaired animals. Large pets or those with thick or long hair are more difficult to flea comb. Give it a try and see if it works for you.

Bathing

Giving your animal companion a bath with a flea shampoo helps. Find a shampoo that is specially formulated for your pet; only use a kitten shampoo on a kitten and an adult dog shampoo on an adult dog. Choose a shampoo that is made from natural ingredients and one that contains a conditioner. See the discussion that follows regarding flea-control chemicals to better help you choose a gentle but effective flea-control shampoo. If you don't use a flea-control shampoo, you lose the residual effect but will still drown many fleas. If you are going to put your pet through a bath, you may as well use a shampoo with a conditioner to add the extra benefit of making the skin a bit softer and prevent it from drying.

When using shampoo on your pet, the directions usually suggest leaving it on for five to ten minutes. This can be quite a challenge for those animals that do not appreciate a bath. But the soap in the shampoo drowns the pests, so don't fret too much.

Dips

Dips can also be used. Dips are just that: a dip in a flea-killing chemical. Most dips use the insecticide Dursban. Dursban is long-lasting and considered a safer chemical than most. Weigh the advantages and disadvantages. A couple of soothing baths in an herbal or natural shampoo seems a bit more pleasant than a dip in an insecticide.

Also, when considering the use of a chemical on your animal, remember that they will lick off the residue while grooming and will ingest the chemical.

Sprays and Powders

If you are going to use a spray on your pets, choose one offering natural flea control. This type repels any new fleas, and most kill the fleas that are on your pet. Repeat the spraying at least three times a week and keep doing it regularly.

Another method of keeping fleas off your pets is using a dusting powder. Several good herbal flea powders are on the market. Find them through catalogs, high-quality pet stores, or health food stores. These have the added benefit of smelling pleasant rather than like chemicals.

With both the spray and the powder, be careful not to get the products in your companion's face. Sprinkle or spray them on your hand and then rub them into the facial area avoiding her eyes or nose. Always apply the chemicals at the neck first. If you start at the back end, the fleas will run to your animal's head. If your dog shakes while around your bird or your dog or cat spend much time around the cage, your bird could suffer.

The sprays and powders intended for cats are the only safe flea control to use on rabbits. Don't apply too much to your rabbit, and try to use a natural or herbal product.

Flea Collars

Unfortunately, flea collars are not effective. Fleas do tend to congregate around the neck of the animal, maybe because this is where the greatest supply of blood close to the surface can be found; however, the collar cannot control fleas on other parts of the pet's body. If you have a large dog, for instance, most fleas will just stay at her tail end. Flea collars that have an effect on fleas do so because they release strong chemicals into the nervous system of your pet. Other collars release poisonous vapors that with prolonged exposure are dangerous to both the pet wearing the collar and the people and other animals of the home. Many of the chemicals used by commercial collar manufacturers are the same chemicals that are used as nerve paralyzers developed by the government for use in the military as nerve gas. Do you want to use this on your pet?

Insect Development Inhibitors

Insect development inhibitors (IDIs), which are safe for dogs and cats, are carried in your pet's bloodstream and affect the flea only after it has bitten your pet. IDIs (as well as IGRs discussed later), which prevent eggs and larvae from developing, help control the flea population in your environment. IDIs are oral products given to your pets once a month. Dogs are given the dosage in pill form; cats in liquid form.

The adult flea must bite your animal companion in order to be affected by IDIs. This flea-control method may help you control the flea population but should be combined with other products. If your pet wanders or visits other places, IDIs may not be worth the expense. Discuss this product with your veterinarian.

IDIs offer no protection for flea bite allergies.

Safety and Efficiency

Never use a dip, shampoo, spray, or collar that has a warning against breathing the fumes or one that says to avoid contact with skin. Why would you want to put this on your animal companion, especially when there are many good products on the market that do not come with such strong chemicals and many that offer effective ways of controlling fleas on your pet.

So what are the safest ways to control the fleas that live on your animals?

- Healthy diet
- Healthy body
- Good grooming habits, including daily use of a flea comb, if appropriate
- Gentle but effective shampoo when needed and in early spring
- Powder or spray once a week

FLEAS IN YOUR HOME

Fleas in your household environment will have to be treated with as much diligence as the ones that are on your pet. Often it is easier to treat the pet because you feel bad about the animal's discomfort — which you are reminded of by the incessant scratching.

The fleas in the environment are usually comprised of fleas in the egg, larvae, and pupae stages. You don't see or feel the effects of these fleas — not yet anyway. So often it is easier to skip this part of the our treatment program or put less effort into it.

Vacuuming

The first step is to vacuum everything, including carpets, along the baseboards, places where the animals jump down from a resting spot, cracks and rough spots on wood floors, as well as the furniture. It has often been suggested to vacuum up some flea-killing powder so that any fleas that are sucked up will be killed, but if you have birds or rabbits, this practice can be dangerous. The dust created by vacuum exhaust makes your more sensitive pets sick. When the vacuuming is complete, throw the vacuum bag away.

Vacuuming kills many adults and eggs, so it is important to your overall program, but as previously mentioned is ineffective on the larvae. Steam cleaning is good for getting the larvae but will also stimulate eggs to hatch. If you have a large infestation, steam clean the carpets, but realize that you will have an outburst of new fleas in a couple of days. With your other methods of control in place, you will get these adults.

Mop and wax vinyl and tile floors and mop wooden floors thoroughly. While your sensitive animals are removed from the house, treat the area that you vacuumed with a flea-killing powder or spray.

Sprays and Powders

Sprays are good for getting to areas that need a highly concentrated effort. The sprays are also very effective because many of them kill the adult fleas and also contain an insect growth regulator, which will be discussed later. A carpet spray product made with a micro-encapsulated pyrethrin is relatively safe and long-lasting.

Powders are better on carpets and furniture because they can penetrate the fibers better than other methods. Like the powders used directly on your pets, use a powder for the environment that is based on natural or herbal substances.

The problem with both of these methods is the airborne fumes and particles. Remove your pets from the area being treated; this may be a good day for sunning outside in their cages. After treatment, air the house completely. Wait at least several hours before returning the animals. Treat first thing in the morning, open all windows all day, and bring everyone back in the house in the late afternoon or early evening.

If the weather isn't cooperating, you can leave the animals in one room at one end of the house while you spray the other end. Do not move the animals back until the next day. The problem with this plan is that if you have the heater or air conditioner running, the toxins will be drawn in and recirculated throughout the entire house. If you must run a central temperature control unit, you can close off the vents to the temporary animal room and open a window for better ventilation. Don't forget to do the other section of the house the following day while adhering to the same safety suggestions.

Foggers

A fogger is often suggested for flea control, but most foggers are highly toxic. Foggers are not effective under furniture or inside closets, so they don't offer complete coverage, and yet they permeate your living space with toxins.

Care should be taken when using foggers. Follow the directions accurately. Keep your pets away from the house for longer than the manufacturer recommends.

The fogger leaves a residue on everything that it touches: you not only need to move your animals completely from the home (a hassle in itself), but you must also remove the cages and play stands.

Some foggers may use natural pyrethrins as an active ingredient. These foggers are less toxic. If you have birds, rabbits, kittens, or puppies, the risk involved in using a fogger may outweigh the benefits.

Bedding

Wash all pillows, blankets, and bedding that your pet uses. The significant part of this washing will be the drying: they must be in a hot dryer for at least fifteen to twenty minutes. Once a week, this bedding should also be tossed in a hot dryer for fifteen to twenty minutes as a precautionary device.

If your pet has a favorite spot where she likes to lounge, you can place an old towel on the area. This towel can then be washed and dried once a week. If you frequently take your pet in the car, spray or dust the seats with your chosen flea control product.

The Follow-Up

As you can see, treating your home is quite a chore when you have a flea infestation. The work that you must do should help remind you to keep up with your flea-control program. You will never want to go through that again! If you delay the second follow-up treatment, you may have to start from the beginning. Make sure that you follow through and repeat the whole process in a couple of weeks; otherwise, you will be doing the treatment again and again all year and never get on top of the problem.

FLEAS IN YOUR YARD

Most fleas prefer not to live in your yard; there is too much sunshine and there are too many predators, such as spiders and insects. They would rather live in your environmentally controlled home where there is plenty of breeding ground (your carpet) and plenty of food hosts (your animals).

"Outside, Flea Bag"

When people find they have a flea problem, they often exile their pets to the outdoors. In theory, this takes the fleas outdoors and out of the house. Unfortunately, this theory is lost on the flea population. They prefer the indoors so much that they will find new hosts — you. Without your pets around as the perfect host, fleas take whatever they can find. There was a time when the "job" of some dog breeds was to sit on the lap of their caretaker and attract all the pests and relieve the person of unwanted body guests. It is much easier to control the pests on your pets and in the environment than to shuffle the problem from one area to another.

Where the Fleas Congregate

Outdoor areas are the easiest to treat, partially because there are fewer fleas there and partially because it's easier to kill fleas outside. Maybe. If you have a very elaborate, shady yard, it may be just as difficult to treat the outdoors as it is to treat the home environment.

Start with the areas that your pets frequent. If they have a dog house or a favorite lounging site, this area should be first. Spray the shady areas thoroughly. Fleas prefer to congregate under pine needles, under a deck, around a shed, and along the edge of the house.

Treatment Efficiency

When treating your yard use only products labeled for outdoor use. Never mix the use of the products, such as spraying your animal with a product that is intended to be sprayed on the lawn, or using a kitten powder on the lawn. It is a waste of your time, inefficient, and dangerous.

Based on several factors, the success you have with these outdoor sprays will range from good to none. The weather, size of the area to be treated, and the animals bringing in the fleas make a difference. If you are often visited by wild animals, they may continually bring in fleas no matter how much time you devote to your flea-control program.

SO MANY FLEAS — SO LITTLE TIME

**Got fleas but little time?
Take these steps.**

1) Take your dogs and cats to the groomers for a bath and brush and comb treatment.

2) Move your birds and rabbits outdoors for a couple of hours.

3) Have a professional company steam clean your carpets.

4) Bring your animals back from the groomers.

5) Use an insect growth regulator spray (see below).

6) Bring your animals back indoors.

7) Have a professional pest control company spray your yard with a synthetic pyrethroid (more toxic than organic pyrethrins).

FLEA-CONTROL CHEMICALS

For many years, potent chemicals were the common ingredients used for flea control. The belief was that the strength and duration determined their worthiness. However, common sense now dictates that people can no longer disregard the health of the environment, animals, or humans in such a manner. No longer are products that hang around in the environment seen as a solution. Making yourself and your pets weaker by chemical poisoning is not going to help fight off the pests that are the problem to begin

with. Consumers are demanding products that contain more environmentally friendly chemicals that are still effective. More choices are now available.

Diatomaceous Earth

Diatomaceous Earth is a product derived from finely ground fossil materials. It dehydrates and kills insects by scraping off their outer covering. This product is nontoxic, but the dust can cause problems by irritating the lungs of people or animals if inhaled. Diatomaceous Earth is commonly and successfully used on carpets.

Insecticidal Soap

Insecticidal soap is a nontoxic product that uses the insecticidal property of fatty acids used to make soap. Read the labels, insecticidal soap can usually be used on your animals, their bedding, carpets, and even the yard.

Insect Growth Regulators

A recent addition to the flea-controlling chemical list are insect growth regulators (IGRs). IGRs stop the development of eggs and larvae; they are unable to proceed to the next stage in their life cycle and so the cycle ends. IGRs do not contain toxins that kill fleas, so they are less toxic to use than other flea-control chemicals. They have even been compared to table salt in toxicity levels.

IGRs on their own are not an effective flea-control method and should be combined with other methods that kill adult fleas. Generally, products that contain IGRs also contain chemicals that kill adult fleas. At this time, there is no method of flea control that kills the flea in the pupae stage, so you must repeat the treatment again in a couple of weeks.

Pyrethrins

Pyrethrins are the most widely used chemical in flea-control products. They are the least dangerous insecticides — they do not last as long in the environment and are less toxic than most chemicals. If you cannot find a product that uses only natural or herbal components, look for a product listing pyrethrins 0.04 percent or less as the active ingredient.

Many products that use pyrethrins also contain the synergist piperonyl butoxide, which may be unsafe and has been blamed for adverse side effects. Look for a pyrethrin product that does not contain the synergist.

Pyrethrins are also the least toxic to birds. If your dog or cat is dusted with other types of chemicals and hangs around the bird cage, your bird may have adverse effects. Fenoxycarb and Precor have also been shown to be safe around birds.

Other Common Chemicals

The following is a list of commonly found chemicals in flea-control products. These chemicals are toxic, and the side effects of each are also listed. Do not use products listing these chemicals as an active ingredient.

Arecoline hydrobromide: vomiting, unconsciousness, diarrhea, depression

Benzyl benzoate: nausea, vomiting, diarrhea, slow heartbeat

Carbamates (carbaryl or Sevin, methyl carbamate compounds): nerve paralysis, profuse salivation, muscle twitches, uncontrolled defecation, contracted pupils, slow heartbeat, labored breathing, vomiting, diarrhea, watery eyes, hyperactivity, rigidity, bluish discoloration, death

Organochlorines (DDT, DDE, aldrin, dieldrin, lindane, toxaphene, paradichloro benzene, dichlorophene): exaggerated responses to touch, light, and sounds; spasms or tremors; epilepsy-like seizures, death

Organophosphotes (malathion, ronnel, vapona, diazinon, dichlorvos, parathion): same as carbamates

Being prepared for emergencies

It seems like the news is full of stories of natural disasters and evacuation circumstances. There is always the fear of fire, but there have also been a number of natural disasters such as floods, hurricanes, earthquakes, and tornadoes. Facing these disasters is always a possibility, so you must be prepared.

When you have a pet, there is more to think about. A multi-animal household presents immense challenges when faced with an emergency. More equipment is required, and greater amounts of food and supplies must be available. The biggest worry to all animal guardians is having to evacuate in a hurry and having enough time and space to take everyone in your family, all your pets, and all the possessions you want to take with you.

Be prepared for any disaster by doing some planning and organizing your necessary supplies. Know what disasters are common in your area and the safety suggestions.

FIRE

Everyone should practice and understand their roles in case a fire breaks out in your home. Plan your escape routes in advance. The people of the house are the first concern. Once all the people are out safely, then you can worry about the pets.

Stickers on the windows and doors stating what pets are living in the home can alert firefighters to search for your animals. Animals that have more delicate respiratory systems, such as rabbits and birds, can quickly suffer damage from smoke inhalation.

Dogs and cats can be carried out, led out, or let out of an open window or door. A small, light carrier for caged pets should be kept near their cages at all times. Your companion may have to stay in her carrier for some time afterward so make it comfy by preparing it with a towel or blanket. Tape a bagged supply of food on the top of the carrier. Remember to rotate supplies to keep them fresh.

Some areas of the country are at risk of forest fires. Have your property appropriately cared for to reduce the risk around your house. Fires are unpredictable and even if you are watching carefully, a sudden change in the wind can send a fire in your direction. Evacuating your pets at the earliest sign of difficulty will save you much panic if evacuation is later demanded. Sometimes residents are allowed merely seconds to leave their homes. Evacuating your pets first means a less traumatic, speedy evacuation for yourself.

EVACUATION

Have an evacuation plan designed before you need it. In emergency situations, the officials of your area will set up an evacuation site and help the residents of the area evacuate. With animals, this becomes more difficult because most evacuation sites will not allow them. Veterinary hospitals and boarding facilities fill up very fast or may themselves be in danger.

If you have pets, you must find an alternative place to evacuate to, such as at a friend's or family member's. If you belong to a club affiliated with one of your animals, you may be able to start an exchange — a group of people could act as an evacuation site for others. They should be close, but not so close that they would also be in danger if you were in danger. Another matter to consider is whether you will be able to reach your alternative evacuation site. Traffic, weather, and road conditions may make it impossible to reach your safety spot: try to arrange sites in several different directions.

Of course, you must check with these people ahead of time to get their permission to let you stay. They must have room for you and your companions as well as welcome you with open arms.

If an evacuation situation presents itself, act early. Don't wait around hoping things will get better. Even if it only appears that you might need to evacuate your home, begin doing so immediately. You can always move your pets to your prearranged evacuation site early and return home until an official evacuation notice is ordered.

Getting an official evacuation notice means you have a matter of minutes to get out. With a number of pets, you need more time. You don't want to make decisions regarding whose safety, yours or theirs, is most important.

NATURAL DISASTERS

If natural disasters are common in your area, then you should already have a general plan for you and your family to follow. For example, people in California should know what to do if there is an earthquake, and those in the southern United States should have a plan in the event of a hurricane.

In an earthquake-prone area, preventatively remove any pictures or anything hanging on the walls behind a cage. Are any cages close enough to a tall piece of furniture, such as a bookcase, that would fall on them? Furniture, such as a bookcases, should be secured to the wall with special hooks purchased at a hardware or discount store.

If dangerous weather conditions should occur, keep your pets away from all doors, windows, glass, and mirrors. If there is danger of flooding, keep all of your pets and their supplies high and above floor level.

Make sure that you are completely prepared for emergencies by contacting your local Red Cross for information or getting a book from the library on emergency preparedness.

EMOTIONS

Your animals will probably be able to sense things that you won't be able to sense. They may become agitated and nervous when a storm is approaching, and many animals may be able to alert their observant caretakers to earthquakes and other disasters by their actions.

Your animal companions will probably become stressed during these tense situations. Their personalities may even change, causing them to become erratic and unpredictable, especially in evacuation situations. Get your pet secure in a carrier as soon as possible, and do not let her out for any reason. If you let your pet out in the car on the way to the evacuation site, even if you normally do, a dangerous situation could be created. She may be very upset and may cause injury to herself or someone else. Keep your pets safe and secure.

Talk soothingly and handle your animals less than you normally would. Too much handling may actually make an animal more agitated. Keep calm — the more excited you become, the more excited they become. Through your words and actions, show them that there is nothing to worry about and that everything will be okay. Just the fact that you know you have to stay calm for your pets' sake may help you stay calm for your own sake.

After an emergency is over and you are able to return to your home, be aware that it takes animals some time to adjust. A sensitive creature may take a week or more to return to "normal." Reassure your pet and let her have her own space for awhile. If your pet is still highly stressed after a couple of days home or suffered any kind of trauma during the emergency situation, take her to see your veterinarian.

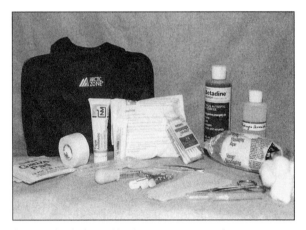

An example of a first-aid kit that you can create at home. You can also purchase pre-assembled kits that come specific for your species of pet.

SUPPLIES

If you are prepared and stay calm, an emergency situation will be less traumatic for everyone. Being prepared means having emergency supplies ready. The following is a list of items to have on hand in the event of an emergency.

Store these supplies in one place. Keep everything in a strong, closed bag or box. Keep all of your animals' supplies together. A separate container for each pet's supplies only makes it more difficult on you.

Make sure that you frequently go through the box and rotate perishable items and that you have everything you need. Change the water and food at least once a month. Sometimes a pet may have started a medication, dropped a medication, or needed a different kind of food — you need to update these supplies. Also replace anything you used out of the first-aid kit. Keep this box easily accessible.

An emergency supply box will seem like quite a chore to create, but your effort will be repaid with peace of mind. The following list should be adapted to your individual animals and situation. You want a sufficient amount of supplies to be prepared, but it must also be easily transportable. You'll have to find a balance that works for you and your household.

- Enough food for each animal for one week, can opener for canned food, bowls, and add some special, favorite treats.
- Bottled water. It is a good idea to have at least one gallon of water in the animal supplies, but you need several gallons of water stored elsewhere.
- Carriers for each small animal. If possible, carriers should be kept near cages. Make sure that your pet is accustomed to the carrier ahead of time. Strap or tape on a few days of supplies in case you have to evacuate due to fire.
- Pet first-aid kit. You can either buy one previously assembled or you can make one yourself for less money (see below).
- Emergency phone numbers. Use the same card that is suggested in chapter 5 for traveling with your pet.
- An extra record book.
- A toy or security item, such as a blanket, that you know helps your individual pet relax.
- Pooper-scooper bags for dogs, disposable litter box for cats, and cage liners for birds. The bird carrier can be lined with several layers of paper; remove each layer as it becomes soiled.
- Extra collar (harness type for cats and rabbits) and leash.

PET FIRST-AID KIT

thermometer
blunt-end tweezers
blunt-end scissors
bandage tape (1 inch wide)
antiseptic soap
antibacterial ointment
activated charcoal tablets
baking soda
3% hydrogen peroxide
lubricating gel (K-Y jelly)
3 inch x 3 inch gauze pads
elastic bandage (vet wrap)
plastic eyedropper
safety pins
triangle bandage
wooden tongue depressors
cotton swabs
measuring spoon
ice pack
gauze

TIPS TO BE PREPARED

- Don't jeopardize your life or the life of other family members: People Come First.

- Keep a full tank of gas in your automobile — you won't have time to stop for fuel.

- Design a preparedness plan in advance including an evacuation place.

- Have food and water supplies together in one area in a convenient carrier.

- Keep a battery-operated radio with your emergency equipment.

- Keep flashlights with working batteries with your emergency equipment.

- Keep pet-care instructions in your house, your car, and with a friend or relative.

Afterword

Reading a book is like taking a journey. The wonderful thing about reading one on pet care is that you get to share that odyssey with your animal companions.

One of my goals for this book has been to provide practical methods for easing caretaker duties. My higher aspiration was to convey that animal friends are not only terrific companions but also important to our spiritual existence.

Spending time with animal friends — whether it is observing, understanding, or caring for them — enables us to experience various levels of appreciation for them. I hope everyone realizes that animals are gifts to us and that we have the opportunity to marvel at the small things that too often go unnoticed. Our ability to share in nature and escape from the pressures of our modern world by sharing time with our pets is truly special. The first time I felt the bond with my animal companions, I knew my soul was nourished and my spirit enriched. I wish all of these opportunities for you.

Throughout the book, I mentioned that each animal is a unique individual and that your relationship with your pets is your own unique experience. In the course of this experience, which ultimately is bonding, no one may be able to give you "the" answer to questions you possibly have — you may have to look to your own loving heart and knowledge of your pet for direction. An open mind is paramount — you must be able to learn from others and adapt that information to your life.

Please take from this book the information that speaks to your heart and use it in the spirit from which it is intended — to better your life and the life of your animal companions, and to strengthen your bond and ultimately your commitment.

I hope your journey through *Creating a Peaceable Kingdom* stimulates your curiosity to learn more about your animal friends, leads you to new ideas about how to interact with and care for your pets, and ultimately enhances your adventure with them.

Relish in the magic of your animal companions and enjoy life in your own peaceable kingdom. Happy tails!

I would love to hear your suggestions, hints, and secrets for making life with your animal family easy and rewarding! Please send your thoughts and comments to:

Cynthia D. Miller
Animalia Publishing Company
P.O. Box 1390
Yuba City, CA 95992
(916) 755-1318
(888) 755-1318 toll free
(916) 755-2695 fax

195

Appendix

The following is a list of addresses and phone numbers of organizations, clubs, and periodicals that can be of assistance to you and your animals. Do not feel intimidated about calling or writing to ask any questions you may have. These people care about animals and their caretakers and will help you any way that they can.

When writing to these organizations for information, send a self-addressed, stamped envelope to help defray costs and speed response.

National Animal Poison Control Center
1220 Veterinary Medicine
Basic Sciences Building
2001 South Lincoln Avenue
Urbana, IL 61801

1-800-548-2423
Credit card calls — $30.00 per case evaluation

1-900-680-0000
$20.00 for 5 minutes plus $2.95 for
each additional minute

In addition to handling emergency case evaluations, you can also write to the NAPCC for information about protecting your animal companions from poisons in and around your home. They will also send you emergency phone number stickers to place near your phone.

Pest Control Information
BIRC (The Bio-Integral Resource Center)
P.O. Box 7414
Berkeley, CA 94707
(510) 524-2567 fax (510) 524-1758

BIRC is a nonprofit organization that offers information on the least toxic methods of pest management. Call or write for information on booklets covering different pest control problems and the actual cost (about $5.00 to $10.00). These booklets are helpful and worth the small cost.

U.S. Environmental Protection Agency
Office of Water
Washington, DC 20460
(202) 260-2090
(Write or call for National Primary
Drinking Water Standards)

DOG REGISTRY CLUBS
American Kennel Club
51 Madison Avenue
New York, NY 10010
(212) 696-8200
(breeders and events)

United Kennel Club
100 East Kilgore Road
Kalamazoo, MI 49001
(616) 343-9020
(breeders and events)

Mixed Breed Dog Club of America
1118 Marquita Avenue
Burlingame, CA 94010-3323
(415) 344-3550
(general information)

American Mixed Breed Obedience Registration
Wilma Z. Riddell, Public Relations Representative
819 Meads Road
Norfolk, VA 23505
(804) 451-0571
(information on trials and registration)

CAT REGISTRY CLUBS

American Association of Cat Enthusiasts
P.O. Box 213
Pine Brook, NJ 07055
(201) 335-6717

American Cat Fanciers' Association
P.O. Box 203
Point Lookout, MO 65726
(417) 334-5430

Cat Fanciers' Association
1805 Atlantic Avenue
P.O. Box 1005
Manasquan, NJ 08736-0805
(908) 528-9797

Cat Fanciers' Federation
Juanita Vorhees
P.O. Box 661
Gratis, OH 45330
(513) 787-9009

The International Cat Association
P.O. Box 2684
Harlingen, TX 78551
(210) 428-8046

Contact these clubs when you are searching for a cat breeder. They will help you locate a local breeder and give you information on activities they sponsor for cat caretakers.

OTHER ORGANIZATIONS

Bird Organizations

American Federation of Agriculture
P.O. Box 56218
Phoenix, AZ 85079-6218
(602) 484-0931

National Parrot Association
8 N. Hoffman Lane
Hauppage, NY 11788
(516) 366-3562

Rabbit Organizations

House Rabbit Society
1524 Benton Street
Alameda, CA 94501

Join the House Rabbit Society and support its efforts to rescue rabbits and educate rabbit caretakers. When you join, you will receive the *House Rabbit Journal.* Order *House Rabbit Habitats* for good information on rabbit housing.

American Rabbit Breeders Association Inc.
Glen C. Carr, Secretary
P.O. Box 426
Bloomington, IL 61702
(309) 827-6623

OTHER ORGANIZATIONS (CONT.)

Therapy Dogs International
6 Hilltop Road
Mendham, NJ 07945
(201) 543-0888

Avian and Exotic Veterinarian Associations
Association of Avian Veterinarians
P.O. Box 811720
Boca Raton, FL 33481
(407) 393-8901

American Veterinary Medical Association
1931 North Meacham Road, Suite 100
Schaumburg, IL 60173
(708) 925-8070
(800) 248-2862

Delta Society
P.O. Box 1080
Renton, WA 98057
(206) 226-7357

The Delta Society will send you a list of bereavement groups that you can turn to for support and counseling. The Delta Society also provides information on training for special needs (such as hearing dogs).

Pet Loss Support Hotlines
University of California at Davis
(916) 752-4200
6:30 a.m. to 9:30 p.m. PST

Alpha Affiliates, Inc.
103 Washington Street, Suite 362
Morristown, NJ 07960-6814
(201) 539-2770

Write to Alpha Affiliates and ask for its *Durable Power of Attorney for Pet Care*. Send a self-addressed, stamped envelope and $3.00.

ANIMAL IDENTIFICATION SUPPLIERS

Microchips
AVID
3179 Hamner Avenue, Suite 5
Norco, CA 91760
(909) 371-7505

InfoPet Identification Systems Inc.
517 W. Travelers Trail
Burnsville, MN 55337
(612) 890-2080
(800) INFOPET

Tattoo Registries
National Dog Registry
P.O. Box 116
Woodstock, NY 12498
(800) 637-3647

Tattoo-A-Pet
6571 S.W. 20th Court
Ft. Lauderdale, FL 33317
(800) TATTOOS

TTOUCH®

The Tellington TTouch®
78080 Calle Estado, Suite 2A
La Quinta, CA 92253
(619) 777-0217 fax (619) 777-0214

Linda Tellington-Jones first developed this method of touch for horses and has discovered the benefit for all animals from dogs to monkeys to dolphins. This is not a form of massage intended to affect the muscular system; it activates the nervous system. I highly recommend TTouch®. It is a wonderful way to bond and is useful for a multitude of conditions. Videos spotlight dogs, cats, and horses.

PERIODICALS

I encourage subscribing to periodicals because of the up-to-date information they can provide. Your knowledge base won't become obsolete if you receive magazines and newsletters on your animal companions. There is always something fun to try, suggestions for ease of care, or advice for solving problems.

Dogs

Dog World
P.O. Box 6500
Chicago, IL 60680

Dog Fancy
P.O. Box 6050
Mission Viejo, CA 92690

Cats

Cat Fancy
P.O. Box 6050
Mission Viejo, CA 92690

CATS
P.O. Box 290037
Port Orange, FL 32129

Birds

Bird Talk
P.O. Box 6050
Mission Viejo, CA 92690

Pet Bird Report
2236 Mariner Square Drive #35
Alameda, CA 94501

Rabbits

House Rabbit Journal
1524 Benton Street
Alameda, CA 94501

CATALOGS

Direct Book Service
Dog and Cat Book Catalog
P.O. Box 2778
Wenatchee, WA 98807-2778
(800) 776-2665 fax (509) 662-7233

Their list of titles is impressive. You'll find what you are looking for and some you didn't expect to find.

UPCO
3705 Pear Street
P.O. Box 969
St. Joseph, MO 64502
(800) 254-UPCO (8726) fax (816) 233-9696

A great catalog for all animal companions. They carry a wonderful rabbit cage with a plastic slat floor.

R.C. Steele
1989 Transit Way
Box 910
Brockport, NY 14420-0910
(800) 872-3773

They have divisions for each type of animal; ask for the catalog(s) you need.

Great Companions
P.O. Box 87
Warren, MN 56762
(800) 829-2138

They carry bird, dog, and reptile supplies.

Drs. Foster & Smith Inc.
P.O. Box 100
Rhinelander, WI 34501-0100
(800) 826-7206

Dog and cat supplies.

Annotated Bibliography

Anderson, Nina, and Howard Pieper. *Are You Poisoning Your Pet?* East Canaan, CT: Safe Goods, 1995. This book describes how common products in your home can be affecting the health of your animal companions (and yourself). You will learn about symptoms that warn you of poisoning in your animals and alternatives to toxic products.

Aslett, Don. *Pet Clean-Up Made Easy.* Cincinnati: Writer's Digest Books, 1988. Those who share their home with an animal companion need this book. Aslett, the cleaning guru, describes the best way to clean every animal mess you'll experience. The book also has great organizational tips and hints.

Association of Veterinarians for Animal Rights. *Canine Consumer Report: A Guide to Hereditary and Congenital Diseases in Purebred Dogs.* Vacaville, CA: The Association of Veterinarians for Animal Rights, 1994. If you want to know what genetic diseases affect the dog breed you are considering for adoption, this twenty-eight page booklet is the perfect source. A series of numbers follows each of the 147 dog breeds covered. Look up these numbers to discover what diseases are associated with your chosen breed. Discuss these findings with breeders and your veterinarian before adopting, and you will have a better understanding of what to expect.

Athan, Mattie Sue. *Guide to a Well-Behaved Parrot.* Hauppauge, NY: Barron's Educational Series, 1993. Athan, a respected parrot behaviorist, will help you understand the psychology of your parrot friend with this valuable book. She takes you through the psittacine learning stages and shines a guiding light on these emotional creatures. Athan also gives great practical advice and suggestions.

Baer, Ted. *Communicating with Your Dog: A Humane Approach to Dog Training.* Hauppauge, NY: Barron's Educational Series, 1989. A straightforward approach to teaching a dog to live in a human family. Baer teaches anyone how to train his or her dog in a gentle, respectful manner. Not a "dog training manual" but a book demonstrating how human and canine can become friends.

Benjamin, Carol Lea. *Second-Hand Dog: How to Turn Yours into a First-Rate Pet.* New York: Howell Book House, 1988. When you adopt an older dog or a dog from a shelter, your concerns are different than if you had adopted a puppy. With her humorous cartoons and extensive experience, Benjamin will ease your mind by offering you appropriate advice. Look for other books by Carol Lea Benjamin; they are all very helpful and entertaining.

Bergin, Bonnie. *Bonnie Bergin's Guide to Bringing Out the Best in Your Dog.* Boston: Little Brown and Company, 1995. Bergin is the pioneer in training dogs to assist handicapped people. Her training methods are meant to instill confidence and the desire to please in her canine students. The most valuable section of the book is her discussion on choosing a dog companion. If you are contemplating the adoption of a dog, you will more than likely be happy with your choice if you read this section. If you already have a dog or have anything to do with dogs and their people, this important information will shed light on the dynamics of human/canine friendship.

Culp, Stephanie. *How to Get Organized When You Don't Have the Time.* Cincinnati: Writer's Digest Books, 1986. When it comes to organizing your life, there are many books on the market. This is my personal favorite because of her friendly writing style and wonderful advice. Although not written directly for animal caretakers, you will find many ideas applicable to your animal care. And if you use the rest of the suggestions, you will have more time for your pets!

Curtis, Patricia. *The Indoor Cat.* New York: Perigee Books, 1981. This fun-to-read book will explain why keeping cats indoors is not only necessary in our changing times but also beneficial to both cats and people alike. Contains a good discussion on multiple cats.

Dadd, Debra Lynn. *Nontoxic & Natural: How to Avoid Dangerous Everyday Products and Buy or Make Safe Ones.* Los Angeles: Jeremy P. Tarcher, Inc., 1984. Now that you understand how easily our animals are affected by the everyday products we use around the house, how do you lessen their effects and eliminate their use? This book will show you how.

Davis, Kathy Diamond. *Responsible Dog Ownership.* New York: Howell Book House, 1994. A wonderful book that covers the obligations that a dog caretaker has to the human community. Barking, roaming, renting a home with dogs, spaying and neutering, and many more subjects are fully covered. A thoughtful discussion on choosing a dog and a section on the Canine Good Citizen Test present valuable information.

DeBitetto, James, DVM, and Sarah Hodgson. *You & Your Puppy: Training and Health Care for Puppy's First Year.* New York: Howell Book House, 1995. This book is organized into sections by the age of the puppy, and you will refer to this informative volume again and again. Although suggestions on training are abundant, you will, more importantly, learn how to keep your puppy from getting into trouble in the first place. The health section is very helpful.

Doane, Bonnie Munro. *The Parrot in Health and Illness: An Owner's Guide.* New York: Howell Book House, 1991. Doane is a veterinarian assistant and bird breeder capable of explaining the most technical jargon in layman's terms. You will have a clear understanding of a healthy bird and one that is ill. It is important to catch illness early, and if you read this book, you will know when your bird friend is not right and will understand your avian veterinarian's diagnosis and suggestions for care.

Frazier, Anitra. *The New Natural Cat: A Complete Guide for Finicky Owners.* New York: Plume, 1990. The title says it all. Every home that has a cat should also have this book. The section on grooming is thorough and with this information you will be able to make even the most reluctant cat more cooperative. A reference for holistic remedies for many feline health situations is offered.

Hammond, Sean, and Carolyn Usrey. *How to Raise a Sane and Healthy Cat.* New York: Howell Book House, 1994. In question-and-answer format, the authors offer advice on almost everything related to cats. If you have a question, it is probably answered here.

Harriman, Marinell. *House Rabbit Handbook: How to Live with an Urban Rabbit.* 3rd ed. Alameda, CA: Drollery Press, 1995. In 1985, the first edition of this book began a revolution in rabbit care. Rabbit guardians brought their rabbits in the house and made them a part of the family. In an effort to educate rabbit caretakers, Harriman began the House Rabbit Society, which continues to grow in numbers and support. This is the book on the personality and emotional lives of rabbits as house companions. Any of the three editions are valuable; each focuses on a different area, so don't pass up an old edition if you come across one.

Hunter, Samantha. *Hop to It: A Guide to Training Your Pet Rabbit*. Hauppauge, NY: Barron's Educational Series, Inc., 1991. This book describes methods of training rabbits to be good house rabbits, but the benefit of this book is the discussion on normal rabbit behavior.

Kushner, Harold S. *When Bad Things Happen to Good People*. New York: Schocken Books, 1981. This popular book is helpful and comforting when dealing with the loss of a beloved animal companion.

Lowell, Michele. *Your Pet Bird: A Buyer's Guide*. New York: Henry Holt and Company, 1994. Lowell offers an insightful description of life with a bird and urges you to evaluate your lifestyle and its compatibility with a feathered friend before adopting. She gives a wonderful description of the various pet bird species. The book is complete with information on purchasing a bird (who, how, where) and bringing your new animal home.

Masson, Jeffrey Moussaieff, and Susan McCarthy. *When Elephants Weep: The Emotional Lives of Animals*. New York: Delacorte Press, 1995. Everyone who loves animals should read this book. (I wish it could be required reading for the entire human race.) You, as an animal caretaker, know your pets feel emotions, but you also know that scientists tell us this is impossible. Masson shows us why the scientific community will not accept this and offers countless examples that prove animals have rich emotional lives. Parts of this book may break your heart or make you angry, but you will look at your animal companions with increased admiration.

Matthews, Andrew. *Being Happy! A Handbook to Greater Confidence & Security*. Los Angeles: Price Stern Sloan, Inc., 1990. This wonderful book will not only make your life brighter, but it will also explain in clear language the concept of how your attitude affects your life. This idea has been used throughout *Creating a Peaceable Kingdom* to demonstrate how your relationships with your animal friends are reflected by your thought patterns. This book is simple to read, straightforward, and pleasant.

McDaniel, Jack, and Colleen McDaniel. *Pooches and Small Fry: Parenting Skills for Dogs (and Kids!)*. Wilsonville, OR: Doral Publishing Inc., 1995. Using the basis of leadership and respect, the authors share the idea that the same parenting skills are successful with children and dogs.

Milani, Myrna M., DVM. *The Body Language and Emotions of Dogs*. New York: Quill William Morrow, 1986. If you interact with dogs, you must read this book. The information will give you insightful knowledge into the relationship you have with your canine friend. Milani also authored *The Body Language and Emotions of Cats*, also published by Quill William Morrow. Both books are invaluable to animal lovers.

Pitcairn, Richard H., DVM, Ph.D., and Susan Hubble Pitcairn. *Dr. Pitcairn's Complete Guide to Natural Health for Dogs & Cats*. Emmaus, PA: Rodale Press, 1982. You will find an abundance of information on natural health and care for your dogs and cats in this book. The section on nutrition and processed pet foods is excellent.

Randolph, Mary. *Dog Law: A Legal Guide for Dog Owners and Their Neighbors*. 2d ed. CA: Nolo Press Self-Help Law, 1994. Every dog caretaker should own this book. Some of the laws and most of the suggestions can be applied to other animal species as well. This is not a dry law book; it is full of helpful information about many animal-related problems.

Rogers, Fred. *When A Pet Dies.* New York: G.P. Putnam's Sons, 1988. This children's book deals with pet loss in a simple-to-understand, practical manner.

Rubenstein, Eliza, and Shari Kalina. *The Adoption Option: Choosing and Raising the Shelter Dog for You.* New York: Howell Book House, 1996. If you are considering a dog, read this book. Even if you haven't decided to get a dog from a shelter, investigate the possibility by reading this wonderful book. The information is thorough, and choosing a shelter dog and getting acquainted are discussed in detail.

Rylant, Cynthia. *Dog Heaven.* New York: The Blue Sky Press, 1995. This children's book, offering a heartwarming and spiritual explanation about what happens to dogs when they die, is just as helpful for adults as it is for children. It was devastating when my dog, Mike, died. I bought this book to help my children deal with the loss, but I found I felt much better after reading it. Despite what you truly believe about the afterlife of companion animals, there is comfort in the possibility of angels in heaven giving our beloved dogs biscuits and patting them on their heads as they pass.

Sife, Wallace, Ph.D. *The Loss of a Pet.* New York: Howell Book House, 1993. This book is invaluable when you lose an animal companion. A complete explanation of the stages of grief and an excellent section on helping children deal with the loss are offered. If you read this book before you need it, you will find greater strength and understanding when the occasion occurs. I encourage you to read this book, especially if you have children.

Smith, Carin A., DVM. *Get Rid of Fleas and Ticks for Good!* Leavenworth, WA: Smith Veterinary Services, 1995. The most complete source on getting rid of the pesky pests I have seen yet. Includes natural alternatives to harmful chemicals. Maybe you really can get rid of fleas and ticks for good!

Tortora, Daniel F., Ph.D. *The Right Dog for You.* New York: Simon & Schuster, 1980. A series of questions regarding your lifestyle and tolerance of various doggie attributes, such as shedding and activity level, help you select dog breeds compatible with your expectations. Use this book to get an idea of breeds suitable for you and your family, and then research other resources, such as clubs and breeders, to further your education.

Warshaw, Jennifer. *The Parrot Training Handbook: A Step-by-Step Guide to Taming and Training Pet Birds.* San Jose, CA: Parrot Press, 1990. The spiral binding of this book helps ease its handling when you are training your companion bird to perform tricks such as waving hello and playing basketball. Gentle, respectful training is a fun way to spend time with your creatures, and this is a great book about training a parrot.

Glossary

avian — Having to do with birds.

aviary — A cage or building housing birds.

canine — A dog.

come/recall — A command requesting an animal to immediately return to the handler no matter what activity the animal was engaged in.

despotic ranking system — A social ranking system in which there is only one absolute leader with unlimited power. The others are equal but have no power.

displaced attachment — In reference to animals, it is the abnormal and unhealthy attachment of a person to an animal where the animal is a replacement for the emotional support of another person.

down-stay — A command requesting the animal to assume a down position and hold that position without moving until requested to release it.

feline — A cat.

field trials — Hunting trials of various types created to test the function of the dog breed. Includes trailing for hounds, pointing, retrieving, spaniel (flush and retrieve), coonhound (treeing), and terrier (finding game animals in underground tunnels).

genetic faults — Inherited physical or behavioral problems.

hip dysplasia — A complex, degenerative disease that affects the hip joint. This condition is often painful and debilitating, and is genetically transmitted.

hookbill — A parrot. Distinguished by hard, strong, curved mandible (the bird's jaw).

leave-it — Command requesting animal to turn away from what the animal was investigating and focus on the caretaker.

lure coursing — Dog sport where sighthounds participate in a "hunt" contest chasing a lure. The lure may be a real rabbit in some states or strips of plastic and possibly fur strung on a cord that is then reeled in using various methods.

moggie — Mixed-breed cat.

psittacula — Slender, small to mid-sized parrots with long, graceful tails and a colored band around neck. Includes Indian ringneck, African ringneck, Alexandrine, moustache, and plum-headed parakeets.

psittacine — Pertaining to parrots.

quarantine — A period of thirty to sixty days of complete and strict separation of a newly introduced animal. During this time, the caretaker observes the animal for signs of illness. The separation continues until good health is verified through observation and veterinary exams and tests. This protects the resident animal(s) as well as the new animals from the spread of disease.

ringneck parakeet — Common name for birds from the psittacula family.

Schutzhund — German for protection dog; also a sport. A highly specialized discipline involving tests in tracking, obedience, and protection. Only physically and mentally sound dogs and responsible, sensitive handlers participate in this sport.

sighthound — A group of dog breeds that rely on their keen eyesight for hunting.

sit-stay — Command requesting the animal to assume a sitting position and hold that position without moving until requested to release it.

skijoring — Cross-country skier pulled by a dog or a team of two or three dogs.

vent — The area on a bird at the underside of the base of the tail where feces are extracted.

Other Publications from Animalia Publishing

Available Fall 1996

Creating a Peaceable Kingdom: Pet Record and Observation Book

Forthcoming in 1997

Canine Adventures: Fun Things to Do with Your Dog

101 Fun Activities for Dog Lovers

101 Fun Activities for Pet Bird Lovers

Special Reports

01 *Personality Traits of an Animal Lover*

02 *Observation and Record Keeping: Getting to Know Your Pets*

03 *Animal Caretaker's Guide to Emergency Preparedness*

04 *Street-Wise Exercise for You and Your Dog*

05 *When You Don't Want to Leave Your Pet at Home*

06 *What to Know Before Adding an Animal Companion to Your Family*

07 *What Do I Do with My Pets While I'm Vacationing?*

08 *Creating a Bond for Life with Your Animal Companion*

09 *The Least Toxic Way to Protect Your Pet from Fleas*

10 *Your Vet — Your Partner*

11 *If It Just Isn't Working — Rehoming Your Pet*

12 *Tips on Choosing the Almost-Perfect Feline Companion*

13 *Tips on Choosing the Almost-Perfect Canine Companion*

14 *Tips on Choosing the Almost-Perfect Pet Bird Companion*

15 *When You're Not There to Care for Your Pet*

16 *Finding Your Lost Pet*

17 *How to Make a Move Less Traumatic for Your Pets*

Photography Credits

Page iii - J.C. Carton/Bruce Coleman, Inc.; H. Reinhard/Bruce Coleman, Inc.; H. Tschanz/Bruce Coleman, Inc.; Michele Burgess/Photo Bank; G. Lawrence/Bruce Coleman, Inc.; Digul/Bruce Coleman, Inc.; Kent Knudson/Photo Bank
Page 4 - J.C. Carton/Bruce Coleman, Inc.
Page 9 - Cynthia D. Miller
Page 16 - H. Reinhard/Bruce Coleman, Inc.
Page 26 - L. Borodulin/Bruce Coleman, Inc.
Page 38 - Cynthia D. Miller
Page 43 - Cynthia D. Miller
Page 44 - H. Tschanz/Bruce Coleman, Inc.
Page 50 - Vaughn Medford
Page 56 - Cynthia D. Miller
Page 69 - Vaughn Medford
Page 76 - G. Kronmuller/Bruce Coleman, Inc.
Page 78 - Michele Burgess/Photo Bank
Page 82 - Kyle Miller
Page 89 - Cynthia D. Miller
Page 99 - Cynthia D. Miller
Page 106 - G. Lawrence/Bruce Coleman, Inc.
Page 112 - Vaughn Medford
Page 119 - Cynthia D. Miller
Page 121 - Cynthia D. Miller
Page 141 - Lewis Litzky
Page 146 - Digul/Bruce Coleman, Inc.
Page 149 - Vaughn Medford
Page 154 - Vaughn Medford
Page 162 - Vaughn Medford
Page 166 - Kent Knudson/Photo Bank
Page 174 - Doug Mazell/Photo Bank
Page 178 - Cynthia D. Miller
Page 183 - Vaughn Medford
Page 192 - Cynthia D. Miller

Index

A